A SCRAPBO
SNOWDONIA

Vernon Hall

ARTHUR H. STOCKWELL LTD.
Elms Court Ilfracombe
Devon

First published in Great Britain, 1982

ISBN 0 7223 1622-4
Printed in Great Britain by
Arthur H. Stockwell Ltd.
Elms Court · Ilfracombe
Devon

CONTENTS

ILLUSTRATIONS

FOREWORD

By the Lord Hunt of Llanfair Waterdine K.G., C.B.E., D.S.O.

It was not until I was 18 that I paid my first visit to Snowdonia, during the Easter holidays of 1929 which preceded my last term at school. My mother had taken my brother Hugh and myself to North Wales, not especially because of the mountains but because she wanted to look at the castles. We took a taxi from Bethesda and knocked at the door of Ogwen Cottage. But Mrs James was fully booked; she sent us down the Nant Francon Pass to a farm, Ty Gwyn, where we stayed for a few days exploring the Carneddau. Our next step was the Pen y Pass and my brother and I walked over the Glyders, taking an inexpert and adventurous route down to the Llanberis Pass on our way. I recollect that Rawson Owen, proprietor of the Gorphwysfa Hotel on the Pass, had only recently given up driving a coach and four up and down the narrow roads; the Inn with its fine collection of copper pans and cauldrons, was under the masterful management of Miss Jones.

It rained nearly every day during our stay. The tops were hidden in cloud but for me, long accustomed to the Alps, the mountains, far from being dwarfed, in my mind seemed larger than life: the mists which shrouded them only added to the illusion of height and mystery.

At Easter-time 1933, while on leave from my regiment in India, I made my first acquaintance with British rock climbing, from a leaky tent. This time it snowed as well as rained upon my companion and myself; even such undemanding climbs as the Horned Crag route on Lliwedd,

Tryfan's Grooved Arete, Route two on Crib Goch Buttress and the Great Gully on Craig yr Ysfa seemed hard enough in the circumstances. Yet these two inauspicious visits sufficed to build a life-long attachment to North Wales.

At that time the Gorphwyfsa Hotel on the Pen y Pass was still the focal point for the climbing establishment. But even if I had been deemed worthy of their attention, I was serving almost continuously overseas in those years; I was not among the favoured few at Geoffrey Winthrop Young's Easter gatherings. It was not until shortly before the end of the war that I next came to Snowdonia. During a week's leave from the European Theatre of Operations, in March 1945, my wife Joy and I travelled by cycle from Knighton-Tref y Clawdd on the Welsh border, for a few days' climbing. We were thrilled about the little house which we had just purchased under Offa's Dyke. A trifle weary we pushed our laden cycles up the hill from Nant Gwynant after spending the night at a bed and breakfast stop-over provided by a Mrs Hughes at Hafod y Rhis, we arrived at the Pen y Gwryd Hotel. It was a welcome haven and we were more than ready for breakfast. But strict food rationing was in force and we were by no means satisfied with the meagre portions of butter, toast and marmalade: we looked covetously at the left-overs of the other guests, without quite summoning the courage to ask if we might finish what they apparently did not require.

That was the beginning of a long and very special association with P.y.G. From 1945 onwards the hotel has become an inseparable part of the Everest saga; a place where we of the first successful expedition have been made welcome year by year and plied with good food by Jo and Chris Briggs: a place where I have been only one among thousands of climbers who have found there the friendly ambience of a club house. It is right and it is timely that the long-standing link between this historic hostelry and British mountaineering should be placed on record and I am glad to introduce Sam Hall's book to the many people who share my love for Yr Eryi, and to countless others who will come in the years ahead.

John Hunt

PREFACE

Gloucester: When shall we come to the top of that same hill?
Edgar: Come on, sir, here's the place: stand still. How
fearful and dizzy 'tis to cast one's eyes so low!
The crows and choughs that wing the midway air
Show scarce as gross as beetles: half way down
Hangs one that gathers samphire, dreadful trade!
Methinks he seems no bigger than his head:
The fishermen that walk upon the beach,
Appear like mice.

Shakespeare. King Lear Act IV. Sc. VI.

It is a well accepted habit for the author to begin his book by making excuses for having written it: for me as I only considered entering the field of literature at an age at which the Bible would have me dead it may seem a bit late for an apology: but I can offer one or two good reasons for writing — at least they seem good reasons to me although to others they may seem poor and illogical.

My first reason was to give myself an occupation during retirement, and this has proved an excellent reason for the necessary research and writing have given me great pleasure.

Then it seemed to me that there were many people who know little of Snowdonia except what can be seen from a car or a coach, and who do not realize the measure of enjoyment to be found in walking, climbing or fishing in this grand mountain region; in an effort to reach the man in the street I have tried to avoid overstressing any special pastime, although this has often been difficult in a book centred on a mainly climbers' hotel. Fortunately, I am no climber myself but merely a mountain walker and so I have not the knowledge to discuss climbing, and the subject has already been well and ably written by many who understand it.

And I am very happy to write about Pen y Gwryd as this seems one of the few remaining inns where all guests are friends and not merely purveyors of pound notes. All too often today even the efficient hotel tends to have an air of remote efficiency rather than one of friendly welcome to a personal guest.

Pen y Gwryd throughout its long history has assembled together those whose tastes are similar and who all enjoy the brooding hills and the rushing waters. Pen y Gwryd remains a place where the frequent visitor can feel confident of meeting old friends and the stranger can feel sure of making new ones.

A great problem of writing about Wales lies in deciding what spelling to use: should it be genuine old Welsh or the half-caste English-Welsh of the Ordnance maps? Encouraged by an ardent and persuasive Welshman I use the spelling advised by the Board of Celtic Studies of the University of Wales hoping that even the benighted Englishman will be able to recognize the meaning.

In obtaining information for this book I have had so much help from so many friends that I need a second volume to adequately express my thanks.

Unfortunately Charles Edward Mathews is no longer with us to be thanked, for without his *Reminiscences of Pen y Gwryd* the history of the period of the Owens would be sparse indeed: and I am particularly grateful to Herbert R.C. Carr for with his generous permission I have pillaged, without remorse, his classic *Mountains of Snowdonia*. Harry Inman has kept intact all the documents and diaries of his uncle Arthur Lockwood and has allowed me full access to them; and he has helped in putting me in touch with Mrs Muriel Green the surviving daughter of William Hampson and she has produced a lot of information.

Mrs Nea Morin has given me many facts about the Ladies

Alpine Club and the Pinnacle Club, and so has Mrs Angell the present secretary of the latter club.

Other helpful friends have been Lord Hunt, Sir Charles Evans who corrected many of my errors and Kevin Fitzgerald. I also consulted the Hon. John Twining, Peter Bicknell and Mrs Graham.

As always librarians have been ever helpful for in libraries at least the spirit of service still remains strong: the Alpine Club Library, the London Library, the Devon County Library, and Miss Gillian Pentelow from my old Medical School library have all helped to look up necessary books and references.

My near neighbour Walter Green has been extremely kind and helpful in making copies of many photographs, while Mrs Hutchins and Miss Shirley Peerless have both demonstrated the excellence of their first class typing.

I must not forget my long suffering wife who put up with my vagaries during the period of gestation of this book; she advised on many points and also read and selected the poems digging them out of their illegibility in the Visitors' Books; she also copied the sketches in the Visitors' Books so that they could be easily reproduced, and she vetted the botanical extracts a field in which I am quite ignorant.

And Chris and Jo Briggs have from the beginning given me every help and encouragement, they have given me full access to their considerable library on all aspects of Welsh life, and they have fed me with anecdotes of the happenings (real or apocryphal) at Pen y Gwryd and in the area round about. There have been many others who directly or indirectly have been of assistance to me and to them I am ever grateful and apologetic at such a sketchy acknowledgement. And I can but hope that each and every one of my innumerable helpers may be pleased to see this book in print and to know that they have played some part in its production: and I wish to remind them that Pliny the Elder said 'It is godlike for mortal to assist mortal'.

CHAPTER 1

THE APPROACH TO NORTH WALES

The seat of the Celtic Muse is in the mist of the secret and solitary hill, and her voice in the murmur of the mountain stream. He who woos her, must love the barren rock more than the fertile valley, and the solitude of the desert better than the festivity of the hall.

Sir Walter Scott.

Mountains, music and men; surely it is these three which together make up much of the magic and mystery of Wales; it is these three enticements which lure the traveller from without into this lovely country. This includes, in particular, the traveller from England, the man who, in days gone by, sometimes was crudely called the Sassenach.

These three charms can be put in varying order according to the taste of the invader: some may put men first even though, or maybe even because, it means Welshmen. Many may put music high on the list for here Wales has always been pre-eminent in the British Isles, indeed some may think in the whole world. Giraldus Cambrensis, sometimes known as Gerald the Welshman, writing way back in the twelfth century remarks of his own country 'Those who arrive in the morning are entertained till evening with the conversation of young women and harps allotted to this purpose'. While in 1770 Joseph Cradock walking with a party which was determined to reach the summit of Snowdon at all costs and was resting worn and weary halfway up the mountainside, notes 'Determined to amuse ourselves in this dreary situation we sent for a harper, a blind man, and a number of blooming country girls to divert us with music and dancing'.

Anyone who has had the good fortune to be invited to a Noson Lawen even in this modern age will know what very excellent music is still to be found in many a Welsh home, and on these occasions the harp is still not forgotten. For the benefit of the uninitiated it should be explained that a Noson Lawen would in England be described as a musical evening at which, before the days of radio and television, many families would entertain themselves by their own skills, but the English edition would seldom rise to the superb level of that found in Wales.

The origin of this delightful ceremony seems lost in the mists of the past, but it may be that it started centuries ago when the unexpected traveller arrived in search of rest and food; the hospitality of that time demanded that such a guest should not only have a meal but should also be allowed a musical accompaniment by song and harp, and in return the thankful traveller was expected to sing or at least to recite for his supper not only as a thank-offering, but to allow him the chance to give a full account of himself. It gave the opportunity to tell his host whence he came from, where he was going to and for what purpose he was travelling; for the unknown wanderer always tended to carry suspicion with him. Even if he could give only an unsatisfactory account of himself (and this might result in a knife in the back during the night), at least honour would have been satisfied on both sides.

As has been said the Welsh Noson Lawen is normally far ahead of its English counterpart in quality, and although today the song-script may not be impromptu it is almost certainly produced for the occasion, and of course rendered with the flourish and harmony that no one but the Welshman can achieve. Although there may be many who have not had the opportunity to enjoy one of these choral concerts there must surely be few who have not had their senses stirred and their emotions aroused at some time by the magnificence of a Welsh choir; and there must indeed be many Welshmen who would not agree with Walter Scott when he finds the solitude of the desert better than the festivity of the hall! Although

Walter Scott oddly enough had at least one expert who agreed with him; for when Mendelssohn made his tour of Snowdonia round about the 1820s he is said to have commented 'Heaven help us! A harper sits in the hall of every reputable tavern incessantly playing so-called folk melodies, that is to say, dreadful vulgar out-of-tune trash' and he also thought the Welsh had rough nasal voices. But the Welsh can at least take solace in the fact that he was equally rude about the Papal Choir in Rome!

The pleasures of the men and the music can often be found and appreciated outside their own country, but it is the mountains and the valleys of this lovely country which can be found only there and so have attracted visitors in large numbers. Here it may be interesting to quote Kenneth Clark (now Lord Clark) who tells us that mountains 'For over two thousand years have been considered simply as a nuisance; unproductive, obstacles to communication, the refuge of bandits and heretics'. He goes on to point out that to any of the early great civilizers the thought of climbing a mountain for pleasure would have seemed ridiculous, while few travellers crossing the Alps in earlier centuries would pause to admire the scenery, but would be more likely to scuttle rapidly away from their sinister surroundings. Lord Clark does, however, exempt the occasional artist and even the odd poet from this censure; for example he quotes Thomas Gray, writing in the middle of the eighteenth century about the Grand Chartreuse neighbourhood: "Not a precipice, not a torrent, not a cliff but is pregnant with religion and poetry." But here Gray was unusual because for the average man the unknown and the unapproachable always suggested the haunt of demons and bad spirits and this bred that strange fear of the mountains which seemed natural little more than a hundred years ago. Even in earlier Victorian times strangers heading for the beauties of Wales kept to the broader valleys with their rivers and lakes; they avoided the remote and more sinister regions of the brooding mountains and for them there was little desire to climb the summits — that was a later enthralment. It gives some idea as to how some pre-Victorians looked at mountains generally and at Snowdonia in particular to see the descriptions given by the Rev. William Gilpin who toured

North Wales in about 1773. He had his own definite rules about scenery and Snowdon did not fit them at all. Of this mountain he says: "With regard to Snowdon, I fear, not much can be said, as it nowhere appears connected enough as one whole to form a grand object; so neither has it any of those accompaniments which form a beautiful one. It is a bleak dreary waste, without any pleasing combination of parts, or any rich furniture, either of wood or well-constructed rock." He admits that he never went up the mountain, or he might have found that the rock was not too badly constructed after all. But evidently he was a man of very advanced views and he might have fitted better with modern art and modern sculpture.

Among the hills and mountains of Wales it has always been the Snowdon area which has attracted the visitors and also many of the writers and talkers. Certainly it has always been the Snowdon massif which has been of great importance to the Welsh people. It is a traditional hub of their universe, maybe largely because it was to such mountain fastnesses that the outstanding leaders such as Owain Glyndwr often retreated when the misfortune of defeat overtook them; and it was from there that, with the guerilla fighter's knowledge of his own difficult terrain they later re-established themselves and advanced when the time was ripe. Knowing every path and precipice, they could hold the field until the invader found the weather and the difficulties of the mountain country too much for him and went away, probably to deal with the dissentients of his own country. Hence the integrity of the highest mountains meant much to the Welshman, and only when the Sassenach started to come in peace and not in war was it permissible to instruct him in mountain worship.

It is quite interesting to read the *Remarks upon North Wales* published in 1803 by W. Hutton of Birmingham: in his preface he starts by saying 'In former ages, the English rarely entered Wales but to destroy it. Her sovereign mountains, beautiful valleys, and surprising cascades, instead of being admired, were tinged with blood. Nor was the eye of the curious fascinated with her wonders till within the last fifty years. The improvement of her roads, and particularly the daily communications between England and Ireland, brought her into notice. The English traveller, at length, ventures to cling to her precipices, descend her glens, admire her curiosities, and now the vast influx of annual visitants enriches her with their wealth. If the fathers oppressed her, their children support her'.

It has been said that the name Snowdon was given to it by the English, who so christened it because it could so often be seen with its snowy cap; in particular the sailors going down the coast of Wales were able to see its snowy crown when some distance out to sea. If this is right then it must have been named towards the end of the last ice-age, for the summit is, in most years, really snow-clad for only brief periods during the winter months, and would hardly qualify for the name. Its ancient British name, still popular with the local folk is Eryri. According to some this name came from Creigiau'r Eryri, meaning the Eagle Rocks, but Thomas Pennant derives it from Creigie'r Eryri, meaning the Snowy Mountain. Most Welsh authorities like to think it comes from the word eyrie or the breeding place of the eagles and for the many writers who described it in previous centuries this was the popular name.

Inigo Jones, who some of the Welsh call Ynyr Jones (claiming that he hailed from Wales although he had the misfortune to be born in London), when painting the scenery for some of the masques in 1619 selected a Snowdon scene which was called Creigie'r Eira or the Snowy Mountains.

To add still more to the confusion, in the mind of the poor Englishman, the very peak of Snowdon is called Yr Wyddfa, and it is marked thus in the Ordnance map and to this is added the height of 3560 feet which no doubt has already been changed to metres. Again the experts in their usual way will each give a slightly different interpretation to this name, but it appears to indicate some form of tumulus or cairn, and the most knowledgeable say that the God of the Mountain has his burial place right on the very top, which is to say immediately under site of the hotel which the vandals of the nineteenth century build; its great weight should guarantee that there is little risk of the ghost of the great God of Snowdon roaming the country around.

The history of the Inn at Pen y Gwryd is so closely entwined with that of the mountains and valleys which encircle it, and these have been so often described by so many writers that it is interesting, and indeed almost essential to start by including some extracts from these writings. If this book does nothing else but encourage readers to go back and study some of these fascinating works again, it will still have served a useful purpose.

Our old friend Giraldus Cambrensis writes mainly about Wales and tells us much about the region now called Snowdonia; he seems to be the only writer to have observed the beavers which in those days were to be found in several places in the Welsh kingdom; they were present, he says, in the Teivy, in some lakes in Montgomeryshire, and in a pool in the Conway not far from Betws-y-Coed. In his view the name Nant Ffrancon means the Vale of the Beavers, and in this idea he was strongly supported in after years by Thomas Pennant; but many experts think that the whole idea of beavers another old myth, and some students of the Welsh language laugh to scorn the suggestion that the name for a beaver, which was 'afangc', could have become Ffrancon. Undoubtedly there are other observations made by Giraldus which make one ponder: the idea that Bardsey Island, named Enlli in early Welsh, at one time housed twenty thousand saints, all of whom are now provided with graves in this Insula Sanctorum seems maybe a slight exaggeration even when talking about such saintly people as the Welsh.

Perhaps even the greatest worshipper of Snowdon may find it difficult to believe what Giraldus calls the vulgar tradition according to which 'These mountains are frequented by an eagle who, perched on a fatal stone every fifth holiday, in order to satiate her hunger with the carcasses of the slain, is said to expect war on that same day, and to have almost perforated the stone by cleaning and sharpening her beak'. Those were the days of unending warfare and perhaps the eagle has found that the death rate from mountain accidents does not supply as many meals as the battles of the past: it may be that she (for this blood-sucking beast always seems to have been a female) has emigrated to lands across the sea looking for a more profitable perch; or perhaps the greatly increased tourist population now found on the summit of Snowdon has driven her away, but in any case the eagle is now replaced by the ever-present seagull looking for the picnic party's scraps.

Giraldus cast his net as widely as did Borrow in later centuries; a strenuous churchman who spent a good part of his life trying to persuade the King and the Archbishop of Canterbury to appoint him Bishop of St David's, he noticed carefully what happened in other ecclesiastical establishments and he tells us 'We have miracles galore. The staff of St Curig is a certain cure for glandular swellings upon the devout application and the oblation of one penny. And the Saint would not take less. A thrifty patient, who invested to the extent of one halfpenny, found himself still with half the swelling. Another who was cured on credit did not meet his engagements on settling day; he had his swelling back until he gave the Saint an apology and a fine of threepence'.

Giraldus has two other most strange observations which still give rise to a good deal of discussion and controversy; for he says 'On the highest parts of these mountains are two lakes worthy of admiration. The one has a floating island which is often driven from one side to the other by the force of the winds; the shepherds beholding with astonishment their cattle, while feeding, carried to distant parts of the lake . . . . The other lake is noted for a wonderful and singular miracle. It contains three sorts of fish — eels, trout and perch, all of which have only one eye the left being wanting'. No doubt this lack of stereoscopic vision has made it impossible for these fish to escape the wiles of the very experienced fishermen found hereabouts, and the survival of the fittest having played its full part and these fish are now extinct! Certainly no modern fisherman confesses to having seen one, let alone caught one.

Despite the gales of hurricane force which frequently beset Snowdon it is difficult to believe that even these winds could have moved islands about the lake; but these lakes can produce some surprisingly strong and solid-looking reed beds, which would undoubtedly support sheep and might support small cattle, and these do get blown across the lake in a severe wind; anyone who perseveres with this book as far as the chapter on Arthur Lockwood, will find some interesting supporting comments by him on the formation of islands of sphagnum moss which appeared in the newly formed Pen y Gwryd lake.

That exceptional man Thomas Pennant comments on these islands of Giraldus and he too reached the same conclusion as Lockwood saying that they were due to 'turvery' which had broken away from the bank.

Of course, Pennant included an ascent of Snowdon on his journeys; after a night's rest at Llanberis, staying at the home of Mr Close, the agent for the local mines, he and his friends set out under the guidance of Hugh Shone, who was considered to be 'an able conductor' and who must be one of the earliest of the guides. As usual at that time, they walked along a path which approximately followed the route later taken by the mountain railway, but they veered away from it going up Bwlch y Cwm Brwynog; this was a place at which those who rode often left their horses for the path soon became very rough and steep. Quite soon they noticed on their right Llyn Goch, the banks of which the fairies used for their revels; and then Pennant nearly lost one of his friends who, wanting a better view of Ffynnon Las, which he calls the Green Well, the friend poised himself on an overhanging rock and was rescued only with difficulty.

However they reached the summit of Y Wyddfa; a name which he interprets as 'The Conspicuous' although many at that time thought it came from the word Gwydd or a wood. On one previous visit he had started out at night leaving about midnight in order to get the best of the view and in this he was well rewarded for 'The night was remarkable, fine and starry; towards morn the stars faded away, and left a short interval of darkness, which was soon dispersed by the dawn of day. The body of the sun appeared most distinct, with the rotundity of the moon, before it rose high enough to render its beam too brilliant for our sight. The sea which bounded the western part was gilt by its rays, first in slender streaks, at length glowing with redness. The prospect was disclosed like the gradual drawing up of a curtain in the theatre.'

He was very exalted with this view and thought it well worth the effort of early rising, but on his day-time journey it was disappointingly misty, and here many climbers will sympathize with him. The way down was not too good, particularly as soon after mounting their horses they suffered from a severe thunderstorm; the over-full rivers worried both them and their horses but they gained the bottom 'with great hazard.'

On one of his trips Pennant, going round Cwm Dyli and struggling up to Llyn Llydaw finally found his way Gorphwysfa or what he called 'The Resting Place.'

Pennant provides many fascinating tit-bits of history which he gleaned on his travels, being rather surprised at the accounts of were-gild in Wales – the fines which the Welshman could pay in order to escape punishment were often very small. It was possible for the sinner to escape further punishment for killing someone on payment of ten guineas, although, of course, this was a large amount which only the wealthy of those days could afford. Similarly the compensation received by sufferers seemed rather poor: a man who lost a finger received one cow and twenty pence, while the loss of a nose would allow the loser as much as six oxen and one hundred and twenty pence. But Pennant was most surprised, and pained by one particular reparation. 'Recompence to a virgin who had been seduced is very singular; on complaint made that she was deserted by her lover, it was ordered by the court, that she lay hold of the tail of a bull three years old, introduced through a wicker door, shaven and well greased. Two men were to goad the beast: if she could by dint of strength retain the bull, she was to have it by way of satisfaction; if not, she got nothing but the grease that remained on her hands. I fear by this, and other penalties for the same offence, that the crime was not held by my countrymen to be of very deep dye'.

The only Englishman who seems to have attempted Snowdon at about the same time as Pennant was W. Hutton, and he gives us a full description of his effort, saying that after he had picked up a guide, he, my servant and I immediately began to ascend. The sun was not hid one moment during the whole day. I asked, "What distance to the top?"

"Nearly four miles . . . ." I ascended about a mile, rather boggy but easy to rise . . . . A prodigious chasm in the mountain was on the right all the way, and the summit in view, which seemed at so small a distance, that a man might almost reach it with the cast of a stone. At the bottom of the chasm were three pools of considerable magnitude. The whole of this road is rough, walking required that attention to the feet which prevented me from viewing an object without standing still . . . The blood was in a ferment, a sickness and giddiness ensued. Travelling a little more than a mile in this fourth or last division I came upon a Green Well. Here we opened our provisions and tapped our brandy'. However this and a rest in the shade got him going again and despite the rough and rugged path they reached the top where 'A man may fairly say he is got above the world'. The journey took Hutton three hours going up and three hours going down and he thought it the severest labour of his whole life: but if he made rather heavy weather of it it should be remembered that he was seventy-six years old when he climbed the peak, and so perhaps he should be excused.

But some of the best descriptions of Snowdonia come from George Borrow, that walker and talker extraordinary, in his well-known *Wild Wales* published in 1862. Although he was usually a sensible man he was not wise enough to start his tour from the Pen y Gwryd Inn, nor did he visit it at any time, but he approached the climb of Snowdon from Bangor. While there he found some very enthusiastic words to say about Beaumaris Bay which he thought more attractive than the Bay of Naples and few Welshmen would disagree with him there. He set out for the mountains accompanied by his wife for a short distance, but his daughter Henrietta went all the way with him and his account of the journey goes as follows: 'On the third morning after our arrival at Bangor we set out for Snowdon; Snowdon or Eryri is no single hill but a mountainous region, the loftiest part of which called Wyddfa nearly four thousand feet above the level of the sea is generally considered to be the highest point in southern Britain'. As can be seen in his estimate of height Borrow was not averse to a slight exaggeration of his achievement. When he had given the accepted reasons for the name of the mountain, he puts a footnote in the book pointing out that in addition to meaning 'eagles' the word Eryri also signifies an excrescence or a scrofulous eruption, and that some maintain that this meaning of a rugged excrescence or eruption on the surface of the earth is the one that should be accepted here; an idea that would not meet with general local acceptance. But what would be very well accepted would be his later declamation 'Snowdon is interesting on various accounts. It is interesting for its picturesque beauty; perhaps in the whole world there is no region more picturesquely beautiful than Snowdon, a region of mountains, lakes, cataracts and groves, in which Nature shows herself in her most grand and beautiful form'.

Borrow continues with a series of historical and pseudo-historical fact about Snowdonia. He tells of how Vortigern fled to the mountain to consult with Merlin when he was accused by his subjects of being too kind to the horrible Saxons; and he tells of Llywelyn ap Gruffith's last stand for Cambrian independence on the very summit of Y Wyddfa; and of how Owain Glyndwr retreated there in face of an attack by Henry IV, and of how from this summit he staged a come-back and drove the invader back with flights of best Welsh arrows. Owain Glyndwr is, of course Shakespeare's Owen Glendower who could 'Call spirits from the vasty deep' to be met with Hotspur's famous reply 'Why, so can I, and so can any man, but will they come when you do call for them'. The kind of spirited reply not perhaps used often enough in answer to our politicians' vapourings. In fact, Owain Glyndwr was a Welsh chief, who claimed descent from Llewelyn the Great, the last of the original, and in his view, the true Prince of Wales. He was born in Montgomeryshire in 1359 and although he combined with Hotspur and some other well-known but unruly characters, he was defeated in the battle of Shrewsbury in 1403, by Henry IV. Never happy unless fighting, he obtained some help from Charles VI of France and kept up a steady, but not very successful, guerilla campaign until his death in 1416.

It was customary in the middle of the last century to have a guide when trying to climb Snowdon, and Borrow engaged a young lad from Llanberis Inn. Then he set out arm in arm with Henrietta for the mountain path singing at the top of his voice the celebrated Welsh stanza:

> Easy to say, behold Eryri,
> But difficult to reach its head;
> Easy to him whose hopes are cheery,
> To bid the wretch be comforted.

Unless the tune is very much better than the words it may be as well that this song is no longer heard on the footpaths leading up Snowdon! When people started looking for the troublesome ways of getting to the top of Snowdon, this following poem gives a better picture, although not many would take quite such a gloomy view. It comes from a Pen y Gwryd Visitors' Book and it was written in 1889 by M.G. Watkins, M.A. while staying at the hotel.

THE THRONE OF SNOWDON
I sit like a Queen

Throned high on mighty desolation, crowned
With mist of stars, we wander by thy base,
Or lay presumptuous hands upon thy face;
And thou remaineth sternly-silent, drowned
In cloud — mysterious vastness; not a sound
But in articulate world-sighs can we trace
Or some deep-hidden brooklet's measured face;
As glad to linger on they charmed ground.
Thine is a treach'rous splendour, one false grip
Of cruel rock where all is beautiful
Upon the shining bents a sudden slip —
The venturous climber o'er the rock shelves flies,
And a poor corpse looks up to saddened skies,
While still thou reignest, grand, implacable.

Borrow is not very explicit about the route he followed, but it was almost certainly the usual one; very rough tracks were not appreciated in those days, for they were taken by walkers and not scramblers. Much of the first part of the path was that now occupied by the railway, and it was very common, particularly for the ladies, to journey the first half or two thirds of the way on the back of a pony, but the Borrows seem to have walked all the way. His next remark is an interesting one for he says 'We were far from being the only visitors on the hill this day; groups of people or single individuals might be seen going up or descending the path as far as the eye could reach'. It is difficult to think of Snowdon as a tourist attraction way back in 1850, but all the writers emphasize the large number of folk who climbed it, at least in the summer. The Borrows found the last part of the ascent very hard going, but they both arrived at the top in good order; looking round him Borrow said 'The Wyddfa is about thirty feet in diameter and is surrounded on three sides by a low wall; in the middle is a rude cabin, in which refreshments are sold, and in which a person resides throughout the year, although there are few or no visitors to the hill top except during the summer. Below on all sides are frightful precipices except on the side of the west. Towards the east it looks perpendicularly into a diffryn or vale, nearly a mile below, from which to the gazer is at all times an object of admiration, of wonder, and almost of fear'.

The Borrows were lucky in getting an excellent view from the top seeing, they thought, Anglesey, Cumberland and with the eye of faith the hills of Ireland. Then George running true to form and as always unable to keep silent recited to Henrietta a poem by Goronwy Owen concerning the Day of Judgement: 'The brow of Snowdon shall be levelled to the ground, and the eddying waters shall murmur round it'. If Goronwy Owen had experienced the ravages of the modern Horseshoe scramblers and the mountain railway addicts of today he would know that it might not be necessary to wait for the end of the world to see the final flattening of the summit of Snowdon!

Father and daughter returned to Llanberis fairly fresh having completed the ascent and descent in about four hours; not a bad time for the inexperienced, but of course, George Borrow was a superb walker and no doubt his daughter had been well-trained in her youth. With his unequalled experience of staying at inns and hotels, it is a pity he did not leave to posterity his thoughts on Pen y Gwryd.

However, a writer of the same period who did know Pen y Gwryd and who fell in love with it was Charles Kingsley; he has given a dramatic description of the Inn and of the surrounding countryside, in which he makes Wales appear a good deal more wild than it does in *Wild Wales*. Kingsley became a constant visitor to the Inn and he left his mark on the Visitors' Books as will be seen later. In 1857 he published a novel called *Two Years Ago*, one chapter of which most suitably entitled 'Nature's Melodrama' gives a dramatic account of the behaviour of a very psychopathic character named Elsley Vavasour. It would be hard to find a better opening for a book on Pen y Gwryd than to show it as Charles Kingsley saw it and his description is worth quoting in full for although somewhat lengthy, it gives a good idea of how it appeared to most visitors and as an accomplished writer he can do it full justice. This is Kingsley's view: 'What has become of Elsley? And whence had he written the fatal letter? He had hurried up the high road, for half an hour or more, till the valley on his left sloped upwards more rapidly, in dark dreary bogs, the moon-light shining on their runnels; while the mountain on his right sloped downwards more rapidly in dark dreary down, strewn with rocks which stood out black against the sky. He was nearing the head of the watershed; soon he saw slate roofs glittering in the moon-light, and found himself at the 'Little Inn' of Pen y Gwryd, at the meeting of three great valleys, the central heart of the Mountains . . . and a genial, jovial little heart it is, and an honest kindly little heart too, with warm life blood within. So it looked that night, with every window red with comfortable light, and a long stream of glare pouring across the road from the open door, gilding the fir tree tops in front: but its geniality only made him shudder. He had been there more than once and knew the place and the people; and knew too that of all the people in the world they were the least like him. He hurried through the doorway, and caught one glimpse of the bright kitchen. A sudden thought struck him. He would go in and write a letter there. But not yet — he could not go in yet: for through the open door came some sweet Welsh air, so sweet that he paused to listen. Men were singing in three parts, in that rich, metallic temper of voice, that perfect time and tune, which is the one gift left to the strange Cymry race, worn out with the long burden of so many years . . he breathed more freely when the sound vanished: he strode hastily in, and down the little passage to the kitchen.

'It was a low room, ceiled with dark beams, from which hung bacon and fishing rod, harness and drying stockings, and all the miscellanea of a fishing inn kept by a farmer; beneath it the usual happy, hearty, honest group. There was Harry Owen, bland and stalwart, his baby in his arms, smiling upon the world in general; old Mrs Pritchard bending over the fire, putting the last touch to one of those miraculous soufflets, compact of clouds and nectar, which transport alike palate and fancy at the first mouthful from Snowdon to Belgrave Square'.

There is much more but too long for quotation: but poor psychopathic Elsley Vavasour then wrote a quick letter, quaffed a quick brandy and water, and rushed into the night, followed rapidly by a couple of Englishmen who were not unnaturally convinced that he was bent on suicide in Cwm Ffynon. There follow several pages of lurid description of his rush up the mountainside towards the little lake, and a sensational account of an unbalanced mind's assessment of a terrific thunderstorm, obviously meant by the Almighty solely for Elsley's destruction, and accompanied by torrents of rain such as had not been seen since Noah's flood. This exaggerated picture of these cataclysms of Nature, which even to the sane mind might herald the Last Trump, produces a horrifying vision such as no man has yet seen even in the worst Welsh weather and with the most fertile imagination. No matter how attractive his picture of Pen y Gwryd may be, no one would be likely to visit it after having read his description of the events outside: and it seems unlikely that many Welshmen would agree that good part singing was the only talent or virtue left to the worn out Welshmen!

Unless one assumes that Elsley Vavasour walked to the Inn backwards, it is not easy to follow Kingsley's account of the way up, but it is correct that Pen y Gwryd stands at the parting of the ways for here the main road from Betws-y-Coed divides into two branches, the southern branch leading to Criccieth, Portmadoc and the other coastal towns, while the right hand branch continues by the Llanberis Pass through the Snowdon range to end finally at Caernarfon.

It seems that Charles Kingsley was not the only one to find the Glyders usually dreary and often terrifying, for in 1883 Richard Harris wrote a poem about the Glyders and inscribed it in the Visitors' Book, and no doubt Kingsley would have agreed with every word of it. It runs thus:

There's not a sound of beast or bird,
  No worldly thoughts intrude;
And all around is wild and weird,
  Majestic solitude.

Here rocks on rocks amid the gloom,
In boiled confusion hurled;
Like monumental piles entomb,
A devasted world.

Here scornful ruin holds his sway,
Nor ever rival saw;
And here shall reign till all obey,
His universal law.

With might unchallenged and supreme,
Beyond all earthly kings;
He'll reign when man has ceased to dream,
Of perishable things.

What mad destruction here has riven,
His temples from their base;
As though the eternal rage of heaven,
Concentrated on the place.

All is seen a sated wrath,
Above, around below;
As though the fiat had gone forth,
Unutterable woe.

This is only a half portion, but the whole poem is given in the Appendix.

Pen y Gwryd, pronounced as Kingsley told his wife, *Pennygourid*, derives its name from the place at which it stands, for it is at the head of the Gwryd river. Every philologist will give a different meaning to the word Gwryd. It certainly means a man's length, and as this was the scene of many battles over the ages some consider it merely indicates the six feet of earth which our English King Harold thought the right gift for any foreign invader. Gwryd also means a chain, and a more pleasant interpretation is that when seen from the top of the Glyder mountains, the Gwryd river runs through the valley like a silver chain. For others again the name indicates a ford, and when joined with the word Pen shows that this spot was the head of a series of fords across the river. The lake in front of the hotel is an artificial one, and before the damming of the river several fords were available there. Still another supposition is that this word is a North Wales corruption of the word Gwaered, which means downhill or steep declivity, and shows that this was the start of the steep declivity; if this is correct there must indeed be few places in Wales which could not qualify for this title. So the choice of the meaning lies with the reader. Pen y Gwryd it has been for many years; and it is to be hoped that Pen y Gwyrd it will remain for many more.

During their occupation of Britain the Romans had a marching camp on the site of Pen y Gwryd, at a height of about nine hundred feet above sea level. This camp covered about nine and a half acres of land and was a rhomboidal structure of about 240 yards long and about two hundred yards wide; it was surrounded by a turf-covered stony bank of three feet high by fourteen feet wide, but these ramparts have been greatly damaged by modern disturbance. There are several sections of the original wall still visible but the construction of a pool behind the hotel has caused parts of it to be submerged in a marshy quagmire. The diagram (page 35) shows where the camp was sited and indicates just how completely it controlled the roads from the military point of view. This camp may have been of some use to the Welsh after the Romans had departed from the land, when they suffered from another invasion. It is reputed that the Irish landed at Tremadoc, followed the lovely Glaslyn valley and settled at Cwm Dyli where, it is said, relics of their houses can still be seen between the road and the Power Station. They stayed there feuding for a long time until one year after an Eisteddfod held at Dolwyddelen an inspired group of Welsh citizens attacked them and they were slaughtered to a man. This happened just below where 'Pen y Gwryd Hotel' now stands, at Bwlch-y-Gwyddel the Irishmen's Pass.

In Roman times, of course, the direct route from Londinium to Anglesea was along Watling Street, now the A5 road, but at Capel Curig there was a branch road leading to Beddgelert and further on to the ports and fortresses lying further south. The diagram shows no lake on the east side of the road from Capel Curig to Beddgelert as that did not exist until the beginning of this century, when it was made artificially. The road via Llanberis to Caernarfon, branching off right at Pen y Gwryd was not a road for chariots in Roman times; it was a well-marked but rough track along which the Legions could tramp without difficulty. This remained little more than a pack-horse track until the early part of the nineteenth century and went behind the present hotel site, and is shown on the diagram as a dotted line.

There seems to be some difference of opinion about the Llanberis road. It undoubtedly was a full coaching road by 1845, but before that the Rev Bingley states that coaches from Caernarfon had no road beyond the bottom lake at Llanberis. Also the Rev Mr Evans comments that Llanberis and Capel Curig are joined only by a terrible horse path, narrow through the Pass and ascending over the craggy rocks behind Gorffwysfa (now the 'Pen y Pass Hotel'). But at the same time John Cliffe in his delightful book on angling in North Wales states that there was an excellent posting road made through to Caernarfon in 1818, and that Dolbadarn Castle and the Hotel Victoria on the shore of Llyn Peris were built there about the same time because the road was so much improved. Undoubtedly in 1832 the Duchess of Kent with her daughter Alexandrina, later better known as Queen Victoria, paid a visit to Llanberis from Caernarfon, and they certainly went some way up the Pass as they remarked that they were most impressed with the view. The probable answer to these differing opinions is that the roads varied from place to place and from year to year; some sections nearly always in good repair, and this might well include the stretch from Caernarfon to Nantperis, but it is very likely that the less frequented section over the pass may have been poorly preserved and often little better than a track troublesome for a wheeled vehicle but quite adequate for a pack-horse. In the early part of the nineteenth century comparatively few roads were good, and opinions about road surfaces depended very much on the toughness of the travelling individual and the springing of the vehicle; coach travel must usually have been very uncomfortable.

The coach road from Betws-y-Coed through the Nant

Ffrancon Pass was constructed about 1795, and when it was complete Lord Penrhyn built the 'Royal Hotel' at Capel Curig; the 'Goat Hotel' at Beddgelert was built in 1802. Even then these roads were terrible and for a long time the 'Ancient Briton' which was the only coach venturing on them had frequently to spend the night at the Pen y Gwryd Inn on the way through from Beddgelert to Holyhead. It took sometimes up to fourteen hours to travel from Pen y Gwryd to Holyhead. Before these roads were made there were pack-horse tracks of about six feet wide, paved only when the ground was particularly boggy. It is still possible to trace some of these tracks.

A considerable amount of the land round about the present site of the 'Pen y Gwryd Hotel' is owned by Sir Richard Bulkeley of Baron Hill, Anglesea. From early medieval times Lord Bulkeley of Anglesea was one of the landowners of considerable areas in North Wales. It was a Lord Bulkeley who tried, without success, to hold Beaumaris Castle for King Charles I during the Civil War and despite his failure he was given the Constableship after the Restoration, and the family has retained large tracts of land in Snowdonia ever since.

In his fascinating book *Bedd Gelert; Its Facts, Fairies and Folklore* D.E. Jenkins says that a cottage was built on the Pen y Gwryd site by John Roberts of Pen y Bryn somewhere about 1810 or 1811. Roberts was either a tenant farmer or a farm agent, and his cottage was also the farmhouse. He did not own the land on which it was built, that was Bulkeley territory, and although Roberts did the building, the money for it probably came from the landlord.

As shown by the double dotted lines on the diagram, the original road or track went behind the place where the hotel now stands, and not on the line of the present road. It went close to a quarry, which was started in 1810 and which was named the Great Snowdon Hone Stone Quarry because from there stones for honing razors and other steel instruments were quarried and cut, and these were sold to barbers all over the world. But even in the days of Queen Victoria imports sometimes ousted home trade and first an Italian stone and later synthetic carborundum stones took the market away from North Wales and the quarry closed down.

It has been suggested that the first cottage was built on the foundations, some of which are still just visible, of the water-wheel and the buildings of the quarry, but this seems unlikely as both places were built at much the same time. Arthur Lockwood, who did a lot of work about the hotel and fully investigated this part of the land, remained convinced that the first cottage was built on almost precisely the same site as the present hotel, and the latter may have used some of the same foundations, although some of the stones from the original cottage may well have been incorporated in the hotel building.

In any case, the cottage farmhouse stood at the parting of the way and so in a convenient position on the long road from Betws-y-Coed to Beddgelert, or to Caernarfon: so although it was primarily a dwelling house for himself, John Roberts must commonly have found riders and walkers who, feeling hungry and thirsty while passing his door, turned into it and looked for refreshments. With the generous hospitality of the times he would find them good, if rough food, washed down by a mug of ale; and in most cases he would get paid for his pains. How long he managed to escape the Licensing Law of 1750, which made a licence compulsory for anyone selling beer or spirits is a matter of guesswork. In that remote place where the arm of the law would barely reach, no doubt all his visitors were friends and not clients! Then some of those calling in would be poor, benighted wanderers anxious for a night's lodging, and he would provide that also. As trade improved the extra income became useful, and, in due course, he evidently succeeded in obtaining a licence from the magistrates thus making his sale of liquor legal.

John Roberts married a local girl whose surname was Close, but there is no mention of her Christian name. Unfortunately for her, she is best known by reason of a tragedy which befell her family. She had a small brother John, aged seven years, who was left staying with his uncle at Betws-y-Coed while his mother went to stay for a short time in Llanberis. Much distressed, the poor boy set off on a lone trip to try and reach her, and on his way across the moors he got lost in a snowstorm. The saddest part of the story is that his cries for help were heard by a passing shepherd, but the shepherd's fear that the sounds were the wailings of a gnome or a wicked fairy prevented his investigating and he fled away in terror. The boy's body was not found until a week later.

John Roberts kept the 'Farmhouse Inn' for about twenty-five years altogether. Even for those days it could not be described as a luxury hotel. G.J. Bennett writing about his tour in Wales describes it at some length as 'A small public house with a sign signifying nothing . . . it possesses a small parlour carpeted, with half-a-dozen hair-bottomed chairs and a mahogany table.' His view is somewhat biased, as he was rather unlucky. After a snack meal, with maybe a measure of ale, he 'ascended by a ladder-like staircase to a kind of cockloft which was divided into two compartments, one for the family, man, wife, children and servants: the other fitted up for travellers. Sleep soon overtook me and I should have continued to sleep no doubt, until breakfast time, had I not been awakened by a trifling accident. "At the mid-hour of the night when stars were weeping and the ghosts of the mighty walk upon the hills" with a variety of interesting objects which poets and nursery maids have described better than I can pretend to do, I was visited by a dream in which the ghost of a lobster popped its head out of a salad bowl, and demanded by what authority I had presumed to make mincemeat of its body, when a loud crash roused me from my slumbers, and I found myself with my knees doubled up to my chin upon the floor, the bedstead having broken in the middle, and deposited me in this unenviable position. I need not say that for the remaining part of the night I was wholly left to waking reveries, and uncontrollable desires for the blessings of daylight, which at last greeted my longing eyes, and hurrying on my clothes I descended and walked forth to scent the morning air in the direction of Llanberis.'

At least the modern traveller staying at Pen y Gwryd can rest assured that he will not be expected to share a room with the proprietor and his wife and family, although with the lavish food followed by the hospitality of the Smoke Room with its famous cheese and onion sandwiches, perhaps it cannot be guaranteed that he will get no visits from a nightmare lobster!

History has it that once, when John Roberts was digging the field round his cottage, he turned up a large collection of old coins. By some they are reputed to have been Roman coins, and by others to date to the reign of Queen Anne. But it is reputed to have been a valuable collection, and that the money he received from the sale of it enabled him to fulfil a life long ambition and emigrate to the United States of America. There he continued his farming in California and he christened his new American house with the same name as that of the house he had left in Wales. What is more, his descendants still live in the same house, and in 1922, some of them paid a visit to the Pen y Gwryd Hotel to see for themselves where the Roberts hailed from.

On leaving, Roberts transferred the lease of the farmhouse to Mrs Hughes who was already the owner of the 'Royal Hotel' at Capel Curig, and she almost at once put in Benjamin Williams as manager, which suggests that Pen y Gwryd had started to get a useful trade as an inn to make it worth while. The legal documents for this sale are still available for inspection at Pen y Gwryd but the full understanding of them would require an expert. In addition to the customarily confusing old fashioned legal jargon, they are made still more perplexing by reason of a plethora of Welsh names; so that Roberts, Hughes, Owen and Williams are scattered broadcast throughout the documents and it requires an expert genealogist to sort them out properly.

One indenture is dated July 5th 1840 and it is between John Roberts of Pen y Gwryd in the Parish of Beddgelert, Caernarfon in the first part, and Sir Richard Bulkeley Williams Bulkeley, Baronet, of Baron Hill, Caernarfon, in the second part, and Elizabeth Hughes of Henar, Llanrwst, Denbigh, widow in the third part. In this indenture it is noted that John Roberts was at this time 45 years of age, while his sons, Robert Roberts, and Humphrey Roberts were 17 and 15 years old respectively. Under a previous lease the boys would have had the property for twenty-one years following the death of their father, at a rent of 15/- per annum and 'certain comforts'. Whether the 'comforts' were vegetables from the farm or beer from the bar is not stated. This indenture also covers the sale of another small plot of the Bulkeley land immediately surrounding the inn; this land went to Mrs Hughes, and she kept her interest in the property for some time; for when Harry Owen took over the lease in 1847 he was still a sub-tenant, and it was not until 1858 that, with the full permission of Sir Richard Bulkeley, he made the first purchase of part of the freehold. By reason of some complicated mortgage arrangements, Owen's purchase of the property continued as a strange series of bits and pieces for some years; in 1858 for the payment to Mrs Hughes of £250, he retained the lease for a period of three lives and twenty one concurrent years. Then in 1873 Harry Owen borrowed £326 from Ellis Griffiths of Gerlan, Bethesda, and from Jones of 5, Pen y Bryn, Bethesda; and in 1878 he borrowed a further £600 from the North Wales Benefit Building Society. As these documents are still with the various leases of the property it can probably be assumed that this money was paid to Mrs Hughes in part payment for the hotel. He did not get the full freehold of the inn and the land belonging to it until 1873, when he had already run the establishment very successfully for nearly thirty years.

It seems impossible to find any record of the happenings at the inn during the seven years that it was under the management of Mrs Hughes; as she was the owner of the larger and at that time, more important hotel at Capel Curig, she probably left most of the problems to the manager in charge at Pen y Gwryd. It must be presumed that from her point of view it was not particularly profitable as she kept it for only seven years, and Henry Owen took over in 1847. He soon married and took his wife there.

To Harry Owen and Ann his wife, and to Mrs Pritchard his mother-in-law, belongs a main part of the credit of starting off the 'Pen y Gwryd Hotel' on the path it has followed ever since: the path which has made it a climbers' hotel, a mountaineers' hotel, a fishermen's hotel and a walkers' hotel of originality and prominence in this county; hence the Owens deserve a large place in this book. One of the happiest of the many tributes which has been paid them is that of John Henry Cliffe when he wrote: 'Barren, solitary, dignified Nature in her ruder aspects is aptly portrayed in the desolate Nant y Gwryd. In the midst of this solitudinous region formerly stood a wretched roadside alehouse, known as the 'Pen y Gwryd Inn' . . . In the course of time this humble roadside pothouse becomes transformed into a very comfortable Inn; here not only the wayfarer meets with civility and attention, but even in the culinary department he will have no cause to complain. The enterprise of the landlord Henry Owen has in great measure accomplished this desirable result, and in a few years more we confidently predict that 'Pen y Gwryd Inn' will occupy a still more important position among the hotels of Snowdonia'.

This was indeed an accurate prophesy, and we can now go forward to recount the rise to fame of this Inn and its early establishment as a centre for the climbers of that era.

ROMAN MARCHING CAMP

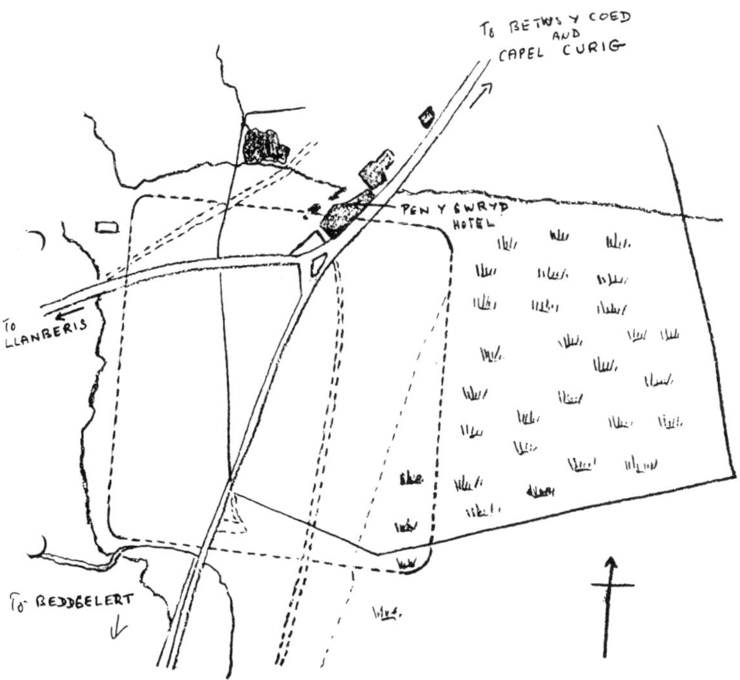

The area marked by the dotted line shows the extent of the Roman Camp, and a number of sections of this wall can still be traced. The lake beside the road, being a man made one, did not exist when the camp was first built.

CHAPTER 2

THE REIGN OF THE OWENS

Thou most beauteous Inn,
Why should hard-favour'd grief be lodged in thee,
When triumph is become an alehouse guest.
Richard II Act V. Sc. 1, 1 13.

Henry Owen was born at Castell Farm, a remote and isolated house lying between Llyn Dinas and Nantmor. At that time, in remote country districts, unless a boy wanted to become a miner or to work in a quarry or was willing to leave home there was little he could do but farming, and so at a young age Harry got a job helping the agent in running Sir Richard Bulkeley's estate. The part of the land in which he was working consisted of four sections each with its farmhouse just big enough for a family. They all lay in Cwm Dyli, which then had no power station with the unsightly twin water pipes feeding it, but in their place pleasant streams carried the water from Llyn Llydaw and Llyn Teyrn down to the Afon Glaslyn. The largest of the farmhouses was 'Gwastad Annas' sited just off the road from Pen y Gwryd to Nantgwynant. Close by was another house called after the valley Cwm Dyli, but this unfortunately was gutted by fire in 1838 and the re-building took a long time. The progress was far too slow to satisfy Sion Prys the tenant's brother, who built himself his own cottage dwelling near by and named it 'Penlan'. The fourth building had been an outbuilding but was converted into a cottage called

'Geufron' or 'Gaifron'. By the end of the nineteenth century the only farmhouse left in occupation was 'Gwastad Annas' and this remained as a small cottage dwelling, housing one family.

By 1847 it seems that Mrs Hughes of Capel wanted to give up Pen y Gwryd, either because she found managing two hotels much too hard work or perhaps because Pen y Gwryd proved less profitable than she had hoped, and the tenancy of this Inn was taken by Harry Owen. His good efforts as Sir Richard Bulkeley's farm worker now bore fruit for in virtue of his help over the years Sir Richard allowed him the use of about eight acres of land adjacent to the Inn and this land still remains the property of Pen y Gwryd.

Oddly enough, this land transfer was not entirely popular with the visitors, or at least with one of them; for according to G.J. Bennett in his book it was 'with a result quite painful to observe; instead of the lively movement of living beings, the sound of the meal-time horn, the crack of the team driver's whip, the neighing, lowing and bleating of horses, cattle and sheep respectively, together with the hundred other features of farm life, we had only a few stray sheep, a cow or an ox here and there, and perchance a living being far from the reach of gesture or voice'. This extract suggests that either the transferred land had previously carried an unusually large and mixed stock, or that it might have been the assembly point where the farm hands collected their flocks and where they themselves gathered for the mid-day meal and rest.

Within a very short time of taking over the Inn, Harry Owen brought off the most important job of his life: he had the good sense to marry Ann Pritchard to whom he had been engaged for some time. This gave him at one stroke not only a charming and very competent wife, but also a mother-in-law who was equally pleasant and who was a first class cook whose meals delighted guests for many years. John Henry Cliffe, that prince of anglers, visiting Pen y Gwryd several years later particularly noted how well the viands were prepared by Mrs Pritchard 'an old dame, who, in days of yore, was a domestic in the service of Thomas Pennant, Esq. of Downing; whose fame at the close of the last century as an antiquary and topographer is so well known and appreciated'.

Ann Pritchard's early history also makes quite a fascinating study. She was already famed for her good looks when she was working as a maid at the large mansion called 'Plas Gwynant', standing about three quarters of a mile from Llyn Dinas. Tradition has it that this house was given by Llewelyn the Great to the Abbot of Conway for some service rendered, but that the Abbot was deprived of it at the time of the dissolution of the monasteries. It then passed into the hands of the Wynne of Gwydir family who were then the Watkins Williams Wynn. At the beginning of the nineteenth century it became the property of one Mr Coventry, and he chose Ann, first as a housemaid, and then later as Lady's maid to his daughter. This seemed an excellent choice as she was a well-trained and intelligent girl, but later he may have regretted it – for Miss Coventry fell in love with a local lad, Wil Jones, who was in the eyes of her father a man of little substance – so naturally he did not approve the match and equally naturally for those days he forbade any thought of marriage, despite his daughter's weeping requests. The unhappy couple may have biased him at the start, for anticipating trouble they had incautiously asked the curate of Beddgelert Parish Church to marry them. He not only refused to do this without the father's consent, but promptly went off and told Mr Coventry. With a degree of independence rather astonishing for that time, Wil Jones and Miss Coventry side-stepped quietly and went through a form of marriage by the registrar, a method one might have thought impossible in that era. During the whole of the love affair Ann Pritchard had played a big part in fixing clandestine meetings, and she helped a great deal in arranging the wedding – for she would do almost anything to assist her much-loved mistress to get anything she wanted. The unfortunate result was that when husband and wife returned, not only was the new Mrs Jones disinherited by the disconsolate father, but for her part of the business, Ann Pritchard was dismissed from his service. However, this was not such a misfortune as it might appear, for Ann was already engaged to Harry Owen. So he was not left in solitude at Pen y Gwryd for very long.

Despite the great labour involved in running a busy establishment such as a hotel, as was customary in Victorian days, the Owens managed to be fairly prolific, having in all ten children, two of whom died in infancy. Five sons survived named Harry, John, Owen, Griffiths and Hugh, but as they played no part at the hotel in adult life there is little record of what happened to them. But more is known about the three daughters. C.E. Mathews in his *Reminiscences* shows great enthusiasm for Catherine and Jane whom he describes as the most willing waitresses who ever tended to the wants of man. In due course, Catherine left to become Mrs Williams and Jane became Mrs Lewis, and although both survived their parents they took no further part in hotel management. The third daughter Annie, although, oddly enough, not so well complimented by Mathews, did an enormous amount of work in helping the Owens, and was a great favourite of several generations of climbers by reason of her constant help and kindness to them. She also married and it was as Mrs Roberts that she died in 1898 at the 'Bryn Tyrch Hotel' at Capel Curig. What happened to the sons of the Owens' is lost in mystery but it is reputed that some of them took over small pieces of land for farming down the Gwryd valley, and when these plots were worked out they went elsewhere. Certainly they had little or nothing to do with Pen y Gwryd in later years.

However, the Owens remained lucky. For when Annie left to marry, they had Katie Owen, the daughter of son John. She had been adopted by her grandmother when only fifteen months old, possibly because her mother died (but this is only surmise). With her long training and experience she was an extremely competent and useful helper in all branches of the work. It is some evidence of her popularity with the hotel guests that when she left to get married (one should not be surprised that she also became a Mrs Roberts) she was given a purse containing the contributions from many of the hotel guests to whom she had endeared herself over many years by her active help and her kindly ways.

Even in the early days of the Owens' ownership Harry was still doing some farming, and although a steadily developing Inn, Pen y Gwryd had something of the farmhouse about it. Betws-y-Coed and Beddgelert were fair-sized villages — each with its own coaching hotel — and Capel Curig had the 'Royal Hotel', of which, if Cliffe is to be believed, the incumbent of the local church was the landlord! The distance between the two villages was only about eighteen miles, which made it a reasonable coaching journey. But if weather conditions were bad, an intermediate stop was often desirable; and when the road to Caernarfon via the Llanberis Pass was made up the picture changes and Pen y Gwryd became an excellent stop for coaches passing the door. It was at once hailed as a useful place for meals and drinks, and although there is no record of it ever becoming a regular changing place for horses, any wayside inn might find itself called upon to provide fresh horses in times of emergency. With the changes in the roads and the steadily increasing traffic, came the slow build-up of services which the long-sighted Owen provided. As the stops tended to become longer and the Inn became better known to the passengers, so its fame spread.

Although this change was slow, it was much too fast for some who found the increasing number of visitors not at all to their liking. Theodore Watts-Dunton, a contemporary and friend of both Rossetti and Swinburne and also George Borrow, said of Pen y Gwryd 'I went to the Hotel at Pen y Gwryd, but there tourists and visitors made life more intolerable still to a man in my condition'. This comment was not made by Watts Dunton himself, but by one of his strange characters, for he was a novelist who wrote a book, now happily forgotten, called *Alywin* about a peculiar gentleman who fell desperately in love with Winifred, the Snowdon maid. She was half-human, half spirit, and apparently normally invisible to Alywin or to anyone else. It was while Alywin was chasing her round Snowdonia in a state of acute nervousness and irritability that he visited the Inn and made this comment. There is a rock which can be best seen on the way up Llanberis Pass towards Gorphwysfa and which looks very much like a human face; it is commonly called the Maid of Snowdon and it may be from this that Watts Dunton got his idea.

It seems strange that several novelists have given the impression that this hotel has been used mainly by people with marked psychopathic tendencies; whereas today, to the casual observer, most of the guests seem reasonable people — even though some spectators do think that those addicted to the hazardous and uncomfortable pastime of rock climbing demonstrate some grave mental imbalance!

Although there are a number of references to the Pen Y Gwryd in literature before the middle of the century, it was not until 1854 that the hotel acquired its first Visitors' Book. By that time Harry Owen felt that the increase in the number of visitors warranted the introduction of a book in which guests could make what comments they thought fit. The first legible note in this book is written by Eben R. Homan of Whetstone, and Arthur G. George of Southgate on July 23rd 1854 (incidentally, the 6th son of Homan was a visitor in September 1936). From then on, the entries are very varied, but almost without exception they are complimentary with regard to the accommodation and the food provided, while the Owens and Mrs Pritchard seem universally beloved by the guests.

This short extract from a poem written in praise of Mrs Pritchard does give some idea how delighted her guests were with her services: it is headed 'To Mrs Pritchard':

Say hast thou found that charmêd leaf,
That lives in fairy dells?
Which makes thee round thy pancakes cast
Such sweet enchanting spells;
For surely with some magic art
Thou must surround thy dishes,
They never tire the weary sense
But gratify the wishes.

As seems to have been the case with all those who bought this hotel, the Owens started with little or no capital; so that changes and improvements had to be made as and when money became available, and this had to come entirely from profits made by the hotel. But they started from the beginning on the right road. First on the list was the cooking, and they provided good and well-presented meals at a fair cost.

Both Ann and her mother were excellent cooks and they did not stint, so that innumerable entries in the Visitors' Book stress the excellence of the food. The Owens, of course, also knew the importance of hot water and of providing first class facilities for drying wet clothes; without which walking in North Wales would be a purgatory. In view of G.J. Bennett's unhappy experience, it is to be hoped that they looked well to the safety factor of the bedsteads. There is no doubt they gave good bedding to put on them. But the time came when they started on some much-needed major repairs, improvements and enlargements; here they were extremely unlucky for they chose a date in the summer of 1859, and this happened to be a time when they had the worst storm ever experienced even in that very stormy part of Wales. Even today, anyone who visits the lifeboat station on whose very doorstep the disaster occurred will see commemorative tablets on the wall, and may hear the sad story of the wreck of the *Royal Charter*, for this was one of the worst tragedies that has happened about our coasts. The ship was carrying many passengers, including a large number of women and children, and she went down off Anglesea in a storm of such ferocity that any attempt to launch a lifeboat was unthinkable. The result was a great loss of life. This storm, which happened in October that year, spread havoc throughout the whole of North Wales and the newspapers and periodicals of the period, and particularly the local newsheets, are filled with stories of extensive damage, of swamped fields, flooded houses, and bridges swept away, among the latter being the Roman bridge at Beddgelert. Extensive repairs had recently been started at Pen y Gwryd, including repairs to the roof and the whole family experienced a night of terror which they spent cowering in a single room, while the menfolk had to go round propping up ceilings and bailing out water. Ann and her mother were expecting the roof to go at any moment and when daylight came Mrs Pritchard's first words were 'Thank God for the Light'. Remembering that she was no stranger to storm and tempest common in Snowdonia, this gives some idea of how severe the weather must have been. In fact, they suffered comparatively little damage; the complete roof of the stable was blown away and there was a bit of flooding, but all in all the damage was quite limited.

Even in 1852 there were only two bedrooms in common use for visitors, and the only sitting room for public use was a small one facing the Beddgelert road, probably the one still used as a lounge. So more bedrooms were put into use, but the most important work was the provisions of what Mathews calls a commodious coffee-room facing the road. At that time the main road was the one from Betws-y-Coed to Beddgelert, for the Llanberis road was quite a secondary one, and the front door and porch of the Inn were on the main road; it is not easy to locate this new coffee-room exactly but probably it was either the present coffee-room opposite the bar, or maybe the room now used as an office; it is just possible that it was the present lounge which would also be termed commodious. These were not the only alteration made by the Owens during their reign: when they took over from John Roberts or rather from his successor Mrs Hughes, they had a very large kitchen, a small sitting room and a slightly larger public room: they divided the kitchen to provide a smoke room and a still room, and they also put in a small office. Also they started with little more than two bedrooms for the use of visitors and they very soon found room for four more; at a later stage a further four bedrooms were provided and a more adequate dining room was opened up. The next three bedrooms did not come into service until the time of Griffith Griffiths, or it may have been soon after the arrival of William Hampson. These were the only changes or alterations for some decades except, of course, for the innumerable minor changes which are always taking place in a busy and lively establishment of this sort.

Again, not everyone found these alterations their idea of improvements, as will be seen later. A constant visitor about that time was Charles Kingsley and in one of his letters dated 1859, and hence just before the alterations had begun, he called Pen y Gwryd 'The divinest pigsty beneath the canopy'.

One of the later alterations made by Harry Owen was the division of the magnificent old farmhouse kitchen, built large enough to allow for the feeding of a battalion, into a new kitchen and a bar. Before that there was no real bar for casual drinkers. But C.E. Mathews's sad epitaph to Harry Owen in his *Reminiscences* shows that Mathews, anyway, did not like this change, for he says 'How well I remember Harry Owen doing Punch for his children; in the same old kitchen was Mrs Owen knitting in the corner, and the collie dog lying on the floor. No hot whisky was ever so delicious as that we drunk over the peat fire while the wind was howling and the rain beating down outside. No talk was ever more manly, no friendships were ever more sincere. Alas the old kitchen where so many honest men spent such happy hours, has been converted into a bar. Half the charm of Pen y Gwryd lies buried with the Owens in Beddgelert Churchyard.'

This may be the time to break off the direct history for a brief time and to consider in more general terms the happenings in and around the hotel and to see what effect these things had on the development of Pen y Gwryd; to do this it is necessary to delve into the Visitors' Books, and local papers, although of the latter few are now obtainable. In addition quite a number of incidents are to be found in journals, particularly the Journal of the Alpine Club and in the Climbers' Club Journal.

As has already been said, the Visitors' Books started at Pen y Gwryd in 1854 and they naturally continue up to the present day. From the beginning they were large leather bound books with first quality paper, and it was not until 1907 that they started to be ruled into the dull columns of name, address and nationality as they are today; up to that date they were intended to carry interesting essays on climbs, walks or the fish that got away: and particularly welcomed special features of the landscape, the birds, the weather and all the many items which can be seen in the country, and which often have greater impact on the town dweller on his rare holiday, than by the countryman who takes them as a matter of course.

Unfortunately, many of the books, especially the earlier ones, were very badly treated by the guests; many of the entries are stupid and badly written; some pages are scrawled over or included drawings some of which, admittedly, are quite good, but too many are very poor; and throughout are innumerable poems, a few good, but mostly of the worst sort. Some of the pages have been torn, and even torn out and taken away should they show entries made by visiting celebrities.

It is not uncommon in this permissive age to think of the Victorian as a rather proper person who always did the right thing, and whose handwriting was of the copper-plate variety; this may be largely true but certainly on holiday he sometimes became rather strange as a glance at these books will demonstrate; most of the trouble was the effort at humour which was not always good and which became very dated; moreover the writing was often surprisingly poor in quality and with age it has become dim and faded so as to be illegible. But despite this the reading of these books is well worth the hard labour; not only do they give a new and different view of the Victorian hotel guest, but in them can be found descriptions of early mountain climbs, of exceptional weather conditions, described in old-fashioned phrases and a long search will produce gems which make the effort very satisfying.

Happily in 1884 one of the hotel's frequent visitors, Hugo J. Young, a future Queen's Counsel, became so irritated with what he rightly described as the flood of inanities found in the seven old torn books, that he presented the Owens with a large handsome, leather bound, quarto volume with five hundred and twenty-six thick pages of almost vellum quality paper: most important of all it had a large brass lock after the manner of some family bibles of that age. This volume was given with the stipulation that the key should be kept by Harry Owen, and by succeeding owners or managers, and that the book should be closely guarded and should be given only to specially selected guests whose contribution to the literature of the hotel, or to climbing, walking, botany or other interesting items would be worth recording. In several ways there were disadvantages to the Locked Book system; Mine Host was not always available and the key was not always easily obtainable; some of the guests who might be able to contribute good material did not know of the book's existence, or in some cases might have been too shy to ask for it. But this method has saved a good deal of nonsense writing and it has served to produce a volume full of very unusual material; it is to be hoped that in due course the Locked Book will find its way to a suitable museum or into the Alpine Club or Climbers' Club Library, and that it will not be allowed to fade into obscurity.

All the Visitors' Books for the first fifty years, and the Locked Book, contain a good deal of interesting and often fascinating information which added to the knowledge of the part played by visitors to the development of rock climbing in this country. Pen y Gwryd had another stroke of luck when the newly formed Climbers' Club agreed to reimburse one of its members, Charles Sayle, Librarian at Cambridge University, for the repair and rebinding of the early and somewhat tattered volumes, so that they are now in much better condition; when this good work was complete, by the courtesy and kindness of J.W. Hawkins (listed in one of the volumes as a Master of the Supreme Court of Judicature), Charles E. Mathews was allowed the use of these books, and on them he spent much time in study. The result was his article in the Climbers' Club Journal in December 1901 entitled 'Reminiscences of Pen y Gwryd', a delightful essay which was later published separately and which has proved invaluable to anyone interested in the history of this hotel; I am happy to confess to having made the fullest use of this great work.

Part of this book is devoted to the facts and fancies in the history of Pen y Gwryd which have been gleaned from the study of the Visitors' Books and particularly of the Locked Book, and so is a mixed brew.

By the middle of the last century British climbing was already beginning to make its mark in the Alps but the technique of rock climbing in this country was in its infancy and bore little relationship to climbing as it is known today. But there was a considerable amount of exploration in British mountains, and plenty of long and arduous mountain walking combined with what today would be called scrambling: this was carried out by those who had every right to call themselves mountaineers in the fullest sense of the word. This period was, of course the golden age of Alpine exploration, the time when very many of the Alpine peaks were climbed by whatever routes seemed most straightforward to the experts of the age. A surprising amount of progress was made in snow and ice work, but much of the expertise in rock climbing was still to come. This meant that when there was snow and ice on the mountains of Wales, and the experienced Alpine mountaineers could use the methods they had recently discovered in Switzerland and France, real mountain climbing was done in Snowdonia; otherwise the tendency was to follow the straightforward tracks which led to the peaks by the easiest route thus evolving what are now called the tourist routes. But there were no cairns built to mark the best way up, nor the multitude of scratches on the rock from many nailed climbing boots; so through mist or cloud the way often had to be pioneered and the tough walkers of those days fully deserved the title of mountaineers. It would be interesting to know who was responsible for the innumerable and invaluable cairns which mark all the routes across so many of this country's mountains, and also when they were built and who suggested them as waymarks which serve their purpose but which do not desecrate the landscape. It is to be hoped that the daubs of paint which are replacing them in some places will not lead on to continuous yellow lines with maybe signs of suggested speed limits!

Why so many human beings have this strange inborn desire to reach the top of any hill they see, is likely to remain a controversial subject for many years to come, although without doubt a number of psychiatrists will be happy to give an equal number of different reasons; fortunately this is hardly the place for a prolonged discussion on such a topic. Is it not enough to suggest that the completion of the struggle to the summit, however rough the way or bad the weather, together with the unusual and often beautiful view which can be seen only from the top of the mountains, combine to give a feeling of pleasure and above all a sense of achievement which is enthralling to most people?

One of the remarkable achievements of those who went to the mountains in the nineteenth century was their performance in covering immense distances; they often took long, steep and difficult paths to mountain tops and often went summit-hopping for many miles: the enthusiasm and stamina of some of these folk deserved much credit for they were the precursors of the climbers of later days. But they did more than aid the development of climbing. They did much to further the dramatic change in the whole attitude to mountains and to encourage the general public and particularly those who did not live in the hills to appreciate the beauty of mountain and valley scenery. For many decades before these travellers went through mountain districts only if it was essential, and they then found them dull and dreary, or perhaps more commonly black and sinister. For example the Earl of Shaftesbury journeying as a young man in about 1820 in the Lake District wrote in one letter 'From there we went to sleep in an odd eccentric hamlet called Shap after passing through country more suited to monsters and deformities of the imagination than to any human being'.

But there was one man living in the latter part of the eighteenth century who was far ahead of his time in understanding the loveliness of mountain country as we see it today: Thomas Pennant may have retained some measure of apprehension but he is one of the first men to suggest that mountains were worth looking at for their beauty. In his delightful *Journey to Snowdon* he gave many splendid accounts of pleasant scenery; on one journey he travelled from Betws-y-Coed to Caernarfon with some friends and he went by way of Pen y Gwryd, where there was not even a cottage at that time; but he was so struck by the landscape that, sending his horses across the troublesome Llanberis track, he took his few companions up Glyder Fawr, an ascent which he found, as many have done since, 'extremely long, steep and laborious, wet and slippery, and almost the whole way covered with loose fragments of rock, beneath which was the continuous roar of waters, feeling their way to the bottom'. He explored extensively along the Glyder ridge and across to Tryfan and he specially noted, as does the modern tourist, the very unusual rock formation; for he talks of 'Groups of columnar stones of vast size, from ten to thirty feet long lying in all directions'. Thomas Pennant was a man whose ability as a traveller and an observer has perhaps never been fully recognized, and some more of his observations will be found in the chapter on botanical problems.

Harry Owen made no claim to be an expert climber and certainly he would not be considered one by present day standards; but he suited well the needs of his time for in common with most of those who had been born in the neighbourhood and had spent their youth there farming and walking about the moors and mountains tending sheep, he had an extensive knowledge of the surrounding country and he walked the hill paths with confidence. This stood him in good stead in the hotel for he could help and advise his guests on routes and footpaths and he was always happy to go on expeditions with them if required, and in this way he soon became quite an enthusiast in finding new ways to the mountain tops. At the same time his expeditions with the visitors had a twofold effect; he taught those who required it the ways he knew and as he often went out with knowledgeable mountaineers he learnt much from them. Geoffrey Winthrop Young quotes from an article by H.G. Willinck (an artist) in the Alpine Journal describing a party climbing Snowdon in quite deep snow; when coming down the mountain they all enjoyed some long glissades in the snow and it was generally agreed that 'It was Harry Owen who showed the greatest amount of centrifugal eccentricity'.

The authors of the latter half of the century helped to popularize North Wales as a beautiful place to visit; of these George Borrow that champion long distance walker probably did more than anyone else; throughout *Wild Wales* he is constantly calling attention to the lovely scenery presented to those who have eyes to see, and unlike some of the earlier writers he did not think of the mountains as the natural home of demons of all kinds. And he helped to make people realize that the Welshman was not a hostile foreigner. He was more kindly and understanding than Charles Kingsley who always retained some of his feeling of apprehension about mountainous terrain, but Kingsley grew to get over this and to love Pen y Gwryd where he often stayed with friends; witness his entry in one Visitors' Book about the hotel kitchen 'The whole family from Granny (Mrs Pritchard) in the fireside corner, to the young Prince of Wales (Harry Owen's eldest son) in the cradle furnishes a happy example of the honest open-hearted Welsh mountaineers'.

And so in many ways the fame of the hotel, and of the hills and valleys of Wales spread and the visitors came in steadily increasing numbers seeking mountain walks and river and lake fishing. They became more and more venturesome, trying new and difficult routes and some even started to carry an alpenstock or a home made replica when required: and the flow of visitors turned into a flood and then towards the end of the century real rock climbing started. But there were still many hundreds who went to Pen y Gwryd simply to absorb the glory of the land.

Of course these increasing numbers encouraged the Owens to improve the facilities at the hotel: during the management of John Roberts the conditions may not have been much better than those described by Gerald the Welshman in the twelfth century when he remarked of another Inn: 'The kitchen does not supply many dishes nor highly seasoned incitements to eating. The house is not furnished with table cloths or napkins; they study nature more than splendour'. It is perhaps surprising to find anyone in the twelfth century speaking of table cloths, and napkins, but Gerald was an aspiring churchman who spent much of his time mixing with kings and with princes of the Church whose standards of table furniture must have been far above the average.

But even from the beginning of their reign the Owens were never at risk of the description which Nicholas Owen gave to another local hostelry 'The catalogue of negatives is abundant; no butcher's meat, no wheaten bread, no wine, no spirits: oat and barley bread, ale, porter and eggs, commonly make the improvident strangers repast'. For the Owens soon built up a reputation of good food and good living, and almost more important, a reputation of good fellowship. Harry Owen still studied nature but he also studied human nature and its requirements were the first thoughts of the whole family.

It was this happy fellowship which brought the Owens their greatest benefactor Charles Edward Mathews; he was probably the most ardent supporter that Pen y Gwryd has ever had, and it has had many. He was constantly encouraging his walking and climbing friends to make it their centre, advertising it as the perfect place from which to start explorations, and extolling it as the most comfortable and hospitable place to lodge that one could find anywhere.

In particular Mathews was the leader of a small group which preferred going to North Wales in the winter months and two or three of these kindred spirits used to stay at Pen y Gwryd in January most years for at that time of year they found that they had the Inn to themselves, with the rivers often in flood and exciting, and snow on the mountains. They were all alpine experts and so found the snow covered mountains easier and more sporting than the bare rocks; perhaps it was a good thing for Pen y Gwryd that the idea of winter sports had yet to be born or that might have taken these happy guests further afield.

Encouraged by Mathews this group in 1870 founded a new

society called the Society of Welsh Rabbits, which undertook to go to Pen y Gwryd every year just after Christmas and to dine regularly once a year at the Inn. This Society lasted until the formation of the Climbers' Club, and it was of considerable importance to the Owens for it meant that they had found a selection of people who were willing to brave the winter climate and to visit the place at the more inclement times of the year so helping to give the hotel the twelve months, all the year round season which it has always retained and which has in great measure contributed to its success. It was largely the excellence of the food which encouraged the Rabbits to make Pen y Gwryd their yearly dining place; after one of their dinners Mathews wrote that 'Mrs Owen provided us with a goose for dinner; it has fallen to my lot to enjoy many of these birds, but never before since have I tasted one like that. Mr Adams-Reilly, who was one of the party, was quite overcome by it, and begged to be allowed to keep the breast-bone as a perpetual memorial of that particular dinner; next morning when starting for Betws Mrs Owen handed him this precious relic!' Unfortunately when they got to Betws-y-Coed, Adams-Reilly carelessly and stupidly allowed the relic to be snapped up by some discerning Welsh dog and this he said caused him 'poignant sorrow'.

Naturally the Owens were delighted with all the efforts Mathews made on their behalf and wished to give him some return so that he would realize his labours on their behalf had not passed unnoticed. So in the late 1880s Mrs Owen gave him a very special present, a roll of tweed made from fleeces of their own sheep, which she thought would make him some excellent climbing clothes, although we do not know if he actually used it for that purpose.

Henry Owen died in May 1891 after forty years robust and loving service to the 'Pen y Gwryd Hotel' which was his life. He was buried in Beddgelert Parish Church, and there stands a Memorial Tablet put up in his memory: this bears an inscription which should be quoted in full as it shows so well how he was regarded by all who knew him and there must be few who would not covet such an epitaph:

To the memory of
HENRY OWEN
For 44 years landlord of the Inn at Pen y Gwryd
and guide to Snowdon.

In business upright and courteous
In service strong and patient,
In friendship, simple and sincere.

This tribute is erected by old friends who knew
and honoured him.

Born April 2nd. 1822
Died May 5th. 1891.

after so many years of unremitting toil at the Inn, and after the death of her husband who she loved so well and whose knowledge and skill had always been the controlling factor at the Inn, and with her own advancing years it is not surprising that Ann Owen found that during the last five years of her life she could not keep the high standard that the Owens had established and which the guests had come to expect.

In October 1896 Ann Owen, the wife of Harry, died and was buried at his side at Beddgelert.

During the decade following her death the hotel tended to pass from hand to hand, without finding any one owner with the ability, time and inclination to keep it going in the manner to which it had become accustomed.

So it happened that during the latter part of the nineteenth century and the first few years of this century some of the climbers transferred their custom and affection to the 'Pen y Pass Hotel' which stands at the highest point of the Llanberis Pass: known in Welsh as Gorphwysfa, this was called by Geoffrey Winthrop Young who was the leader of the group which adopted it 'the highest roosting place in the country' and it became a famous climbers' haunt for many years. At about this time Gorphwysfa passed into the ownership of some Owens, a husband and wife who were no relations of the Pen y Gwryd folk; but they were in many ways similar, being equally competent and friendly and well able to seize the opportunity presented to them of making the 'Pen y Pass Hotel' another well-known lodging place for the rapidly increasing circle of climbing addicts who infested Snowdonia.

In many ways Rawson Owen was a very independent individual and there are several stories indicating this faculty; on one occasion he was asked to take the horse and carriage to meet the train by which Winthrop Young and friends were journeying up from London. He duly met the train but his guests were not on it, neither was there another possible train that night, so he went home. But Winthrop Young was a man of influence and he had arranged a special train arriving much later: it gives some idea of the marked effects money and influence had, and of the comparatively low cost of railway transport to think that one man could order a special engine and carriage at short notice so as to reach a holiday resort immediately after finishing his work. After some hours he managed to get to Pen y Pass and had the greatest trouble in knocking up Rawson Owen, who however in response to a request replied: "Take your own bloody luggage upstairs."

On one occasion a very smart carriage arrived at the door of Pen y Pass and a superior being lent out of the window and said, "My man, will you get our lettuces washed for our lunch?" Owen touched his cap and said, "Yes, sir." He washed them thoroughly and then sprinkled a few drops of paraffin on each, and returned them apparently in first class condition; the result of the lunch party is not recorded. But, of course, for most of his guests he was very kind and helpful, and despite their one dispute Winthrop Young became his warm friend and supporter.

In the day of the motor car one is apt to forget the importance of distance; the nearest of the other inns or hotels available for climbers was four miles away, and many others were still further from the Llanberis Pass which is the foot of Snowdon. Four miles on foot is quite a way before a day in the mountains and horse or vehicle travel to sport was not easy to arrange: so it was natural that two good hotels in such pleasant and convenient situations would have a head start in attracting a contingent of keen visitors seeking exploration in the mountains.

And after the manner of things it was natural that as the

years went by these two hotels would go up and down in popularity after the way of a child's see-saw, and this is what in fact happened. Winthrop Young served much the same purpose for Pen y Pass as Mathews did for Pen y Gwryd as he was a recognized leader of climbing of his day and so attracted the ever growing climbing community; and for the first fifty years of the twentieth century both these hotels played a considerable part in the encouragement of climbing in this country.

Perhaps it should be emphasized again that this book makes absolutely no claim to be a history of climbing or of its development, but merely tries to introduce a few thumb nail sketches which can be found by reading the hotel Visitors' Books. Inevitably climbing sketches are numerous, for an Inn in this position has attracted a very large number of those who climbed mountains and many of them have written details of their feats in the Locked Book, for indeed this is largely what this book was meant for. But already many books have been written on climbing and climbers and they have been written by those who have a real knowledge of this controversial subject, whereas I can only profess ignorance of its development. The Lake District, Scotland and North Wales have all made great contributions towards producing the present level of rock climbing in this country and probably each has reason to claim priority during some stage of its evolution. Undoubtedly 'Wasdale Head Hotel' with its many groups of experts would not think of allowing the lead to go to any Inn in Wales for providing the men and terrain needed for the growth of the techniques of climbing!

Let great credit go to all these centres for they have all played a full part in putting this country into the forefront of climbing. It is no purpose of this book to allot praise or to cause controversy; for it will have served one of its main intentions if it succeeds in persuading some of its readers to delve further into the massive and pleasant literature which has gathered round the subject of climbing and mountaineering, much of which has been written by experts not only of climbing but also of literature.

CHAPTER 3

THE SUCCESSFUL INVASIONS

And finds a changing clime a happy source
Of wise reflection and well-timed discourse.
William Cowper. Conversation. 1.387

Ann Owen continued to hold the bar licence until her death in 1896 when it passed to Griffiths Owen, her son; he held it for a year, and it can be assumed that he took charge of the hotel, but whether personally or by using a manager there is no way of telling. In 1897 Pen y Gwryd was put up for auction, and it was bought by someone of the name R.G. Lund, for the sum of £1625; the lease from Sir Richard Bulkeley having still twenty-one years to run.

Lund was in partnership with Griffith Griffiths, who worked in London, as a solicitor, but neither of them played any personal part in running the hotel; the bar licence was in the name of a manageress Dorothy Brookes who held it for four years until 1901 when it passed to James Holding, who it may be assumed took over the managership.

In 1901 the mortgage passed from Lund and Griffiths to Alfred Hoare, bankers of London and Algernon Augustine de Littel Strickland; sad to say despite this magnificent name which would have decorated Pen y Gwryd so well had they remained its owners, they put it up for sale the following year and in 1902 it was bought by Elizabeth Ann Roberts who already owned the 'Royal Hotel' at Capel Curig. It seems that she paid £750 for the remaining sixteen year lease and this appears a more reasonable sum than the £1625 of five years ago; it is of course possible that this change in price in a short period indicates the running-down of the hotel and the quick reduction of profits on the departure of the beloved Owens.

Thus over a period of nearly ten years Pen y Gwryd was under constantly changing ownership and management and this in no way helped its reputation. Perhaps they should have experimented with other methods such as following the example of the Inn at Capel Curig where during the early days of the nineteenth century the Landlord of the Inn was also the incumbent of the local church. Or they could have spread their net even further for at this time the landlords of three of the principal Inns in that part of North Wales were also engaged in duties in Law, Physic and Divinity!

Elizabeth Roberts put in Catherine her sister as manageress and the bar licence remained in the name of Catherine Roberts for the next four years. It is not easy to get any idea of how successful the hotel was under this management; the Visitors' Books were kept in a very desultory manner until 1907 when normal hotel entries began giving dates, names, addresses and nationality: so it is not possible to estimate the number of guests staying at the Inn. But what little evidence there is suggests that Pen y Gwryd had begun to pass out of its worst period and that the Roberts were more successful in their trade than had been the previous owners. Soon after they took over they had a stroke of luck for the building of the Cwm Dyli Power Station started; this meant that only about three-quarters of a mile down the road was a small clutch of thirsty navvies available to help the bar sales, while the senior staff and visiting inspectors of the Electricity Company used the hotel for meals and for lodging.

The isolated position of Pen y Gwryd has meant that during most of its life it has never had the normal local bar trade; in the last couple of decades the growing number of climbing huts round about has meant a considerable influx of young climbers who crowd into the bar, particularly at week-ends and over the spring and summer months, and naturally the great increase in car traffic has produced many hungry and thirsty motorists. But in the period 1904 to 1905 a sudden expansion in the number of local inhabitants wanting bar service was very unexpected, and at once some alterations in the layout of the hotel were required and the cellars were converted to form a still room and a tap room. The use of the front door, at that time on the Capel Curig to Beddgelert Road, was denied to the navvies who had to use the back door. Why Elizabeth Roberts gave up the hotel can only be guesswork; it may be that the work became too heavy or the economic return too slight: or it may be that the increasing trade gave the chance of selling at a good profit, but in any case she sold it in 1906 and it became the property of William Hampson, of Four Oaks, Sutton Coldfield and he remained the owner until it passed to Arthur Lockwood in 1921.

William Hampson was born in 1858, and at the age of twenty-one he joined in a saddlers business in Walsall in partnership with his great life-long friend John Scott. The business had been founded in 1794 and when Hampson joined it the manager was Samuel Cox, but quite soon Hampson and Scott became the owners and under their management it obtained a world wide reputation. Whittimore Street, Walsall, can still show a large four storey, somewhat dreary buidling, badly in need of a coat of paint, on the outside of which big letters announce 'Hampson & Scott established 1794 building rebuilt 1890'. So some slight aura of William Hampson still lingers in Walsall. In the early part of the twentieth century the saddlery and harness business began to suffer from the inroads of the motor car as a method of transport, and this made William Hampson very worried about future prospects; it is reputed that he played quite a big part in forwarding the rule by which the motor car had to be proceeded by a man carrying a red flag, which was in force for a year or so. William Hampson moved from Walsall and spent much of his working life living in Sutton Coldfield; for a short spell much later on he removed to Beaulieu in Hampshire, but this did not last long and he spent the latter part of his life in North Wales.

When he bought Pen y Gwryd in 1906 he was clever enough to choose Florence Bloomfield (later Mrs Lockwood) as manageress and her influence on the Inn was very considerable; Hampson must have found the hotel business lucrative or at least interesting for in 1908 he took on the lease of the 'Lake Vernwy Hotel' which had been built by the

Liverpool Corporation when they had converted the Lake into a large reservoir to supply water to their city. The leasing arrangement, which still holds, was that although Hampson owned the furniture and took the profits, the building remained the property of the Corporation. At the present time the ownership of the building has passed to the Severn and Trent Water Authority who draw the rent, while the furniture and effects still belong to the present proprietor who manages the business and runs the fishing and shooting for the use of the guests. William Hampson ran both hotels for about twelve years dividing his time between them according to how busy each one might be, and often shifting staff from one to the other according to the requirements. Hampson himself was a keen fisherman and he also hunted frequently with the South Staffordshire Hounds so he must have been a busy man: but this did not prevent him from spending a lot of time water colour painting and sketching, hobbies at which he showed considerable skill. His surviving daughter, Mrs Muriel Green who lives in Colwyn Bay has several of his paintings and they are first class amateur productions. William Hampson put in train many alterations to Pen y Gwryd; he built the billiard room, unfortunately employing an architect who had little knowledge of the wild Welsh weather, and the structure suffered for some time from leakage. But presumably it was the architect who put in the massive stone fireplace which decorates one end of the room and which started the sport of 'Traverse of the Billiard Room': in this sport climbers had to work their way round part of the room using the natural handholds and footholds provided by the stonework. For many years this had been a popular after dinner entertainment and was still going strong until at last Chris Briggs decided that although he could do little to prevent the erosion of Snowdon summit he could reduce the wear and tear on the billiard room and that the famous traverse should cease.

In addition to the billiard room Hampson enlarged the end of the house to make a proprietor's flat, which has very recently been enlarged by Chris Briggs. John Hampson also decided to build a cottage for his groom John Hill who had a flock of eight children, and this was the origin of 'Hafod y Gwynt', which was increased in size again by Arthur Lockwood and which for years went under the name of 'Lockwood's House'. In addition to the buildings, Hampson was responsible for creating the walled garden on the south west side of the hotel, a garden which Lockwood afterwards despised as very small; indeed it was according to his standards if the large park attached to 'Hafod y Gwynt' is a specimen! But Lockwood always thought on a large scale about land and when he was working at Cwm Dyli he tried to persuade Hampson to create the lake which he afterwards made himself: they went as far as getting a visit by a Mr Twigg an engineer from the Liverpool Corporation Waterworks at Lake Vernwy to make an estimate. Twigg and Lockwood thought they could get the job done for £130 but William Hampson was unwilling to consider the project, even though he must have had capital at his disposal for his saddlers business was a flourishing one, and with Lake Vernwy Hotel and Pen y Gwryd he had considerable investment in the hotel business also. However he did a good deal for Pen y Gwryd for he installed Florence Bloomfield in office and her hard work and experience did much to get the place back to the standard it had reached in the better times of the Owens. It seems that he was a good selector as the couple he had at Lake Vernwy also served him well. As a business tycoon he was not slow to use advertisement and he produced some large bedspreads which advertised his leather business by having large leather insignia on them as a coat of arms in the middle; they carried the name of 'Lake Vernwy Hotel' but they were also installed at Pen y Gwryd, and there were still some in use there when Chris Briggs took over in 1947. Florence Lockwood (née Bloomfield) has never had the full credit she deserves for the part in the redevelopment of Pen y Gwryd; there still exists a letter written by William Hampson in which he points out that for eight years she had sole control of the business, and during that time she gave full satisfaction to the visitors. It appears that one of her visitors found her particularly attractive for he married her in 1909 and early the following year the licence for the bar was taken out in the name of Florence Lockwood instead of Florence Bloomfield; she continued to hold this licence in her married name until 1918 and it seems very likely that Arthur Lockwood had considerable influence on the running of the hotel for much of this time even though he held no official position. But, it is evident that Florence Lockwood was an extremely competent woman, for even after Arthur had bought the hotel she continued to be almost entirely responsible for the internal working of the place while he spent a lot of his time, not only walking, climbing and fishing but also in damming rivers and breeding trout. Before her marriage there were two periods only when her name is not listed as holding the bar licence, one in 1914 when it was in the name of Charles Price, and for the years 1918 to 1920 when it was held by Florence Ada Holt; both these were times when the Lockwoods were away for long spells in the East.

Athur Lockwood was born at Bolton-in-Deane, in the district of Barnborough, Yorkshire, on 18th March 1885; so despite the years he spent in Wales he was a true Yorkshireman and remained proud of it. Although he was away from his native county for three-quarters of his long life, he never lost his Yorkshire accent. He spent his infant school days at a Church school, and then he was transferred to a Board school of the kind which had only recently come into being. At the age of thirteen he went to the Grammar School at Penistone where he worked hard, as indeed he did throughout his whole life, and he did very well for he had considerable intelligence; at the age of sixteen, taking the advice of his headmaster, he became an apprentice to the electrical engineering firms of Flather & Co. in Leeds, and he remained there for six years. At about this time he was fortunate in getting a small legacy from his grandfather's estate, an amount apparently of just about four figures which was quite a bonanza at the time: with his careful Yorkshire upbringing he doubtless invested it wisely.

As an apprentice he had to work for fifty two hours a week, for which he was paid two shillings a week rising to five shillings a week in his third year, which in today's currency is ten pence a week, so that his yearly income was £5.20; but for this he received a very wide training in all branches of electrical engineering.

His boss in the firm must have been a person of very advanced views for those days, for he and his wife Lavinia used to spend their weekends taking trips on a tandem bicycle; for this exercise Lavinia used to wear bloomers which had only just been invented, and when they went out they had to be careful to avoid meeting the local mill girls going to work or they suffered a good deal of jeering and rude remarks. Lockwood was an enthusiast in all forms of sport during his youth. Surtees has said that a Yorkshireman, like a dragoon, is nothing without his horse, and Arthur accepted this dictum for during much of his schooldays he kept a pony acquired from his grandfather and for some time he rode on it to school every day; there were occasions when he got mixed up with the local hunt and on seeing the hounds the pony took control. But later in adolescence he joined the Y.M.C.A. and took up the more usual sports such as football and cricket. All through his life he was a keen and vigorous swimmer, well versed in first aid and rescue; he once put it to good use when the friend he was with got into difficulties in the river, and Arthur Lockwood extricated him and by using artificial respiration managed to bring him back to life.

He had no trouble in gaining the necessary certificates of merit as an apprentice and at the end of his time in 1903 he started work with the Leeds City Lighting Department, a post he held for three years. In 1906 he obtained a post with the Durham Collieries Power Company which was later taken over by the Newcastle Electric Supply Company; this year proved a most important one in his life because for the first time he took a holiday in Wales, spending it at Bangor, and he evidently liked the country he saw. For in August 1907 he applied for a job with the North Wales Power and Telegraph Company; this entailed a visit to the Company's office at Llanberis; and from there he was taken to see the site of the new power station they proposed building in Cwm Dyli for the erection of which he would have some responsibility. This was the occasion on which he took his very first lunch at the 'Pen y Gwryd Inn'; but sad to say he made no comment on the Inn or on the food provided.

Arthur Lockwood was what would now be called a good mixer; he had a sound Yorkshire sense of humour, and although no great talker what he said was blunt, direct and sensible and he got on well with most people: but underneath he was a thoughtful man who took his work seriously and performed it zealously. During his years as an apprentice he had joined any number of extra courses, and acquired several certificates outside his work in order to improve his skill and so he usually found it not too difficult to get the kind of work for which he was looking.

He got the job at the Llanberis office of the Company and soon started work superintending the building of the Power Station at Cwm Dyli and supervising the installation of the machinery. Then in 1908 he was offered and accepted the post of Station Superintendent there and this proved to be a turning point in his life; for it not only brought him to Pen y Gwryd but it brought him to Florence Bloomfield.

For the information of those who do not know the neighbourhood the Cwm Dyli Power Station was a small hydro-electric scheme; a couple of large and not very pretty tubes run down the mountainside from Llyn Llydaw just below Snowdon; the electric current produced covered only a small area and the station was closed down when the full grid system was introduced; unfortunately the twin pipes still remain.

As superintendent in charge of the Power Station he lived in a bungalow close to his work and soon he started to roam the countryside; it will give some idea of how quickly he showed his delight in that kind of life in that by the end of his first month there he started a climb from the bungalow at 1.30 in the morning in order to reach the top of Snowdon in time to see the sunrise. He continued to spend much of his spare time exploring the countryside of Snowdonia and he must have learnt the terrain quickly for by May 1908 he joined a search party from Pen y Gwryd looking for a lost German guest who had disappeared while wandering round Crib Goch; history does not reveal if this search was successful.

A month later he accompanied Frederick Morshead round the Snowdon Horseshoe, and this must have taught him a good deal for Morshead was one of the most advanced climbers of the time. Then only about two months later Lockwood climbed the chimney in Clogwyn y Bustach which has been known as Lockwood's Chimney ever since; this gave him a reputation as a climber maybe slightly greater than he himself would have claimed, for he was never an advanced rock climber at any time and probably climbing always came second to fishing in his thoughts.

One very pleasant story is told of Lockwood's Chimney, and that is the one of a lady, who although slightly plump in build was quite a good climber. Unfortunately, when she tried this Chimney she found herself stuck at one well-known, narrow place; she does not impart the information as to whether the trouble was due to what the farmers sometimes call 'a satisfactory fleshing of the hindquarters', but probably not, for after many ineffectual struggles she had the happy idea of discarding her corsets — which she promptly did, although how this feat was accomplished while stuck in a chimney is not divulged. But unhappy she — her figure was such that without her corsets she took up rather more room than with them and was quite unable to wriggle through the small gap, so that in the end she had to be rescued in an undignified manner, feet first.

This may be the adventure which brought forth this poem about Lockwood's climb; it was written in July 1911 by Rufus Glethicke and Truda H. Crossfield but this does not suggest in any way that Miss Crossfield was the lady in, or out of the corsets!

One fine week in mid July,
   We came to Pen y Gwryd,
The skies were blue the turf was dry,
   The climbs we did were lurid.

We four soon reached the Marble Arch,
   Midway on Lockwood's climb,
We thought our throats were caked with starch,
   Or rather caked with lime.

Here Mr Lockwood filled the gap,
   And kicked and wriggled through it,
It felt exactly like a trap,
   Stout people should eschew it.

A traverse and a scramble now,
   To us girls proved a toil,
We climbed a steep and turfy brow,
   Our nails were black with soil.

But Oh! as nothing proved these woes,
To that which followed fast,
Within the crack our leader rose,
How would his foothold last?

Within the chimney's blackened gloom,
By lateral pressure merely,
He crawled up barely finding room,
And taxed his powers severely.

With trembling limbs R. then began,
He hauled her from above,
George lends a shoulder whilst he can,
And then resorts to shove.

The chimney measures scarce a foot,
In width you seem to smother,
At times we found we could not put,
One foot before the other.

When out of this at last we got,
We rested on a narrow spot,
And down three hundred feet or more,
Gazed on the valley's emerald floor.

R's trembling heart became forlorner,
As she surveyed the last dread corner,
And calling "pull" she rose at length,
But chiefly due to Lockwood's strength.

And when upon the top we lay,
With hearts once more sublime,
Though bruised and aching we could say,
"Hurrah" for Lockwood's climb.

Quite soon after starting his new job Arthur Lockwood acquired the hobby of meteorology and this remained with him all his life. He met Dr H.R. Mill, at that time President of the Royal Meteorological Society, when he was travelling through Wales investigating the climate in general and the rainfall in particular; Lockwood went round with him quite often, at first in order to show him the way, but soon because he had become very interested in the subject himself. This interest was not unrelated to his work, for rainfall and the level of the small lakes up in the mountains which supplied the water to run his hydro-electric plant were matters of considerable concern to him; moreover he spent a good deal of time repairing faults in the electric supply caused by thunderstorms and flooding. The level of water in Llyn Llydaw had a major effect on the power station of which he was in charge, and he worked out the possibility of building another dam to increase the water supply, hoping in that way to produce more electric power and so be able to supply the local quarry with the current they required; however, Head Office decided that the scheme would be too expensive and might be impracticable, and they rejected it.

This in no way curbed his enthusiasm about rainfall and climate, and he added another one to the fourteen rain gauges already scattered round the Snowdon range, and putting a maximum and minimum thermometer on the top of Glyder Fach at a height of 3262 feet. Using these instruments W. Cliffe Brown wrote an interesting article which was published in the Quarterly Journal of the Royal Meteorological Society; among other things it demonstrated that there had commonly been long periods of surprisingly mild winters, interspersed with sequences of cold ones: for example between 1867 and 1876 the recorded minimum temperature varied only between 14 and 18 degrees Farenheit which at that height is very reasonable; while on Glyder Fach the minimum temperature reading was 26.9 degrees in the years 1876-77 and only 9 degrees Farenheit in the year 1891-92.

With his interest in weather one can but hope that he looked into the back numbers of the Visitors' Books and found the poem written in 1891, by someone who did not dare to give his name, but who said he wrote it after two days of hideous rain and under the depressing influence of indigestion; it was entitled 'The Imprisoned Soul's Lament'.

Spit forth your vapours leaden skies
  And let your turgid fountains rise
And burst their iron chains;
  Let ice and hail and freezing snow
Dash on the swelling plains below,
  And let the turgid torrents flow,
  Full gorged with rushing rains.

With joy we left fair England's soil
  Prepared up Snowdon's heights to toil
Leaving the city's care and moil
  To rest our fevered souls.
Imprisoned in these weary walls
  Nothing we find but screaming squalls
Loud belching winds, rock blasting brawls
  The sky a parchéd scroll.

Oh sun send forth thy gladdening light
  And beam upon our fainting sight
Smile one poor dim ray.
  Let thunders make the welkin ring,
Crack skies, let earth with storm blasts sing,
  But grant us one bright day.

Like all walkers before and since, Lockwood enjoyed traversing the strange and fascinating Glyder ridge, with its unusual rock structure; once again Thomas Pennant is worth quoting for few people can describe it better. 'The plain which forms the top is strange, covered with loose stones like the beach of a sea, in many places crossing one another in all directions and entirely naked. Numbers of groups of stone are almost erect, sharp pointed and in sheaves; all are weather beaten, time eaten and honeycombed, and of a venerable gray colour. The elements have warred against the mountains, rains have washed, lightnings torn, the very earth deserted it, and the winds make it the constant object of their fury. The Shepherds make it the residence of storms, and style a part of it Carnedd y Gwynt or the "Eminence of Tempests".' Surely anyone who walks it today will recognize the beauty and truth of this description.

With his interest and scientific knowledge of rainfall Arthur Lockwood had the best possible subject for conversation among visitors who were very susceptible to the question of rain; he enjoyed telling stories about remarkable rainfalls, and talking at length about local flooding, and living in North Wales he had no reason to draw on his imagination. He would tell of the flood of August 1906 which among other destruction swept away the old Roman Bridge at Beddgelert; all these incidents were fully documented in the local Press; he would tell of eighteen inches of rain which fell in five days in the Llydaw area in 1908, a fact which he entered in the Locked Book with full scientific glee. And he would crown all by the story of how in 1911 a man was actually blown into Llyn Llydaw and was drowned.

As had already been mentioned Lockwood's bungalow at Cwm Dyli was but a short walk from Pen y Gwryd, and while he was in charge of the Power Station, the hotel was an obvious port of call for meals and drinks at the Bar. William Hampson, the owner, had installed as manageress, barman and general factotum Miss Florence Bloomfield; she was not a Welsh native having been born in Ipswich in 1875; in spite of the efforts of the Roberts sisters which had done something to upgrade it, Pen y Gwryd had fallen on hard times since the Owens died and she must have found it very heavy labour. Miss Bloomfield was a quiet unassuming lady who preferred not to be seen too often; she was a stern disciplinarian and kept her staff in good order. If she thought one of the staff to be ill no one could be more attentive than she was, and it is reputed, maybe unfairly, that to her illness meant a temperature; if you had no temperature you went back to work, but even a slight temperature meant bed, the doctor and the very best of treatment. But there is no doubt that it was her work that played a very large part in bringing Pen y Gwryd back to its old high standards.

For almost the only time in his life Arthur Lockwood failed to display the real North Country caution on which he usually prided himself; indeed it must have been a case of love at first sight for having started work at Cwm Dyli in August 1908, behold in May 1909 he married Florence Bloomfield at Beddgelert Parish Church; nine months incubation for matrimony from start to finish must be almost a record for a Yorkshireman.

Always early risers they were married at 9 o'clock in the morning, but even this was not early enough to avoid trouble for the roadman was already at work and he fired some explosive charges, maybe in celebration; but these naturally frightened the horses drawing the married couple's carriage. Then some counterpanes hanging out of the window in Beddgelert, again to express jubilation did not help to calm the horses, but in due course they were got under control without accident. In one document it says that during the ceremony Tinker went into the church, but it is not clear if Tinker was a dog or a horse; it was probably a dog and if so they may have had the opportunity to use the Gefail Gwn or dog tongs which had been found on the Lleyn peninsula; these tongs had points with serrated ends, and were specially made to expel dogs from church during divine service. Lockwood does not give many details and strangely enough there is no mention of climate or rainfall on his wedding day; he must have regretted missing this chance.

But Arthur's quick thinking before marriage brought its reward for there is no doubt about the wisdom of his choice, for his new wife had already shown her competence in looking after the hotel. During their many years in charge, although he was always at hand to advise, it was undoubtedly Florence who was the guiding hand in the day to day management of the hotel, in the supervising of the staff, the bed-making and the dozens of little things which go to make a first class establishment. And above all in the cooking because in her younger days she had taken a course in cookery at a London catering house and throughout her life she took special pride in the excellence of her cuisine; the entries in the Visitors' Book show that her pride was not misplaced.

One of the many visitors who wished to show their great appreciation of the treatment they had had at Pen y Gwryd, and who decided, as unfortunately some did, to give it in bad verse, was R. Antrobus who in 1906 wrote:

I love the mountains, love the hills,
The rivers great and small;

The good attendants, home-like life;
  But Miss Bloomfield best of all.

Whichever way you look around,
  You see the fussy stream,
Tumbling down the rocky slopes,
  They mingle in your dream.

And when you wake, refreshed with sleep,
  One cannot well feel worried;
For smiling faces, friendly words,
  Greet all at Pen y Gwryd.

Perhaps the best to be said of Mr Antrobus was that he wanted to be most complimentary and he tried!

While his wife could cope with the hotel so well, Arthur Lockwood had plenty of time to devote to the important outside work; he could give help and advice to walkers, climbers and fishermen, and could accompany them if wanted; and above all he could find time to make the Lockwood Lake and to look after his pet trout hatchery. So in temperament and ability the two of them slotted in admirably together and under their combined management the hotel was guaranteed to regain its full popularity. It is impossible to separate the share each made towards this end, but they followed the best tradition of the Owens, and the same pattern of turning a hotel into a home was followed.

Although the Lockwoods married in 1909 and undoubtedly they both took a share from then in improving the hotel, it did still belong to William Hampson until 1921, and a good deal of their influence was behind the scenes. Soon after the wedding Lockwood got permission from his employers to live at Pen y Gwryd although still working in Cwm Dyli, and not long afterwards he took over the house adjacent to the Inn for a seven year lease at a rent of 2/6 per annum on condition that he repaired it at his own expense; he could almost be called the first of the squatters. He claimed that these repairs cost £120, a fairly large sum for those days with him doing much of the work himself; afterwards the landlord paid him £108, but some of this may have been for other procedures or for work in the hotel itself; when the repairs were finished the rent for Hafod y Gwynt became £12.10 a year.

At about the same time Lockwood also rented a small piece of land next door to the hotel and his house at 5/- per annum for use as a hen run; he was allowed to use it for that purpose only on the understanding 'that any sheep entering are not abused'. He then agreed to the sheep using the hen run provided they had no objection to the fowls' droppings!

Lockwood was still in charge of the Power Station when the First World War began and in that capacity he was in a reserved occupation; but he did make some enquiries about the possibility of joining the Caernarfonshire Volunteer Regiment, the First War's edition of the Second War's Home Guard. A reply from the Adjutant says that a Motor Battalion was being formed, to be attached to the Portmadoc Company which in turn was attached to the Lleyn & Eifionydd Infantry Battalion with headquarters at Pwllheli. Among Lockwood's papers is an application form for joining and it has been filled in by Lockwood in December, 1915. In it in view of his work at the Power Station he calls himself a munition worker, states that he has already had slight military training with the Caernarfon Volunteer Regiment, that he owned and could drive a car and ride a bicycle; he also says that he is accustomed to horses, and if so required he could dig trenches; all these replies are in response to the questions on the paper. There is no indication that he was ever a member of the Motor Battalion, but later in the War he was addressed in official letters as Major Lockwood so he must have put in a good deal of service locally.

The beginning of 1917 inflation started to worry him and he asked the North Wales Power Company for a rise in salary; he was then earning £200 a year which was the maximum for his particular job. His case was an excellent one and he called attention to transport difficulties for supplies, the extra emergency work involved and the extra duties involved because he lived over the shop. He got a bonus for the duration of the War of £30 per annum. This kept him satisfied until November, 1918, when he again asked for an increase, remarking in a surprisingly up-to-date way that his bonus had meant a rise of only 29% whereas his own workmen had been given increases of between 60% and 100%. On this showing he did manage to extract another rise of £24 per annum in April 1919, but he evidently thought this was not adequate for in August 1919 he sent in his resignation, as in the meantime he had found another more remunerative appointment.

Perhaps feeling that he would like a complete change of scene, in 1919 Lockwood took on a job in his own type of hydro-electric engineering work in Burma: he landed at Rangoon in December that year and went to a lonely hill station called the Mansam Falls in the Shan States. It is possible that he acted mainly in an advisory capacity for he did not stay there very long; later the same year he was appointed by Messrs Boving & Co., Hydraulic Engineers as supervisor to the erection of a hydro-electric plant at Simla, India. This was in fact a transfer as the firm was the one he had been working for in the Shan States.

It was while he was abroad that Pen y Gwryd quite unexpectedly came onto the market, but he managed to arrange to buy it and he officially took over in October 1921, having sailed home from Rangoon earlier in the year. He records in his usual very full detail that the licence was transferred to him in July that year and so from that date he could sell at the Inn 'Spirits, Wine, Sweets, Made Wines, Mead, Metheglin, Beer, Cider and Perry; also tobacco and snuff, except for Cavendish or Negro head', nor was he allowed to add certain named chemicals to the snuff. So evidently there were problems even before the days of L.S.D. and marijuana.

Both he and Florence were well acquainted with the Inn and doubtless they had very definite ideas on what changes they wanted to introduce; the Lockwood's records say most about the large works he started outside the Inn and very little about what happened within, but he may have completed the construction of the billiard room; he certainly introduced the full-sized billiard table which adorned it for so many years. In those quiet friendly days before the often unwanted blare of *soi-disant* music was considered to be an essential accompaniment to any gathering, the billiard table requiring skill and concentration was a common fixture in many hotels.

But this large room gave plenty of space round the table for other quiet activities and it had a very big fireplace of local stone in which logs up to half a tree trunk in size could be burnt; round the fireplace was an ingle-nook in which it was just possible to keep out of the worst of the draughts which blew steadily round this unheated hall. It was not until the 1950s that the billiard table was removed and replaced by dart boards, and ping pong (Oh, No! Table tennis) tables and the room was called the Games Room and was very popular with the younger visitors. In still more recent years it has been fully centrally-heated and furnished and has become a much needed extra lounge. But for a hotel which has frequent large meetings, and large scale dinner parties and other forms of entertainment this very large room is invaluable. Lockwood also built the outhouse behind the Inn which in time became the bunk-house.

Harry Inman, Lockwood's nephew remembers clearly helping his uncle to instal some wash basins in some of the bedrooms, thus starting early on a new fashion of the time; another of his recollections is that of climbing on the roof of the hotel and assisting in putting up a red electric light on the end of a metal curtain rod which would serve as a guiding light to climbers trying to get off the mountains after dark.

Lockwood also carried out many improvements to the stabling, converting much of it into garages for cars; it is not easy these days to remember that cars for visitors were still in their infancy and relatively few and far between; at the time of the Owens and of William Hampson, guests still arrived by coach or if they were of the wealthy type they may have had their own *chaise*. For many years just outside the front door of the Inn could be seen a couple of short ladders which could be put against the side of the large high coach to help the outside passengers to dismount; one would imagine that in many winter days in the mountains these passengers needed lifting down as they must have been frozen into blocks of ice. Some years after they had ceased to be used, these two short ladders still ornamented the side of the front door, but unhappily they are now lost.

Arthur also began making improvements in the garden, starting with a kitchen garden reaching from the hotel window to the wall on the Llanberis road. During one of these excavations he found a large bell, some fifteen inches across the mouth, buried in the Owens' ash pit: cleaned up this bell proved to be in very good condition and it was soon handed back to its rightful owners, the local Britannia Copper Mine. Its use there had been to call the miners to their meals or to signal the end of the shift, but some Cambridge undergraduates staying at the Inn had removed it for a joke and not wanting to steal it they had, somewhat illogically, just left it behind when they went home. It was found by Ann Owen who was too frightened to say anything about it and she buried it in the ash pit.

Despite all this work the Lockwoods continued to run the hotel to the satisfaction of their guests, but even the most popular of landlords sometimes go astray and a few visitors felt they were not getting full attention as this short verse will show: It was written in June 1940 by Alan Molesdell and he called it 'The Lockwood Lament'.

If you want a drink at Pen y Gwryd
　Don't be cross and don't get worried;
For Mr Lockwood's at the garage,
　Or fixing up the Snowdon barrage.
A pint of beer's perhaps what you're wishing?
　Though Mr Lockwood's still out fishing;
Someone else could serve a drink:
　Oh! foolish one, for thoughts like these
For Mrs Lockwood's lost her keys!

It has already been mentioned that soon after Lockwood first went to Pen y Gwryd he noticed that the land in front was very boggy and he conceived the idea of forming a lake there; this suggestion he put up to William Hampson who proved not very interested; but when Lockwood got back as full owner he revived this scheme. It was in 1923 that he started to think again about this major work which in the end produced a lake across the road from the Inn and which was immediately christened Lockwood's Llyn. Undoubtedly he was keen on this project not only because of amenity value, a phrase not even coined then, but he thought of it mainly from its practical use for the fishing. He received a good deal of help from another ardent fisherman, W.E. Corlett, one of Pen y Gwryd's most constant visitors, and whose name appears frequently in the Visitors' Books signing descriptions of new climbs and explorations, and who appears to have been a business man of considerable means.

Corlett was particularly useful in the first step of this plan, which was to buy the necessary land; although it was merely bog, Sir Richard Bulkeley seemed unwilling to part with it, and it needed many letters and negotiations, and much persuasion by Mr Corlett before Lockwood found himself the proud possessor of the necessary ten acres. Even then Sir Richard retained the mineral rights and this complicated the construction somewhat as a special valve had to be incorporated in the construction so that the lake could be drained at any time if required. However, the deal was completed in 1925 and in March that year the work started on building the dam.

After surveying the site Lockwood started putting in the spillway; he did a great part of this work himself although he persuaded a number of friends to help him; he also cajoled other passers-by with a small *pourboire* to do some work and these included the local postman and a succession of tramps and beggars. His remarks about these are worth full quotation thus 'A tramp E. Worthington by name (a name still very well known at Pen y Gwryd today but in reverse!) put in three days, then he succumbed to the urge and call of the road'. Also 'I and the postman fixed one straining post for the new fence, and pushed in some portions of the banks of the Gwryd stream so that floods would bring along some well-washed gravel for use in the spillway concrete'.

'April 25th. Another tramp, a rather useful type of man asked for a job. He stayed two weeks and did some work alongside me, collecting gravel, blasting about forty tons of rock, pulling up the old fence and re-erecting it on the new boundary line'.

'May: carrying gravel and stone to site. Resurveyed the whole site and decided on a still larger lake and to make dam as natural as possible'.

'June: Started Patrick Reddy, a tramp. Marked out the course of the dam, finished excavations for the spillway and commenced concreting on the 18th. On the 22nd started Jim, a tramp, dirty beggar, and on the 25th both Pat and Jim jibbed so I paid them off. Some interested guests, Messrs Carlisle, Henderson, Watson, Arnold, Rowntree got in some good work digging and Henry Hollingdrake came to help me generally and I made him foreman'.

'By the end of the month the spillway was up to the last step, reinforced by Ford axles, bedsteads and any old iron I could get hold of, and quite a fair stretch of dam thrown up on both sides. The position of the spillway was chosen on account of natural rock and to look as much as possible a natural waterfall'.

Finding enough material for the dam was more troublesome than might have been expected and the items used were as varied as was the labour; they even got some parts of a German submarine which was being broken up at Portmadoc. The spillway was finished by July 10th. and the dam completed by November 3rd., so that by then the river bed was closed. Lockwood was sufficiently content with the result that he and Florence sailed off happily for a six month spell in Burma.

As might be expected there were minor troubles soon afterwards. Round about Christmas an old hip bath was carried down by the floods and choked the outlet and caused some damage to the dam, and a perhaps slightly larger lake than anticipated; after the usual manner of village rumour the word went round the houses, growing as it went, until it was said that "Lockwood's Dam has burst". In fact, the damage was soon repaired and the dam survived a much greater flood in April.

The final result was a most successful piece of work; a good-sized and attractive lake has replaced some dull, boggy marshland, and it not only looks better, but having now been stocked with trout it has produced some much improved fishing. This was possibly the main cause for Lockwood's enthusiasm for the creation of a lake, and it certainly was as far as Corlett was concerned. The lake was then stocked with trout and an angling club was formed, which was lucky in being presented with a thirty foot punt, and in due time other boats were provided for the members.

In addition to fish they liberated a pair of barnacle geese on the lake in 1927; these unfortunately did not last long as the foxes were too active, but the provision of the stretch of water helped to improve the general bird life; moorhens, mallard, teal, snipe and sandpipers all started breeding there in quite fair numbers. Later on more stocking was done with brown and Loch Leven trout, and although it was an expensive process they flourished exceedingly. To reduce the cost Arthur Lockwood started his other venture, the hatchery, of which more anon.

In 1927 soon after it was finished the lake provided an unexpected treat for it froze over completely and about this Arthur made a strange comment when he said "the ice was so slippery it was nearly impossible to walk on it". Surely this aligned him with Mr Winkle in his remark to Sam Weller when contemplating skating at Dingley Dell "How slippery it is, Sam", and the Weller reply: "Not an uncommon thing upon ice, sir." But Lockwood's best Yorkshire instinct of betting only on a certainty, showed up when he offered to give a shilling to anyone who could ride a bicycle across the frozen lake; needless to say he did not have to pay anyone. But a considerable number of skaters arrived including students from Bangor University and the lake was voted a great success.

It was in the following year that he first noticed floating islands in the new lake, and spent a good deal of time and thought investigating the cause for them. The results of his investigations proved most interesting in view of the observations of Giraldus Cambrensis about seven hundred years before. For the islands proved to be beds of sphagnum moss which had grown to a large size on the boggy area before the lake was formed: when there was some flooding and the lake rose in level and became a bit turbulent, the islands of moss lost their attachment to the bottom, broke free and floated on the surface, although in some cases they were still slightly attached by long streamers of root partially fixing them in place. Some of these islands were two or three feet thick, and one at least was six by eight yards in area. Lockwood started cutting the roots free by using an old dragoon sword, but later he had made a special tool with a disc of sharpened steel attached to the end of an eight foot length of three-quarter inch galvanised pipe. When he had freed the moss a garden fork was driven in and the whole island was dragged to the edge of the lake by a rope. He soon thought of an even better idea. Several islands were towed together until they grounded in a shallow part of the lake, and willow sticks were pushed through them to anchor them to the bottom; then galvanised iron sheets were put on top so that they would bear a man's weight and with earth put on top the structures became steadily more and more solid until grass and finally trees began to grow and the artificial islands became real ones which still exist. All the islands to be seen on the lake today were made in this way. It is not difficult to see how Giraldus Cambrensis could have seen such floating islands as were formed when the moss was first released from the bottom of the lake; these would almost certainly have supported sheep and the bigger ones might have carried small cattle and been pushed about by the strong winds.

There must be few people who have produced a new lake complete with islands as did Arthur Lockwood, and one result was an amusing article in the *Daily Herald* of 1933; they reported seeing a lake which had apparently escaped the notice of the usually very observant Ordnance Survey engineers, made some enquiries and came up with the answer 'Host Lockwood of Pen y Gwryd made this lake with his wheelbarrow and another good man'. 'Did you', I asked 'get permission from the Home Office, or the Prince of Wales or the policeman at Capel Curig?' 'I asked no one', he replied, 'I just made it'. The final phrase in the article 'An Empire Builder'.

There is another story on which Pen y Gwryd used to pride itself: about a mile up the road to Llanberis is the 'Pen y Pass Hotel', originally called by its Welsh name which is now coming back into use, of Gorffwysfa: this was owned by another Owen who was no relation to Harry but who in his early life had been a coachman to King Edward VII when he was Prince of Wales. When Owen gave up that post he took on Pen y Pass and managed it for fifty years; but he remained madly attached to horses and very fond of carriages and his hotel outbuildings contained a collection of landaus, carts, traps and other vehicles, and this collection was not finally dispersed until after his death. It was reported that during his time working for the Prince of Wales he drove the Boss on a journey round Caernarfonshire, and they stopped at Pen y Gwryd for a little refreshment and the Prince alighted and went into the Inn for a drink; but history does not relate what he consumed. At that time brandy and soda was a very usual drink for the 'upper classes' while whisky was more often reserved for the 'working man' in general and, of course, for the Scottish working man in particular who found it such a cheap drink that it was not uncommonly consumed at breakfast: how times change!

Arthur Lockwood's next great work was the creation of the trout hatchery of which more details are given in the chapter of the angler; and he went on working in the garden at Hafod y Gwynt.

During the whole of the Second World War while the hotel was occupied by an evacuated school Lockwood remained in his house and acted only in an advisory capacity as far as the Hotel was concerned; and then when the School left he sold the hotel in 1944, but retained Hafod y Gwynt his favourite house and garden and also the lake he had built. Much as he enjoyed working in his garden, as time went on even Arthur Lockwood found its sloping, rugged and overgrown nature too much for him to cope with and then when his wife died even the house became rather derelict until finally he went into a nursing home at Llanrwst where he died in January, 1973.

Mrs Lockwood lived well into her 93rd year and died on 3rd March 1969; had she lived a month or two longer, until 10th May, Florence and Arthur would have celebrated their diamond wedding. There is no doubt that her contribution to the growth of Pen y Gwryd was considerable and she does not always get her full share of the credit. Arthur Lockwood had owned and run the Pen y Gwryd Hotel for twenty-five years and his wife Florence, sometimes with his unofficial help, had managed it for ten years before he bought it. Throughout his reign he had seen Pen y Gwryd serving the sport of rock climbing while this was passing through its period of maximum development and while it was changing from what would now be considered to be merely mountain scrambling to a scientific and gymnastic achievement.

Lockwood's first love was fishing of which he had

considerable knowledge and experience, and much of his time and thought was occupied in finding ways of advancing its facilities. He gave much background help and advice in the furtherance of climbing, but he was wise enough to make little effort to keep himself in the forefront of the rapidly advancing skills needed. He knew much about the mountains and their strange ways and his fellow enthusiasts fully appreciated his great knowledge and help, so that throughout his life he had a wide and happy reputation among the mountaineering fraternity.

CHAPTER 4

THE MISFORTUNES OF WAR

A handsome house to lodge a friend,
A river at my garden's end.
Alexander Pope. *Epistles*.

The Second World War had an effect on Pen y Gwryd completely different from that produced by the First War; on inspection of the Visitors' Book between the years 1914 to 1918 it is very surprising what a large number of guests still went to stay at the hotel for holidays even during the worst and most frightening periods. During the time when according to Douglas Haig, who should have known, Britain's Army had its back to the wall there were still quite a large selection of people staying at the Hotel; they were mostly the older ones, for with the hundreds of thousands of casualties which that fearful war produced the slaughter among the young men had an effect from which it took a generation to recover. But from the hotel point of view things went on much as before except for difficulties in getting rationed food, but even these troubles were nothing like so well-marked in the remote parts of the country as they were in the town. Every farmer knows of the strange and sudden deaths to which pigs are prone during war time, while the mountain ewe is always liable to the fatal accident!

But during the Second World War the Hotel was taken over lock, stock and barrel by the Lake House School — evacuated from Bexhill-on-Sea in the general evacuation programme for schools from the southern parts of Britain. This school had spent the first term of 1940, or part of it, at the large and fashionable 'Royal Hotel' at Capel Curig, but it was soon evident that forty or so small boys together with two matrons and several schoolmasters were not entirely happy or suitable guests for a very large luxurious hotel.

The Headmaster was Alan H. Williams who had enjoyed some mountain climbing experience in his younger days, and this may be why he looked for a place in North Wales; later in the War he joined the Navy and unfortunately he was drowned at sea. When he joined the Navy he left the School in the control of Mr Dougal.

When the School arrived at Pen y Gwryd it experienced a considerable change for after being rather lost in a spacious hotel they now found accommodation rather tight. The headmaster's office was in the present hotel office just inside the front door, and the masters' common room was appropriately sited in the Bar. The top form was taught in the small lounge, two other forms used the dining-room and the smallest boys' classes used the billiard room. There is no information about the sleeping space but the boys must have been three or four in a bedroom, unless some outhouses were used as dormitories. It is interesting to remark that when at Bexhill in their proper school building the dormitories had been given mountain names; one of the former boys (The Hon. John Twining) remembers that while there he slept in the Matterhorn dormitory, as he clearly remembers the cry of "Matterhorn Bed" which went up when the boys in that dormitory were due to retire for the night.

It proved almost impossible to provide the sporting activities normal for boys at a preparatory school; the mountainside was no place for a cricket pitch, although they did manage to create a rough and rocky football pitch on the other side of the Betws-y-Coed road next door to Lockwood's lake. In warmer weather swimming could be arranged in the small pool behind the hotel, which may sometimes have been not much colder than the sea at Bexhill: and naturally a good deal of rough walking and scrambling was possible and was enjoyed, parties going up the Glyders behind the Hotel by varying routes, and some boys managing the Pig Track to the top of Snowdon, but no attempt was made to teach rock climbing, probably because there was no one available to teach the art. But a very enthusiastic scout troop was formed, and although ill-equipped for the job, the troop used to scurry round the mountainside. Some more advanced exercises were attempted by the Scout Troop the high spot coming when the troop joined in a one day exercise with the local Home Guard, which set out to hold the Cwm Dyli Power Station against the assaults or invasion by the scouts. The long legged Home Guard scattered over the hillside, managed to pick up the boys as they tried to get by, but they missed one important group: the smallest scout was hidden under the Home Guard Commander's car rug at the back of his car, and when the car reached the Power Station the boy quickly nipped out and 'blew up' the building and so presumably won the War. A suggestion has been made that the Commander concerned was Major Arthur Lockwood himself but that has not been substantiated!

But they did invent a game of their own, which appears to have been very complicated, but slightly verging on baseball, and it could be played on rough ground. Also they started a 'small school (sic) newspaper' which included news items such as the building of a new cruiser, and they used to put on school plays.

John Twining has been good enough to look up some old letters which he wrote while he was there, and which have been carefully preserved by parents and grandparents. He has also been kind enough to allow them to be quoted, and for schoolboy's letters they are of a high standard.

In one he enquired solicitously after Granny's health and tells her how he climbed Snowdon on a very hot day, and afterwards suffered from a boil on the back which he thinks occurred as he was bitten by a fly! One of the best of his letters is to his father and is deserving of a full quotation; it reads as follows:

'Dear Daddy, I am sorry I have not written for such a long time. In half term marks I was top with 2040 marks. In Latin I came top, in maths second in French, English and Scripture 3rd, 2nd in history and 5th in Geography. If it was not for maps I would be 1st or 2nd in Geography.

On Monday last we went up Moel Siabod. Last Monday we had a flag game. On Wednesday before last we had tea at the huts. Last Wednesday we had a flag game. On Saturday before last we . . . (left blank). Yesterday we cut stakes. Tuesday and on both Thursdays we did drill. On Friday before we stayed in. Last Friday we played a game of football which our side won 1 – nil.

We are having a play at the end of term here is the cast:

Sarah Upheart	– Elaine Dougal
George Upheart	– James Carr
Rodney Upheart	– John Williams
Rupert Delco	– Michael Watson
Jones	– John Mosse
Beth	– George Bayley
Owen	– David Bateman
John Arthur	– Me

Elaine Dougal is the daughter of one of the masters.

The plot is this; the Upheart family is staying at a 'mountain inn' in Wales; Jones is the proprietor, Beth the Housekeeper and Owen the Boots. An atmosphere of mystery surround the hotel and Rupert Delco and another guest is the centre of it. Rodney disappears and in the end I come along as a detective and arrest Jones and Delco who are in conspiracy to get gold out of an old secret mine behind the hotel.'

Then follow full details, with diagram of the famous flag game; doubtless father was able to follow it!

With the dearth of transport the boys had little chance of seeing anything much of the surrounding country or of the towns and villages: probably their best treat was a heavy fall of snow in January 1941 which cut them off from the world for ten days or so. There was added excitement when the headmaster's car which had been for provisions got stuck in the snow at the top of Llanberis Pass and the car had to be abandoned, although the boys had a great time rescuing the provisions. It may be that some of the boys acquired a taste for the mountains while they were there, at any rate it is to be hoped they did not miss this opportunity; certainly some of the masters revisited Snowdon in later days.

It is unfortunate that 'Lake House School' did not long survive the end of the War: for a few years after the School had closed the building at Bexhill was used as a local 'Girls' Brigade Training Centre'.

By the time the War was over Lockwood was beginning to feel his age a little and perhaps having been freed from hotel management for four years showed him how pleasant retirement could be and so he felt unwilling to start again, particularly in view of the troubles and difficulties produced by post war shortages of staff and supplies.

In 1941 Owen Riddett had suffered a severe illness and during his long convalescence he and his wife had stayed at a farmhouse near Capel Curig; they had always known that part of the country fairly well for his parents had spent their honeymoon in North Wales and they themselves had enjoyed several holidays thereabouts; during one of these they had met Arthur Lockwood. Before his convalescence was over the Riddetts had visited Lockwood who told them he was not happy about reopening the Hotel because of doubts about getting enough staff; but he added that he certainly meant to reopen the bar to ensure keeping the licence and also to make sure of his own whisky ration! Moreover he pointed out though the boys had behaved very well four years with schoolboys about the place and without any repairs to speak of were bound to leave their mark; as there seemed little chance of finding adequate staff to get the repairs done properly and to run the hotel he was seriously considering selling the place.

In due course Owen Riddett went back to work, but his wife carried back with her the germ of an idea, so that when his doctor suggested that Owen should think about a complete change of occupation and surroundings she inoculated him with the thought of how pleasant life at Pen y Gwryd could be. Why should they not try running a hotel for a change? So they got into touch with Lockwood and started negotiations. These were successful and so in August 1944 they bought Pen y Gwryd. But Lockwood kept Lockwood's Llyn and also his house Hafod y Gwynt, and he continued to live there and deal with his garden and contemplate his hatchery.

The Riddetts were living near Birkenhead when the sale was completed, and they borrowed his parents' car to drive to

Wales. They were not allowed enough petrol to get the car up there, but they finally managed to arrange to have it sent up by train to Betws-y-Coed, and hoped their troubles would then be over. Not a bit of it for only after prolonged argument by letter and telephone and finally going in person to Caernarfon to see the Fuel Officer were they allowed the small ration of fuel needed to go the ten miles from Betws-y-Coed to Pen y Gwryd. They also had some trouble about the telephone at the hotel, but as Lockwood was still the Commander of the Home Guard and had a telephone to use for Home Guard affairs he let them use it for emergency. But very soon the Home Guard was disbanded and then a lot more time and energy was needed before the telephone business was finally sorted out.

No one who had not experienced the conditions at the end of the War would realize the immense difficulties and problems which arose on trying to restart a hotel business at that time. The Riddetts started at Pen y Gwryd with only their own personal supplies; guests who went to stay there had to use their own ration books, which were called emergency ones, and when the guests left the management had to endeavour to make up the supplies of food from these cards. As always the various local authority offices were well entangled in red tape and the regulations said that they could assess the future needs of the hotel only on the amount of food it had used during the past years; as during the past years it had housed a boys Preparatory School this was neither helpful nor logical when the Riddetts wanted to reopen a hotel, and build up a trade for normal adult visitors.

They also had the problem of the bar trade which was bringing in some much needed cash; in this remote spot the day-to-day bar trade was very small, but it did help. But even here they were short of supplies, although Arthur Lockwood allowed them some of his personal allocation. But from all sources they managed to get only two dozen bottles of whisky and one dozen bottles of gin a month, which was nothing like enough for their clients' needs. But they had a stroke of luck for one passing visitor was so pleased with his whisky and with the happy reception he received that he offered to send them a present, and quite soon afterwards they were delighted to get from him twenty 8 lb tins of jam; not very helpful for serving thirsty climbers but useful for those looking for large teas. Even better, this good friend turned out to be a baker from a local village and he became a regular visitor and on one occasion he took as a guest the local Food Officer; after a little gentle hospitality things eased up at once and the food supply improved a good deal!

Naturally staff was a big trouble. They were told about one stalwart retainer named Blodwen Griffiths who had been a housemaid to the Lockwoods before the beginning of the First War, when she went to other employment. She might have returned to Pen y Gwryd if she had been approached, but unfortunately they did not contact her and it was not until the Briggs took over several years later that she went back. So for a long time the Riddetts had to manage on their own, but as the number of visitors was not very large they could just cope with the work.

There was an Approved School close to Betws-y-Coed and they got into touch with the Mother Superior in charge, and from her they employed several boys aged about fifteen years or so who were allowed to work for the small wage of 17/6 a week and their keep, provided they were well looked after. In all they employed fourteen of these boys at varying times and as might be expected some were quite good and some were quite bad and most were idle; but they were useful in those troublesome days. Most people will realize nowadays that it is far from easy to keep staff at a place which is far from towns and villages, and where there is practically no public transport. Some months after the Riddetts started running Pen y Gwryd a desultory bus service was instituted but it was so slight as to be useless to them. At times they managed to hire a cook, but as cooks go they went so that they were frequently without anyone to help with the meals. They had one welcome helper in the village postman, a helper on whom so many villages have relied in the past. Driving his van from Caernarfon to Beddgelert via Pen y Gwryd and Pen y Pass he was in turn newspaper boy, milkman and a cheerful carrier of as many other goods and chattels as required.

After nearly five years with a Preparatory School in residence, and with little chance of getting even normal repairs done it may be imagined that much repair work was urgently needed; damp, doubtful plumbing, loose slates and lack of regular painting all showed, and the outbuildings were in a particularly bad state. Owen Riddett had to do nearly all the repair work himself, and this was not easy as most builders' materials were either in short supply or unobtainable. However, he got through a lot of the most necessary repair work, including putting on new chimney pots and cowls, re-cementing the outside and the inside of some of the chimney stacks, repairing rotted floorboards, sweeping chimneys and, of course, repainting.

Accommodation was difficult and they started by using the proprietors' flat consisting of four rooms and a bathroom at the back of the hotel. But later they felt that they needed to be nearer the working parts of the hotel and moved into a downstairs room. They completed a lot of repair and redecoration to the billiard room and made this into the dining-room as it was very convenient for service from the kitchen; the old dining-room then became the lounge and that gave much more room for the guests, and it looked cheerful as it had two working fireplaces: it should be remembered that there was no central heating and all heat came from open fires, electric fires or oil stoves. The electric power supply came from Cwm Dyli Station and was limited to seven kilowatts and was meant for lighting only. Owen Riddett himself built a fireplace in the hall and placed in it a solid fuel stove which helped to heat the Bar and the coffee room. Fortunately the water heating system was first class with efficient coke fired boilers and two beautiful copper tanks in a room upstairs, which with pegs and shelves made an excellent drying room, perhaps the most essential feature for a mountain hotel in North Wales. The Aga cookers, although past their prime, were adequate for the purpose but the rest of the kitchen equipment was old-fashioned and badly kept; the years of wartime neglect had taken their toll.

As there was only one downstairs lavatory the Riddetts had little trouble in getting planning permission for putting in two more off the passage leading from the bar, and they persuaded a builder to do the work for them. Pen y Gwryd has always been somewhat exceptional in having no special residents' bar, and seldom having enough staff to serve residents their drinks in the lounges. This meant that everyone, resident or outsider, had to stand at the same counter which was fine when the numbers were not too great but with a large invasion from outside things became crowded and noisy. This has been changed today as residents only are allowed to use the Smoke Room which has wooden panelled but strangely elastic sided walls so that it seems that all residents can always find room there!

One of the Riddetts' earliest groups of visitors were some old friends of the hotel, Gladys Young, an actress well known at that time, with her sister Mrs Daniell better known as E.H. Young the novelist. At Christmas, Easter and Whitsun more visitors arrived and they managed to stage some merry parties; and some organized groups from outside and from overseas arrived including such gatherings as the British members of The Swiss Alpine Club. And although the Climbers' Club and the Pinnacle Club and other climbing groups were beginning to get their own huts in which to stay they were still very happy to get back to their birthplace, Pen y Gwryd for drinks and meals and pleasant meetings with old friends.

So fairly soon after the war many old favourites started to drift back to the Inn and these included such well known climbers as John Hunt, Geoffrey Bartram and Bryan Donkin of the Alpine Club, and others soon to reach the peak on climbing circles in such men as R.L.G. Irvine of Winchester and Wilfrid Noyce; and surely the lady climbers must not be forgotten as they included well-known names such as Nea Morin, Jo Fuller and Brenda Ritchie.

Then as always the Pen y Gwryd Visitors' Books show some famous names of those outside the mountaineering groups and the hotel had as guests among others that great pianist Moura Lympany, the artist John Piper and his wife, a photographer called Doucher well known at that time; also Eric James, now Lord James and Mr Justice Thesiger.

But the most notable visitors who however did not stay at the hotel although they may have crossed the threshold, were His Majesty King George VI with Queen Elizabeth when they paid a visit to North Wales to view the proposed Snowdonia National Park before it came into being in 1949.

The restriction on foreign travel, largely occasioned by the limited amount of British currency which could be taken abroad, was slowly eased, and at the same time the new package tour industry began to take shape. At once climbers were eager to visit the Alps and the Dolomites again; while skiing became cheaper in the hands of the tour operators and this popular pastime reduced the number of winter visitors to British hotels. With this went the constant demand for more money for repairs and alterations to the Inn, staff difficulties and the rigid rules of the new Catering Wages Act which made staff more expensive. All these problems together persuaded the Riddetts that maybe the time had come to give up the unequal struggle and to sell the hotel. They were anxious that it should not become a tied house of one of the breweries, so it was put up for auction, but it did not reach the reserve price and it was withdrawn. Very fortunately for the Riddetts and still more so for the 'Pen y Gwryd Hotel' the advertisement was seen by one Leslie Mather, who — as will be seen later — was looking round for a place in the country: he arrived at the psychological moment and with great foresight and without further ado he bought the Inn. Thus it finally passed into the enterprising hands of Chris and Jo Briggs in 1947 and with this family it still remains, and with them it still continues to be the same Pen y Gwryd.

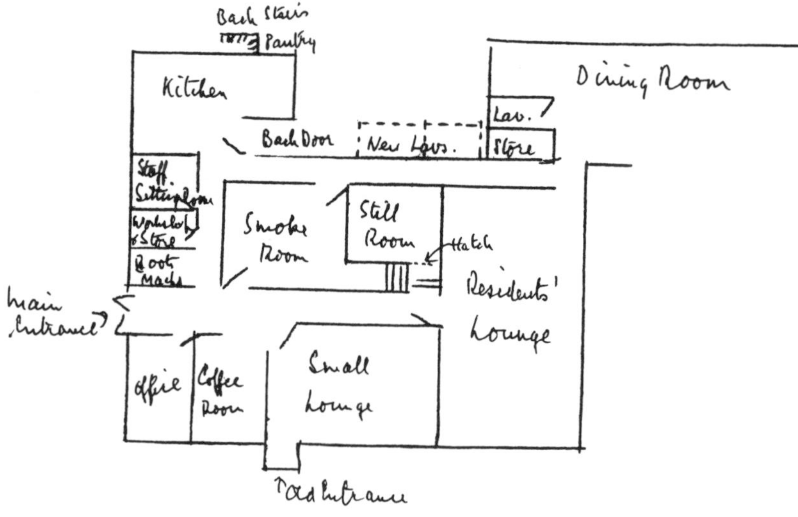

Rough sketch of the ground floor at Pen y Gwryd as it was at the time of the Riddetts; the major changes now are that the room marked Dining-Room is now the Games Room; the Residents' Lounge, large, is now the Dining-Room and maybe most important of all the small Staff Sitting Room, Workshop and Boot Room have together been converted into the Everest Room.

CHAPTER 5

A YORKIST TAKE OVER

Now is the winter of our discontent
Made glorious summer by this sun of York:
And all the clouds that lour'd upon our house
In the deep bosom of the ocean buried.
Shakespeare. King Richard III

We are now entering the present era of the 'Pen y Gwryd Hotel' and fortunately this is an epoch which has had more of its incidents recorded than most of the previous ones. All institutions have their ups and downs and hotels are no exception: after the death of the Owens, Pen y Gwryd had fallen from its position as an exceptional climbers' hotel into a more ordinary plane. Arthur Lockwood very ably assisted by Florence, had done much to raise it to its former level of attainment. Although he had to deal with the difficulties caused by the First World War these were on the whole less troublesome than might have been expected and he fairly easily weathered the storm, but inevitably the Second War caused a major set back. The hotel was closed for five years and somewhat ravaged by schoolboys, while during and after the War few repairs were possible. Immediately the War ended, Lockwood sold the hotel and the Riddetts, working against great odds, tried to guide its first tottering footsteps back to normal. But they were there for only two difficult years when there was little let up from the restrictions of war-time and they made no claim to be well versed in hotel management of which they had no previous experience and which was well outside their usual course of duty.

When Chris and Jo took over Pen y Gwryd the whole country was still suffering from the aftermath of war: there had been practically no easing up in the severe food rationing, in fact for the first time bread was put on the ration list, which it had escaped all through the fighting! Petrol was still as strictly rationed as at any time: and worst of all was the fact that a hotel had its food ration calculated on what it had used in the previous months or years, a method by which any increase in the amount of nourishment provided as the number of guests went up seemed an impossible feat: and of course there was still the greatest difficulty in getting staff. However, by a combination of shrewdness and very hard work the Briggs, using every handhold and foothold, slowly fought their way to the summit and under their control Pen y Gwryd once again came back to the form which it had reached during the best years of the Owens, and after this short early struggle it rapidly climbed to the pinnacle where it has remained ever since. For Pen y Gwryd was not merely the centre for walking and mountaineering in Wales, but it also became recognized as one of the important centres at which the new style British rock climbing was developing. It soon established a close connection with the mountaineers who made history by their achievements in the Andes, the Caucasus and to crown all, with those who reached the summit of Everest and of other Himalayan peaks. And so it became known as a hotel where climbers and mountaineers of all ages and from all over the world could visit with the certainty that they would meet others with tastes and abilities similar to their own.

This is not to denigrate in any way the Lakeland mountains and the superb summits in Scotland for together with the hotels that serve them they have played a great part in the encouragement of climbing in this country. He would indeed be a brave man who would try and estimate which of these groups or areas has had the greatest influence on the growth of modern rock climbing, for all have played their part and each group has its admirers. Small bunches of experts have tended to assemble first in one place and then in another and one locality has shown a spurt in the evolvement of technique for a year or two, and then the lead has passed elsewhere. But there are many who think that over the last quarter of a century Pen y Gwryd has managed to keep in the forefront and to remain a nucleus for all those keenly interested in walking, scrambling, climbing, mountaineering, fishing, the study of flora and fauna and the multitude of activities which take people to mountain districts and to the land of the rivers and lakes. With all this it has maintained an aura of companionship which has made it a home for many; and at Pen y Gwryd many friendships have been made and many have been kept.

Naturally Pen y Gwryd has been fortunate in some ways and unfortunate in others. It has lost some competitors and gained others; for example the 'Royal Hotel' at Capel Curig was turned into a centre for the training of youth in all forms of outdoor exercise from climbing to canoeing and it is now under the direction of the Central Council for Physical Recreation and has been named 'Plas y Brenin'. This change may have brought some more visitors to Pen y Gwryd, and it has given many of the young a taste for the mountains and might bring them back again in later life. A more recent change has been Gorffwysfa the hotel at Pen y Pass. Pen y Gwryd was already a successful climbing centre when someone from Capel Curig decided to build another Inn higher up the Pass to rival it, and so Pen y Pass came into being, and the two of them see-sawed up and down in popularity for many years. Rawson Owen leased Pen y Pass from the Vaenol estate for sixty years, and finally it was put up for sale with only a four year lease to run, and so the estate appointed a tenant for the short time: then it was sold to the Youth Hostels Association and a large extra wing was built on, and thus it remains, and so Pen y Gwryd gains and loses as it does for Plas y Brenin.

But the greatest change which has taken place during the last fifteen years or so has been an enormous increase in the number of climbing huts available. Practically every climbing club, every university and educational authority has taken over some cottage or small house and has turned it into such a hut; and there the young who are willing to live a bit rough can spend their holidays or weekends very cheaply; and many of the young of today seem to prefer this kind of rather uncivilized life where washing and tidy clothes are not expected.

Christopher Bastin Briggs was born in Scarborough in 1913 and at the age of seven years he went with his parents to live in the Manchester neighbourhood; in due course he went to school at Stand Grammar School; he now remarks that the school motto was 'They stand to serve' which he feels that he has fully lived up to as he has spent so much of his life standing and serving behind the bar. The school's best known pupil was Clive of India, who was expelled from the school, but despite this they now have a plaque put up in his honour. Chris was usually late for school and seldom did his homework but did not quite succeed in gaining expulsion; and he did not realize then that the time would come when he would get to know and love India.

A very enthusiastic scout who became assistant scoutmaster, he has no doubt that what he learnt as a scout has stood him in very good stead, and he says that not a day passes when he does not use some art or craft that he learnt as a scout; but he does not emphasise the craft!

When he left school he went to his first job with the Mark Fletcher Dying and Printing Works, and later moved to a post with the Manchester Chemical Agents where he stayed for eight years. So Chris can claim to have essentially Yorkshire genes trained in Lancashire; surely a mixture which can be guaranteed to produce that steadfastness of purpose (never to be confused with pig-headedness) which is customary in all those with North country blood: one northern county is adequate for most people and a combination of both must give a blend impossible to beat and certain to reach success in any walk of life.

Joyce Briggs née Fletcher, (and hereinafter, as the solicitors would say, always called Jo which is the name by which she is known throughout the United Kingdom), was born in Manchester, but her parents took her to Newfoundland at the age of two years; there she went to school and there she acquired a view of life very different from the one which would be gained had she spent her youth in this country. The physical side of life was harder and she thought of the ski, the snowshoe and the dog sleigh as the normal method of winter travel.

At the age of sixteen her father sent her to this country to take a business course at Pitman's College in Manchester. For a short time her mother was also in England but she went back home when the war started, but despite her father's protests Jo could not be persuaded to return to Newfoundland. She had recently started a secretarial job in Manchester which she liked and moreover she felt she would wish to help this country in its hour of need. So she remained and shared a flat with her sister, and she also joined the Red Cross and took part in some part-time nursing at the Northern Hospital. Later she was appointed Assistant Secretary to the Board of Cotton Control, a Government Department which was important under war conditions. Soon after the end of the war her father died and her family moved to British Columbia where they have lived ever since.

The flat sharing was not very long lasting for in 1940 she and Chris were married and set up house on their own, staying in Manchester where their jobs were. It was in 1943 that Jane was born and she was their only child; it was for this reason that naturalist James Fisher, when he knew her well at Pen y Gwryd, christened Jo 'Mrs Gannet' for the gannet normally hatches only one chick: surely James Fisher should have known that the penguin also lays one egg and it is a much more attractive bird to be called after!

During their engagement and after their marriage, Chris and Jo spent their holidays and all their weekends at the 'Brotherswater Hotel' in Patterdale at the foot of the Kirkstone Pass. This small area is in appearance of mountains, rivers and lakes very similar to that round Snowdon and Pen y Gwryd and both the Briggs are sure that these holidays did a lot to create their great love of the mountains of North Wales.

One of their family friends was Leslie Mather, a batchelor who was an accountant and a company secretary. He and Chris Briggs had been friends for many years, and both had received in the first few years of life that cerebral implantation of business acumen which is normal for the child brought up in Manchester. Leslie Mather also shared the love of the country, and together they started to investigate the possibility of finding some kind of part-time occupation which would take them into the country at weekends or for some days in the week, preferably at a place near the mountains which they both enjoyed. With the optimism of youth they thought it might be possible to find a country post office, shop, a bakery round or something similar in which they could share the work and which could be run on a part-time basis and largely by remote control! Neither of them had any intention at that time of giving up their very good and enjoyable jobs in town.

This hopeful exploration did not start until the end of the War and it was not until 1947 that Leslie Mather saw an advertisement in a Manchester paper about the sale of the hotel at Pen y Gwryd and in a moment of great inspiration he rushed off to inspect the premises. Chris and Jo were away on holiday when this happened and on their return they were somewhat surprised to get a telephone call from Leslie asking if they were prepared to run a country Inn; while they were considering this sudden and unexpected suggestion and may have been showing signs of hesitation and even perturbation Leslie pointed out that he had already bought the place so one of the three would have to like it and go and look after it. Chris and Jo had had no previous intention of leaving their regular work so they suffered a lot of heart searching, but Mather was unmarried and as a man and wife were almost essential for the running of such a venture, the Briggs decided that it was up to them to take the not inconsiderable risk. It was a choice they have never had any reason to regret throughout their life. Very little thought was needed to show them that an inn could not be run from a distance and that they would have to live on the spot.

Pen y Gwryd had endured five years of war and although the Riddetts had done some rehabilitation there was still a long way to go as things could not be hurried in the troublesome post-war world; there was still much repair work to be done, much more equipment to get, and so far the staff problem had proved insoluble. The Briggs had very little capital to start with, and very meagre knowledge of the hotel business, but with what proved to be justifiable optimism they felt they would like to try what common sense and really hard work could accomplish; a very brave decision.

If it worked, any profits were to be shared on a fifty-fifty basis with Leslie Mather and they had decided that between them they could lose about £2,000 before being declared

THE OWENS' VISITORS DEPART IN 1892
Note the ladder for dismounting from coaches

PEN Y GWRYD
Old and new

WOMANS' FIRST STEPS?

THE SUMMIT OF SNOWDON
About 1860

CHRIS BRIGGS   JOHN HUNT   TENZING
(LORD HUNT)

KING GEORGE VI AND QUEEN ELIZABETH
King George VI and Queen Elizabeth survey the area of Snowdonia, soon to be proclaimed a National Park. Their guide on the map is Clough (later Sir Clough) Williams-Ellis, background Pen y Gwryd and the Glyders

MR AND MRS HARRY OWEN

THE OWENS

WILLIAM HAMPSON
With wife and grandchild

THE LOCKWOODS
Married at Beddgelert

CHRIS AND JO BRIGGS
With daughter Jane and son-in-law Brian

CHRIS BRIGGS, EVEREST CELEBRATION 1953
Follows the Yeti's footprints

ARTHUR LOCKWOOD
With cuckoo whose broken leg he had mended

THE SMOKE ROOM
Heart and soul of Pen y Gwryd!

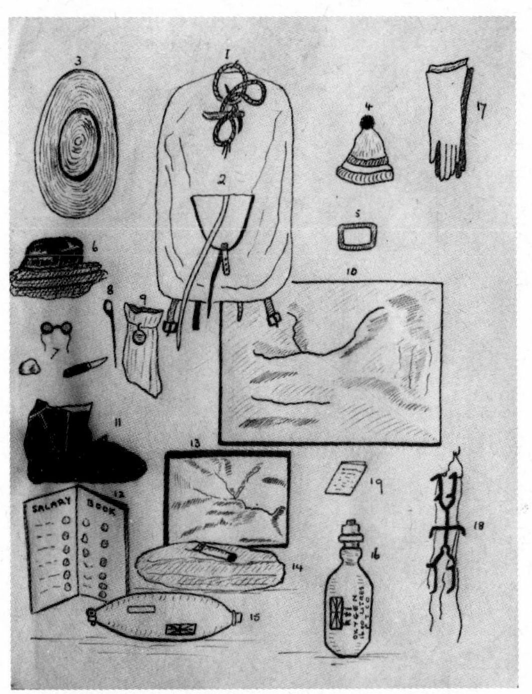

THE SMOKE ROOM EVEREST CABINET
Climbing kit used by Everest team

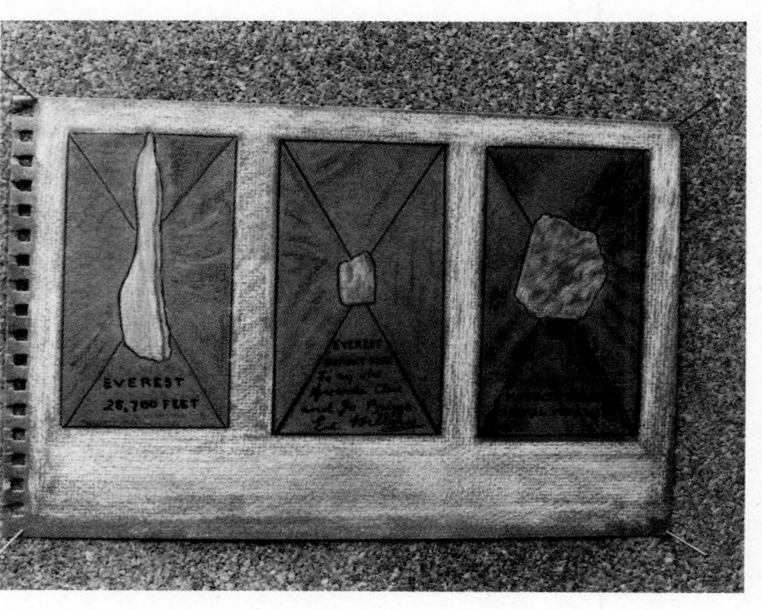

THE SMOKE ROOM EVEREST CABINET
Rock from summits of Everest and Kanchengunga

bankrupt and having to start life all over again. As it happened by doing almost all the work themselves and working seventeen hours a day for seven days a week they lost a small amount in the first year, made a few shillings profit in the second, and in the third year they started to pick up and show signs that the scheme might succeed. Once the decision had been made they started to consider their stock in trade; Jo had many times catered for large private dinner parties for a dozen or so guests, and she well understood the art and science of cookery so that to apply this knowledge to larger numbers should not prove impossible. Chris was a one-time secretary of a rugger club, was used to running a bar on Saturday nights, and knew something of the beer and spirit trade and he was not inexperienced with dealing with some rowdyism should it occur. Fortunately they were starting before the days of vandalism and mob rule and the number of cases of departure from normal civilized behaviour were few. His experience of hotels came entirely from staying in them, but this had taught him that good food, a good fire, good beds and plenty of hot water went a long way towards making most guests content. So on this amount of experience they had to build using the bricks of common sense and the cement of intelligence. Again on the credit side was the fact that the hotel was still not going at anything like full stretch and was rarely full up and this gave them that bit of extra time to learn as they went along and it was easier to cope with a slow build up, to provide more pots and pans and furniture as the money came in and the number of guests increased. But on the debit side was the post-war restriction and disorganization; food rationing was still very strict and so was petrol rationing, and it was not a place where public transport could be used as that did not exist. But they never reached a stage at which they seriously contemplated giving up the struggle; this result was achieved by their hard work and natural capacity, their willingness to tackle anything however new to them and their great talent for friendship with people. That is to say in the realization, apparently almost unknown today that the real pleasures of life come most often from success resulting from work and effort and enterprise; and in giving happy service to others; and for many folk this counts for far more than mere financial gain.

To organize the transfer of the management it had been arranged that they would spend one whole day with the Riddetts for full discussion. As bad luck would have it their aged car broke down on the way and they had to spend the night in a hotel near Chester so they reached Pen y Gwryd only at about five o'clock the next day; as the Riddetts were off early the next morning everything had to be fitted in during the evening, and most of the work was done over dinner. Among those dining at the hotel that evening was a couple of near neighbours to whom they were not then introduced but who they were to know very well later; Esmé and Peter Kirby came from the large sheep farm next door called 'Dyffryn Mymbyr' a place which had already gained fame from Thomas Firbank's book *I bought a Mountain* published and avidly read during the disconsolate early weeks of the War.

Looking at their farm today it is interesting, if slightly off the track, to remember that John Leland in the sixteenth century, speaks of a certain grove as being 'very unlike the great woods which clothed this place "Dyffrin Membyr", Llanberis and parts of Snowdon'; by the time Thomas Pennant had got there he notes that the woods had gone.

For domestic help the Briggs had to start with some of the boys from the Approved School at Betws-y-Coed that the previous owners had employed; these often changed and soon they struck a bad batch and they found that when they were bad they were just delinquents. Some apparently found pleasure in torturing animals, and for Chris and Jo this was intolerable and the boys had to be sacked. They managed for a time to get some sporadic help from the local villages, but such folk usually had to be fetched and taken back daily. A married woman with one child acted fairly well as a housekeeper and manageress for a time, but she is now remembered only by her nickname of 'Cuckoo'. One cook who came from Llanberis had to be fetched daily from the bus stop in Nantperis and taken back each evening just before dinner was served in the hotel; Chris not uncommonly noticed the delightful aroma of roast lamb or pork chops coming from the lady's bag as a bit of illicit food was taken away for home consumption!

But this was not the only trouble which arose about illicit food. Rawson Owen the landlord of the 'Pen y Pass Hotel' proved very kind and helpful to the Briggs when they first arrived, for he realized fully how complicated were the rationing laws to those relatively inexperienced in the catering trade, and he also knew that the Briggs as newcomers to the neighbourhood had little access to the local farmers whose sheep and pigs, although disease free, sometimes died suddenly if not entirely unexpectedly. So Owen would give them an odd joint of meat from time to time to help them on their way. On one occasion he rushed down speedily to Pen y Gwryd to make certain that the joint of mutton was already in the oven and that the blue rationing stamp was obscured, for the inspector was on his way! While another time Chris had a very narrow escape when the inspector arrived to look round Pen y Gwryd; he popped his head briefly into the small workshop on the ground floor but in his interest in the tools and the tricouni nailing equipment he failed to notice the illegal half carcass hanging from a ceiling hook just behind the door!

But luckily they did manage to get hold of Blodwen Griffiths, mentioned earlier as having worked at Pen y Gwryd in the time of the Lockwoods, and having left only when the School moved in during the War. Jo had little difficulty in persuading her to return to the fold and there she remained in good and faithful service until her final illness at the age of eighty four years. The great Blodwen had quite adequate English but she still thought in Welsh, and she took the hotel under her wing in the way common for the family retainer of those days, and she remained a pillar of Pen y Gwryd for the next twenty-five years; she was known and welcomed by many generations of walkers and climbers and more about her will be found later in this book.

After a period of tentative efforts with several cooks, they decided that in future Chris should take over the cooking of the breakfasts, as bacon and eggs seemed within his boy scout training. Chris also took charge of the preparation of the packed lunches but opinions differ as to whether he did those well or not; at least one of their best friends who still visits Pen y Gwryd frequently regarded as a 'hollow mockery' their slogan of those times of 'Packed lunches a speciality'. But this was the wrong terminology for even if a mockery the sandwiches were certainly not hollow and they might have been more tasty if they had been: but this friend will be glad to hear that in their newly acquired son-in-law, Brian Pullee they have found a superb sandwich filler, and now the slogan could be readopted. Jo took over the lunches and dinners and this delighted the guests who got excellent food well cooked and well served. With growing numbers and with sparse kitchen equipment and hardly any help in the kitchen it was very hard work but Jo stuck to it with outstanding success for many years.

Pen y Gwryd had gained its reputation not only as a comfortable Inn but also as a magnificent centre for climbing and walking, and fairly soon after the War there was some clamour for more accommodation particularly by the young climbers. For half a century before the War the most constant customers, apart from the Church, were the reasonably well-to-do graduates and undergraduates from Oxford and Cambridge, and the schoolmasters and senior boys from the public schools, together with a sprinkling from many of the professions. The War gave rise to very marked financial changes; cash shortages struck the professions and the undergraduates so that cheaper holidays were essential and very soon the surprisingly cheap and attractive holiday abroad became popular. But with this change the newer Universities were adding to the student population. In this happily classless sport of climbing, the professional men were being joined in some numbers by artisans, apprentices and manual workers from industries in the Midland towns and cities, all within easy reach of North Wales for these people began getting better wages and holidays and could afford to go into the country.

Chris Briggs had great sympathy with anyone who wanted to explore the mountains, and he always looked for ways in which he could help them in this desire. As a good busines man it was sensible to give them aid, for the less well off young worker of today may be the better off family man of tomorrow, and if he kept his liking for the hills and valleys he would wish to introduce his wife and family to them also; knowing Chris there is no doubt that this was a minor factor and the major one was the desire always in the minds of the Briggs to bring everyone into the fold and to make them look on Pen y Gwryd as their second home. So with a flash of inspiration and some ingenuity Chris converted an outbuilding contiguous with the Inn into a dormitory, from then on known as the Bunkhouse. This provided eighteen comfortable bunk beds and something of that camping atmosphere enjoyed by the young; meals were served for them in the hotel in the usual way, but the whole arrangement gave the occupiers a cheaper but very enjoyable holiday and it proved to be an immensely popular institution. The charge was only four shillings a night, and even this was not always collected, while it was not impossible to get breakfast free if the landlord found the case a worthy one. The Bunkhouse was started in 1950 which was before the great increase in private and institutionally owned climbing huts now scattered broadcast throughout Snowdonia and which are always crowded with young people: it was full during the summer and on most weekends in the spring and autumn and when it was completely occupied it meant that the hotel had a total of fifty guests staying there.

Unhappily, by 1970 the shortage of staff quarters had become acute, and the popular Bunkhouse was converted into staff bedrooms and later into a manager's self-contained flat. In many ways it was a sad loss both to the hotel and to many keen climbers who lacked access to the huts as they belonged to no club; but whether the Bunkhouse could be kept filled now when there are so many cheaper facilities for holidays in the way of caravans and tents can only be guessed.

But this is only one illustration of the thoughtful outlook which Chris and Jo Briggs took to Pen y Gwryd; undoubtedly their most important influence came from their natural genius, for they had decided from the very beginning to make sure that the hotel should return to its original glory and become a homely Inn, such as it had been in the days of the Owens; an Inn with a friendly atmosphere where each guest soon found that they were adopted as kith and kin, and where they felt themselves members of the house party of the Host and Hostess, and not merely staying at a hotel where the food was good.

Each evening after dinner the Smoke Room was filled, indeed usually overfilled, with a crowd of happy people evidently enjoying life, and prolonged discussions, grave or gay, were routine. Jo soon established herself as a superb discussion stirrer, proving as adept at mixing the ingredients in the holdall of humanity as she was in mixing those in the kitchen pots. A natural raconteur with an able and rapid wit she had no difficulty in making sure that talks and friendly arguments on every variety of topic were the order of the evening; hence the Smoke Room after dinner was never dull.

All this meant that anyone going to stay there was likely to find an old friend or to make a new one; many real friendships must have started at Pen y Gwryd and probably this factor more than any other has guided this Inn to its immense success.

As the influx of visitors increased so did the amount of work involved. There was no improvement in public transport facilities and the relative isolation of the hotel made it less attractive to some would-be helpers, and so the staff position became desperate. This gave Jo *her* chance for a little bit of inspiration and she jumped at it: she approached a number of schools and technical colleges asking if they had any girls who had not yet decided on a career and who might be interested in having training for hotel work as an occupation. Any who showed interest were interviewed and if they seemed suitable they were offered a two years' course at Pen y Gwryd in all aspects of hotel management, in cooking, meal service, care of bedrooms and linen and so on: and they were instructed in all the many ways in which a guest could be made comfortable. At the end of the two year stint they could stay if they so wished, or go for other posts. Not surprisingly a large proportion got engaged or married before the two years were up, for after all there was always a good sprinkling of tough young climbers there and in time there were added some of the Royal Air Force Rescue Teams, and units of the Army on exercise so opportunities for matrimony were quite abundant. For many years this venture supplied the hotel with a competent and pleasant staff which helped to make the visitors content; but for many years Jo continued to do the cooking herself and she also had to do practically all the secretarial work and so when the other jobs were finished she found that many long hours had to be spent clattering on the typewriter, a task at which she was also an expert.

One of her friends from educational establishments was Ann

Babcock who was trained in the art of cooking by Jo and who by degrees took over the whole of the culinary art, proving to be an extremely able chef. Then in due course someone called Douglas Verity arrived; he went to Pen y Gwryd to climb mountains but he offered to help serve in the Bar where he saw Ann Babcock, and promptly approached Chris to ask if there was any chance of a permanent job. This was found for him and Ann and Douglas were married. For some years they stayed with Ann still as cook and Douglas as assistant manager and barman; but later Douglas found himself a post as secretary to a golf club. After a few false starts the Briggs managed to get another first class chef in the person of Jack Williams from Blaenau Ffestiniog who arrived in 1965 and stayed with them doing admirable work until 1974.

Snowdonia has fourteen mountain peaks which reach a height of over three thousand feet, of which more will be said later. Fortunately, even if fortuitously, Pen y Gwryd has fourteen bedrooms for guests and the Briggs hit on the idea of naming each bedroom after one of these special peaks and this was done in 1952. It can only be guessed what would have happened if the number of bedrooms had been wrong, but it is not impossible that they would have adopted a procrustean method for making things right. These names are well-liked by the guests, partly because they are pleasant and unusual names and partly because it gives the poor Englishman some simple instructions in Welsh pronunciation, and for the first time perhaps they meet such words as Yr Elen, Pen yr Ole Wen, y Garn, Crib y Ddysgyl on the room doors. But the idea did have some teething troubles for on one occasion Jo met a large and rather unhappy looking Lancashire lass scuttling round the corridor and she said to Jo with great concern "Eh, lass, which of these names means lavatory?" History does not relate if Jo took the opportunity of introducing her to Pen y Gwryd's notorious compartment which is believed to be the lavatory of the smallest size and the strangest shape of any in the British Isles.

Within very few months of his arrival poor Chris Briggs ran into one of the constantly recurring and most troublesome problems of running a climbing hotel in Snowdonia. Paul Hermansson an experienced climber who had been visiting the hills in North Wales for twenty years or so, set out on a solitary mountain walk and failed to return.

This at once introduced Chris to the immensity of such problems: firstly had he told anyone where he was going? His wife was staying in the hotel but she did not know the mountains well and had only vague ideas as to his route. Then which way did he start off, and had he any intention of coming back by another route? All these points needed clarification before a search party started to look for him. In this case Chris organized a rescue party and they spent the whole of the next day exploring Cwm Glas, and the complete Snowdon Horseshoe as that was supposed to be his intended way; they continued until nightfall without any luck, and it was not until noon the following day that his body was found at the foot of Lliwedd down a precipice of which he had fallen to his death.

My wife and I had visited Pen y Gwryd in the times of the Lockwoods and of the Riddetts but this happened to be the first visit we had paid to the hotel since the Briggs took charge, so we were somewhat surprised, if not alarmed, on going through the front door to find the hall decorated by policemen's helmets suggesting that the new owners were already being arrested. But they have just managed to avoid that up to the present and the cause of the trouble was that we had arrived at the precise moment of the Coroner's inquest on the death of Paul Hermansson. Perhaps it is as well that we never claimed to be climbers but mere mountain scramblers or such a welcome might have put us off Snowdonia for life.

But to Chris and his family the mountains held no terrors; in 1950 during what was called the last guest free days before Christmas, a tribe consisting of their great friend John Disley, later of Olympic Steeplechase fame, Ralph Jones, Jack Henderson, Mr and Mrs Briggs and their seven-year-old daughter Jane all set out for the summit of Snowdon. Despite newly fallen snow, in places several feet thick, and which sometimes meant the use of the ice axe for the final passage, they all reached the top; then they returned by the same route, glissading down the zig-zag slopes.

There is no end to the steady alterations required in a go-ahead hotel to keep it up to new standards; Pen y Gwryd had had a number of changes but they were mainly minor ones as it had been an Inn for over a century and a quarter, and was a solid, well-constructed stone building. Such buildings were put up to meet the needs of the time not of the future, and they were built to ensure that they remained wind and weather proof for centuries if necessary. But it is not always easy to work in old-fashioned places which may appear a bit cramped according to modern standards, also it is usually impossible to modernize the design fully without spoiling the old world appearance which is one of the attractions of many hotels in this country.

Chris and Jo did much to counteract these disadvantages by making their guests fit in with the landscape of the hotel; or perhaps more accurately by making sure their selection of guests came from the groups that would enjoy the surroundings found in the hotel, and the atmosphere created by the host and hostess, and in this they were supremely successful. Most of their visitors went there by reason of their love of the mountains and the rivers and lakes, whether they wished to climb or walk in the hills, to fish in the lakes or just to stroll round and admire the beauty that enveloped them. Of course, they wanted good food and good beds, and hot water; and perhaps most important of all in North Wales good drying facilities and in all of these Pen y Gwryd excelled. Although there are some who think the drying facilities, excellent though they are in these self-service days, are not up to the standard which the Briggs first introduced: for then each bedroom had its small heap of numbered discs and safety pins, and decorated with these the wet clothes were hung outside the bedroom door and in due course they were collected, dried and returned. This shows the natural Briggs standard of service which they would still be happy to provide were it possible nowadays. The very rare visitor who expected a valet or lady's maid constantly in attendance, a television room and a variety of lounge space, and to be served with meals at any time of the day or night, strangely enough frequently found that the hotel was fully booked when they wanted to make another visit.

Among the first of the issues to be dealt with was lounge accommodation; the small lounge was emptied and furnished for its correct use for guests, and the dining-room facilities were reinstated. Then the Billiard Room arrangements were tackled; a full-sized billiard table and a lack of real heating did not produce the comfort required for a lounge, and so the billiard table was removed and the installation of table tennis tables, card tables and a dart board converted it into a Games Room for both active and passive exercise. The large stone fireplace was reorganized and brought into use and the installation of electric radiators there and in the passages gave some real heat. Later full central-heating was installed and then this very large saloon proved invaluable for large dinners and receptions; parties could be arranged there so easily and they happened so commonly.

Another necessary alteration was in the addition of two more bathrooms, ingeniously built into the thick walls in an obscure way but one which does not take up other useful space. Happily the famous Pen y Gwryd bath was not removed; this magnificent Victorian contraption, apparently built of battleship armour plate, with a shower enclosed by the same material, which squirts water from above and from all sides at once if so required. The whole thing incorporates an instrument panel worthy of a large steam locomotive, and it is one of the great sights of North Wales. Many a guest would visit the hotel just for the pleasure and excitement of bathing in this device.

Many of the alterations were carried out by Chris Briggs himself, and throughout his time there he has continued to do much of the unending repair work constantly needed. This includes a good deal of electric wiring and once when he was lifting the floorboards in the room above the kitchen for wiring purposes he put his hand in the gap and felt a strange object; when extracted this proved to be a small child's button boot of Victorian variety, very dried up and showing multiple patches and mends, suggesting that it had been worn by more than one generation of children and that it had been buried under the floor for many years: keeping this boot company was a black tin canister which might at one time have contained powder or perhaps oil for carriage lamps. Some one hundred and fifty years ago it was quite common, particularly in Wales, when building or doing repairs to leave behind a boot or other receptacle containing the 'Luck of the House', and there is no doubt that this find was one of these; the objects are still to be seen but no attempt has been made to date them. The still existing habit of burying coins and documents under the foundation stones of new public buildings is mainly for the purpose of leaving details to those who may pull the place down in the centuries to come; may it not also be for the 'Luck of the House?'

To give the right atmosphere to Pen y Gwryd the Smoke Room was made the hub of the wheel; oak-panelling purchased from the Derbyshire Education Authority came from a chapel being demolished in that county in order to make room for the first outdoor pursuit centre in the country. This panelling was as old as Pen y Gwryd itself and it was used to line the Smoke Room, and minor alterations to the bar, and the installation of ventilation fans completed the structural alterations. Then the Briggs had a stroke of luck. It may be remembered that on their take-over visit they found Peter and Esmé Kirby dining and that they were the owners of the sheep farm called Dyffryn just down the road; in fact, Esmé was responsible for the farming side of the business, a mere three thousand acres or so of mountain, bog and moorland, while Peter, an expert craftsman in woodwork and cabinet making spent most of his time providing oak furniture for churches and public buildings including the wonderful Bard's chair at the National Eisteddffod, thus scattering his superb craftsmanship broadcast through Wales; in this task he was helped by Alan Crosier and an apprentice named Bernard Pettifer.

In 1951 Peter Kirby presented the Briggs with a magnificent oak settle, made and carved specially by him and his team; it was made from a single oak tree felled on the Duke of Westminster's Norfolk estate and reputed to be one of the largest trees of its kind in the British Isles. Naturally this settle was made in the best seventeenth century manner without nail or screw but jointed and dowelled with absolute precision. Carved at the ends are the initials of Chris, Jo and Jane Briggs and in the middle is the device now accepted as the Pen y Gwryd coat of arms, a coiled climbing rope, with crossed ice axes and the letters P.Y.G. in the centre. This addition has graced the Smoke Room ever since and has accommodated the haunches of many generations of delighted guests. Moreover, the following year a matching oak table which still occupies the middle of the room was also presented by the Kirbys, thus completing the grand oak furniture of this much-frequented room.

For this is the great gathering place of the house; this is where all the guests meet together and where they meet their host and hostess every evening, thus keeping alive the family feeling on which Pen y Gwryd has always thrived. For one of the blessings of mountaineering, climbing and mountain walking is that it is perhaps the most cosmopolitan of sports and pastimes, and one which suffers hardly at all from social barriers. Fishing has its addicts in all walks of life and shows a great deal of happy mixing; but there is a line of demarcation between fly fishing and coarse fishing even if this indicates a more sporting snobbery than a social one. But it can truthfully be claimed that the barrier of rank and riches has completely left the climbing world; the thrill and risk of the gymnastic exercise of rock climbing, the essential need to reach a high degree of efficiency so as to keep one's neck in safety, and the real joy of attaining the summit of the mountain, all these appeal alike to the factory worker, the plumber and the clerk, just as they do to the barrister, the clergyman and the doctor. Many things are now levelling the financial barriers, better transport is available for all, even if too expensive for most, and in climbing and mountaineering, all that matters is the skill on the rocks. Grammar and dialect prove unimportant when the conversation is of routes, footholds, belays and the technique of rock work. And so in the Smoke Room the High Court Judge will discuss the country's problems with the garage mechanic, the business executive will chat with the building worker and the schoolmaster or doctor will talk to the university student about either mediaeval history or the best place to climb in the Dolomites. Ideas and ideals of all kinds can be freely exchanged and all ranks are on equal terms when tomorrow's weather and tomorrow's climbs are the only really important matters. Not that discussion never becomes a bit heated and heaven forbid that that should happen; wordy arguments usually on a friendly basis are a constant feature. But the blandness of spirit which comes to all after a day of strenuous exercise in wind, rain or sun, followed by a good meal and a mug of beer taken in warmth and comfort, demonstrates clearly that those who love the mountains seldom lose their own unique friendliness and companionship.

It was at about the same time, in 1950 that Chris and Jo became involved in another campaign; for they were engaged in fighting battles with the Government of the day who planned to build a pump-storage water scheme in the Snowdon area by which the whole of the inside of the Horseshoe would become practically one large lake, and with a tunnel burrowed through the bottom of Lliwedd the water could be pumped backwards and forwards thus creating electricity. The Briggs started a 'Save our Snowdon' campaign and among other items the Committee produced a small ice axe badge which was sold widely and so helped to produce a fund for the fight. After the civil war was over, and happily won, (although probably the main reason for the abolition of the pump-storage scheme was because it happened at the time when there was much enthusiasm for nuclear power instead) the Briggs decided to continue supplying the ice axe badge but in a different guise; a Snowdon Club was founded and the badge, with an added S.C. on it was given as a reward for young people who had climbed Snowdon for the first time. Many young children went in for this competition and Chris Briggs was the one and only judge. When Everest had been climbed he added to the mere physical climb a small test of mountaineering knowledge and this test was given in the Smoke Room in the presence of all the guests who wished to be there. The candidates were asked simple questions including the one of — 'who climbed Everest?' If successful the candidate was given a drink of his choice (but presumably non-alcoholic) in a silver tankard from the hook behind the bar and which had on it the signature of one of the Everest team, and then the medal was pinned on.

Chris tells of one boy of seven who was so anxious to earn his badge that father was dragged up Snowdon in the most appalling weather, but when they got to the final stretch father could take it no longer and they turned back. In spite of their entreaties the son was not allowed the badge and there was nothing for it but they had to try again the next day; the next day the weather was little better, but nothing on earth would restrain the seven-year-old who dragged a screaming father up the PYG track and the boy refused to be taken back. This time they made it, but father needed bed rest and a lot of reviving when he returned, while the seven-year-old was quite fit, and happy to get his badge.

How did the silver tankards with the initials of the Everest climbers come into existence? The answer is as follows: soon after his arrival, as part of the efforts to stimulate competition Chris acquired a set of good silver beer tankards, and these were hung at the back of the bar and each one was made the property of a climber who had earned it by making a first ascent, or who had found a new climb or who had explored the first route up some mountain or cliff either in this country or overseas. The tankard could not be taken away even by the owner but was always used by him when he was staying at the hotel. Such was the memory of Briggs the Barman that he could without hesitation recognize everyone who had such entitlement and would automatically reach up and select a tankard of the right metal when one of the rightful owners came into the bar.

It is almost certainly correct to say that this select band consisted of men only at the time when it was going strong; there may have been some women who had suitable qualifications by a first ascent but to find one who, at the same time had also a palate for beer and the different kind of courage needed to persuade her to claim her right to a silver tankard in such surroundings may have been asking too much even in the mid-twentieth century. But this year is 1976 and last year saw the passing of the Sex Discrimination Act; now poor Chris may have to sort out some very awkward decisions about the ownership of these tankards, unless inborn North Country conservatism stops him taking any action. It is probably a good thing that so many mountains have now been climbed in so many ways and by so many methods of approach that except for some very distant peaks, the recording of first ascents becomes daily more unlikely.

In fact he will be able to get out of this troublesome situation in another and a better way: when Everest was successfully climbed Chris arranged that each of these tankards should be engraved with the facsimile signatures of a member of the team, and that in due course each member should be presented with his own tankard. This was given to him not to take away but to give back immediately to Pen y Gwryd where it would continue to grace the bar fittings but where each year on the anniversary of the Everest success the owner could claim his right to have it filled with beer at the expense of the house. These goblets are still on view and any one of the surviving qualified first ascenders is allowed, indeed is encouraged to use one. It is to be hoped that as long as Pen y Gwryd remains, these trophies will remain on view behind the bar; and should they at any time or for any reason have to leave their rightful places may they be found some equally suitable home at such places as the Alpine Club, the Climbers' Club or in due course the Pinnacle Club! Or the Royal Geographical Society's premises; they well-deserve a place of honour and they would not seem unworthy in the British Museum itself.

By 1953 Pen y Gwryd had undoubtedly returned to its commanding position among the climbing fraternity, and certainly it was entitled to the next honour which came to it. The Everest Expedition was in its preliminary planning stage and those concerned with making the arrangements for the climb, and also those under consideration as possible members of the final chosen party obviously were all regular and well-recognized mountaineers; and this meant that many of them looked on Pen y Gwryd as their second home. So about six months before the starting date for the expedition experts in all aspects of climbing went to stay at Helyg hut partly to try out new and suggested equipment, and for those who had not climbed together recently to renew the knowledge of each other's techniques: many discussions took place over meals or drinks in the happy surrounding of Pen y Gwryd where arguments about climbing had been the custom for over a century.

Among the things fully tested out in January that year, were some varieties of breathing apparatus which might be useful on Everest and the methods of carriage and the facepieces were investigated on Tryfan; according to the entry in the Locked Book this proved to be a dismal business and this comment is signed by George Band, Tom Bourdillon, Charles Wylie, Wilfrid Noyce, A. Gregory, Charles Evans, John Hunt,

Anthony Rawlinson, John H. Jackson, Ralph Jones, Michael Westmacott and David Cox! As will be seen not all of these were members of the final team but they can all be recognized as stars in the climbing firmament whose opinions are respected on all mountaineering matters and all of them have at some time helped in the success of British climbing. Perhaps it is as well that their gloomy views on this trial were not accurate!

Other neighbouring peaks were climbed by this party and were used to experiment not only with different types of oxygen equipment but also with varieties of clothing and equipment to ascertain which would stand up best to the weather and to the strenuous work involved. Once again it gave the chance for members of the team to climb together and to share notes; the ultimate success of such an expedition may depend on the personal and intimate knowledge that the members have of each other.

Pen y Gwryd generates gaiety rather than gravity and so not many weeks pass without some reason being found for having a celebration dinner and it may be as well that not all of these have been recorded so that the lesser ones have escaped notice. But one which took place on April 25th 1953 does appear in the Visitors' Book: it was an interesting one as it was held to remember the fiftieth anniversary of the successful climb of the East Face of Lliwedd; twenty-seven men attended although it seems unlikely that they were all involved in person on the assault fifty years before. It is only in very recent years that the Welsh peaks have been attacked in such large numbers and what is more if some of those at the dinner were actually on the first climb they must have been carried in rucksacks on their fathers' backs, a habit which had not started fifty years before.

But it was June 2nd 1953 which saw the unique event which will not be forgotten as long as Pen y Gwryd lasts; the hotel had a fairly large number of guests staying and there were about twenty-six at dinner the night before; a mixed bag, but mainly habitués of the hotel. Then, to quote the Locked Book 'News reached Pen y Gwryd at four minutes past one on the morning of Coronation Day that Everest had been climbed by Hillary the New Zealander and Tensing under the leadership of Col. John Hunt'. The book does not mention that in fact the news came from a telephone message relayed by the *Times* newspaper, and one which Jo, who took the call, at first thought probably a hoax and she needed a good deal of persuasion by the caller to believe the truth.

Chris acting the perfect host went round the hotel hammering on the door of each guest that had gone to bed and shouting that Everest had been climbed and anyone who was not down in five minutes to drink a toast would have to leave the hotel before breakfast; with this threat in mind everyone went down. Almost at once a telegram was started on its way to the Everest party giving the congratulations of all at Pen y Gwryd; it was a very long message and it was addressed to the British Embassy at Katmandu for forwarding to John Hunt. About two hours later the telephone rang again and the voice of the local operator said "Oh, Mr Briggs, can you please tell me, where is Katmandu?" No doubt surprised that there was a place in Wales which was not listed in the telephone directory.

One of the guests tore in half a sheet from his bed and on it drew an excellent picture of the Everest Massif and this was promptly flown from the hotel flagstaff and stayed there for a few days; this flag is still in existence in the hotel. This decoration and some rather more artistic paintings on the lamp-shades were all done by one of the establishment's most staunch friends, Jack Nelson, a headmaster, who with great regularity took teams of eight boys aged between 8 and 11 years to introduce them to the mountains in the hope of inspiring in them some of the love that he himself enjoyed.

Then in order to prove that it was not only the Everest team which was tough and resilient among those who frequented mountain places, a party of six set out from Pen y Gwryd at 1.30 a.m. to climb Snowdon, the top of which they reached at 4 a.m. There a Loyal Toast was drunk and another telegram concocted to send to her Majesty the Queen with double congratulations; first on her Coronation and then on the success of some of her subjects in at last reaching the summit of Everest.

They were not alone on the top of Snowdon for other enthusiasts had arrived there from all parts roundabout and the P.Y.G. party had the great pleasure of telling them of John Hunt's success, and this of course gave the opportunity for more toasts to be drunk. The now very happy collection set sail again at 5 a.m. and got back to the hotel by 6.20 a.m. with a request that still another telegram should be sent to the Everest team with the congratulations of all those who had congregated on the summit of Snowdon; and this was duly done.

A rather sad postscript to the affair is seen in an entry in the Locked Book, signed by J.P.N. Watson to say that he personally had slept throughout the whole proceedings; this apparently is true but he had not been allowed to sleep in bed and he snored his way through the celebration in a chair in the corner of the lounge; surely this feat qualifies for a place in the Guiness Book of Records.

Chris and Jo decided that some permanent memorial to the Everest success was essential, and this led to the brilliant idea of the Everest Room. Just inside the front door at Pen y Gwryd and next door to the Smoke Room there had been for many years what can only be called junk rooms, albeit very useful ones; these consisted of a very small and unused office, a room containing a work bench with bootrack and tools for boot repairs, and one with hooks supporting a remarkable collection of climbing gear of every known type and age and sign of decay, some of which may have been in use on Mount Ararat.

This whole space was gutted and completely restored and refurbished; it was then lined with polished split logs to resemble those used in the Austrian type log cabin and it was given good wooden benches and tables and a heating stove; this room was intended to be used by climbers to get booted and spurred before going up the mountains, and to rest and drink a mug of beer after getting back, and for the latter purpose it is in constant and pleasant use. After a Celebration Dinner for the Everest team held in October that year, Sir John Hunt (now Lord Hunt) officially opened the Everest Room by cutting a nylon climbing rope stretched across the entrance. A second bright idea came to Chris which he had learnt from a visit paid to an Inn in Vienna which was frequented by students for there some well-known musicians had signed their names on the ceiling in memory of their visit. So thereupon the official members of the Everest team signed their names on the ceiling of the newly opened Everest Room, one or two such as John Hunt and George Band being able to reach the ceiling from the floor without using supports. This ceiling was then covered with a sheet of plain plastic to preserve it for posterity.

After some thought Chris later extended the qualification for having a name on the ceiling; two Olympic runners John Disley and Chris Brasher have added their signatures, Roger Bannister (now Sir Roger Bannister) the first four minute miler and his worthy assistant on that run, Chris Chattaway have signed there while Derek Ibbotson adds to the list of track athletes. This being an Inn in Wales naturally some Rugby footballers have earned a place, and to prove that the ceiling is not reserved only for those with advanced physical attributes a certain degree of literacy and artistry has been added in the names of Bertrand Russell, H.V. Morton and Russell Flint: Chris is still hoping to add the footprints of the Yeti to the ceiling signatures. The names of Sylvia Cheeseman and Madeline Wooler show that the list of exceptional athletes visiting Pen y Gwryd is not limited to the males, while that of Geraldine MacEwen among others, graces the artistic side of the balance.

The First Everest Celebration Dinner at Pen y Gwryd was as might be expected a considerable affair, the tremendous preparations were made for it. Very unfortunately Norgay Tenzing was not able to be there as he had fallen sick in London, maybe by reason of a plethora of celebrations, but the other members of the expedition were present and mainly correct. To make certain that the party found its way to the dinner table, replicas of the footprints of the Yeti done in white paint led all the way from the Smoke Room to the Games Room where the dinner was held and in the centre of which was a model of the Everest Massif up which went Yeti footprints of gradually reducing size until they reached the two small flags on top; the British and the Nepalese flags were flown.

Just twenty-five years after the event on May 27th 1978, John Hunt and Edmund Hillary and most of the members of the successful Everest team assembled at Pen y Gwryd for what is anticipated to be their last celebration dinner. A sad absence was that of Tenzing who was at a similar function, organized at the same time by the Indian and Nepalese governments. Altogether there were about eighty people present as families were invited and also some who had not been members of the team but who had played some conspicious role in organizing previous expeditions, and whose experience had contributed to the final success. Among them was Professor Noel Odell still fit and alert at the age of eighty seven and still a keen follower of all climbing enterprises. His still remains one of the most remarkable exploits on Everest, for he was in close support of Mallory and Irvine at the time of their fatal accident within a few feet of the summit. His lonely vigil at about twenty-seven thousand feet, and with little oxygen as that was seldom used then, was a remarkable achievement.

The thoughts of the party went out to Tom Bourdillon and Wilfrid Noyce, both killed in later climbing accidents, and their widows were affectionately welcomed in their stead.

As always with Everest reunions the buffet supper was on a lavish scale in which the centrepiece was a boar's head carefully accoutered to represent the Yeti. Edmund Hillary commented that everyone 'ate well, drank moderately and talked of everything except Everest'. It is possible that the last statement is not absolutely accurate, but few disagreed with John Hunt's remark that he found it 'a very moving experience'.

A specially commissioned picture of Everest was presented to Chris and Jo Briggs: John Hunt and Edmund Hilary planted a Canadian maple in the hotel garden to remind future generations of climbers that the first conquerers of Everest always thought of Pen y Gwryd as their home.

Although Pen y Gwryd managed to find a reason for celebration almost weekly, August 29th, 1954 can claim to be an exceptional high light: for nearly seven years Leslie Mather had continued his interest in running Pen y Gwryd and his financial investment in the hotel and he had made visits to help with the accounts and to consult on future planning, taking the opportunity for a day in the mountains at the same time. But in 1954 he expressed a wish to sell his share of the business, although always willing to continue his help when required. So on that great day the ownership of the 'Pen y Gwryd Hotel' passed to Chris and Jo Briggs in its entirety and from that date belonged to them only. This meant that starting from scratch and with little capital it had taken Chris and Jo Briggs seven years to gain full possession and to bring this Inn back to its full former glory and beyond, as a haunt of those who loved the mountains: an exhibition of the results of effort and efficiency which should be more widely studied today.

Needless to say this achievement gained its rightful place in the Locked Book, and it takes the shape of a facsimile of the legal document, properly signed, and also sealed with a small section of frayed climbing rope and a blob of sealing wax, the latter incorporating a tricouni nail!

One of the signatories on this document was Marjorie Crutwell and this is the first time this name had appeared. She had put an advertisement in the magazine *Hotel and Caterer* seeking a post as secretary or manageress in a hotel with the stipulation that it should be south of a line through Birmingham. Chris saw this advertisement and with true Yorkshire second sight realized that this was someone worth having and so invited her to fill a vacancy at Pen y Gwryd; he added that though they could not claim to be south of the line she mentioned, they were only about an inch north of it, as indeed was true if the right scale of map was used for the calculation.

Marjorie Crutwell accepted the invitation and became an immediate and lasting success, as she was a competent and friendly person whom walkers and climbers found very approachable and helpful. When she left, as a momento of her years there, Marjorie Crutwell gave to the hotel a very large brass gong, still sounded regularly for meals.

In January 1955 Charles Evans (now Sir Charles Evans) spent a weekend at the hotel with a large selection of those who were with him on the Kangchengunga climb, or who had taken some part in the organization of the expedition.

On another occasion he took up to Pen y Gwryd two of his Sherpa helpers, Dawa Tenzing (not Norgay of Everest fame) and Changjup, and their visit produced some amusing stories. One event as told by Charles Evans runs as follows: "I took them one day with friends to climb on Clogwyn y Ddisgl. They did not want to climb so I told them to go round and meet me where the Clogwyn y Person ridge joins the Horseshoe Ridge. It was misty at the time. They went off on their own and my friends and myself did some climbs on Clogwyn y Ddisgl and then followed the ridge until we reached the crest of the Horseshoe Ridge where I expected to meet them. We were in cloud and there was no sign of them so we sat down for a bit. After an interval they turned up from the direction of Carnedd Ugain and I asked them if they would like to go along the ridge to the top of Snowdon: the reply was 'Do you mean that place with the little hut on it and a train? We have just been along there and back again'." Full appreciation of this episode needs local knowledge.

One other day some other friends from Pen y Gwryd took the two Sherpas to Black Rock sands where they had some enjoyable bathing. They were astonished by the saltyness of the waters. Nepal imports practically all its salt, at one time from Tibet and in more recent years from India, and it is a not uncommon sight in some of the Himalayan passes to see baggage trains consisting of sheep each carrying a couple of small saddle bags containing salt. So the Sherpas filled bottles with this odd salted water to take back to their villages.

Another delight for the two Sherpas was when they were given a cuckoo clock each and a lawn mower. Naturally the differences in farming techniques impressed them: soon after their arrival they felt impelled to round up a flock of sheep wandering at large round the hotel as they were worried about the possibility of incursions by wolves. Another great surprise was the milk yield of the cows in this country, for the idea of five or six gallons a day when they thought more in pints astonished them greatly. On this they consulted with Charles Evans of the possibilities of taking back a fine bull to their own country to produce better cows; the idea of crossing a bull with a yak was even discussed; but finally it was decided that the task of carrying a bull with them in an aeroplane might prove too troublesome!

The Briggs had met the Sherpa party when it arrived at Heathrow and tried to show them something of the sights of London: Buckingham Palace the visitors thought too small and unimpressive as a dwelling house for the Queen of England; also they found London a very unfriendly 'village' as none of the villagers stopped to talk to each other.

The Locked Book now shows a period of two years without any event being celebrated; this seems such an unlikely state that one can but assume that the numbers of dinners must have been so large that the book became invisible in the haze. But in January 1957 a reason was found that could not possibly be questioned; for in the New Year's Honours, Christopher Bastin Briggs was awarded the British Empire Medal; the formal letter telling him of this award had to be dragged from Chris by force, but rightly it is now pasted in the book, and many friends have added their signature to the page. This honour was meant as some recognition of his excellent work on behalf of the Mountain Rescue Service: he had put in ten years of safe, sure and courageous work dealing with mountain accidents and personally accepting not merely inconvenience but often considerable risk which on one occasion at least caused him serious injury. And his administration had facilitated the organization of this Service of which many more details are given at the end of this chapter.

In September 1962 was announced the death of O. Rawson Owen landlord of the 'Pen y Pass Hotel' for over sixty years. This delightfully situated hotel was always a strong rival of Pen y Gwryd as *the* climbers' hotel of North Wales; there were times in the ten years after the death of Harry and Ann Owen when the climbing fraternity tended to transfer their affection to Pen y Pass and a selection remained faithful to it. Geoffrey Winthrop Young was very keen on Pen y Pass as a climbing centre and as he was a man of great influence in climbing circles at that time many expert mountaineers and also budding climbers used to gather round him at Pen y Pass to listen to the most advanced discussions about rock climbing. But it would be unfair to suggest too much rivalry between the two hotels; both have given outstanding service to British climbing, but undoubtedly Rawson Owen deserves to rank with Harry Owen and Arthur Lockwood in a contribution to the popularity of Snowdonia; although oddly enough he was no climber himself, and indeed thought those who did climb were strange folk and perhaps a little mentally deranged.

It is very cheering to see one whole page of the Locked Book in May 1963 devoted to one subject; it is a small subject but none is more deserving of the page to itself for the whole page is occupied by the signature of Tenzing written in his own language and in English. He was at that time staying at Pen y Gwryd for the tenth anniversary of the Everest triumph. On one of Tenzing's visits he was accompanied by his delightful wife Daku, who has been a porter and has carried baggage and equipment to a high altitude in the Himalayas; he has also been accompanied by Gombu now a famous mountaineer who has reached the summit of Everest on two expeditions. Tenzing is always a popular and well-loved guest at Pen y Gwryd; he is full of wonder for what he sees in Britain and despite the efforts of a small number of Press representatives he has remained happy and unspoilt by the paeons of praise rightly accorded to him.

It was 1966 which saw Chris Briggs reach the acme of his career, for that year he was appointed High Sheriff of the County of Caernarfon. Only those well-acquainted with Wales and the Welsh will realize how great was the honour for a Yorkshireman to reach this position in a County in which Welsh Nationalism ran strongly: it demonstrates as nothing else can, the respect and affection with which he was considered in the County.

This appointment added a good deal to the amount of work the Briggs had to do for not only was there the routine labour of the Office, the entertainment and protection of the judges on circuit, but also an additional amount of involvement in social engagements of varying kinds. But as always Chris and Jo took these extra commitments in their stride and carried out all the duties expertly and well; it widened still further their circle of friends and they both found much interest in the duties. At the completion of his term of office Chris Briggs was appointed Deputy Lieutenant to the County, a position he still holds.

In the year following his retirement from office as High Sheriff, Chris Briggs for the first time in history gave a dinner party for all those still living who had held the position of High Sheriff to the County of Caernarfon; there were sixteen present at the dinner and in addition the Under Sheriff was present and the Sheriff's Chaplain, the Rev Alun Jones who doubtless said Grace for the daily bread provided. Another grace was provided by the presence throughout the dinner of a beautiful lady giving an accompaniment on the Welsh harp. A full list of those present is to be found in the Appendix, and also a copy of the menu which gives an illustration of a Welsh snack meal.

There was another happening of exceptional interest during the year 1969; for quite unexpectedly there arrived at the door of Pen y Gwryd asking for Chris Briggs none other than Lord Snowdon; he was engaged in escorting Prince Charles on an incognito tour of the jousting fields at Caernarfon Castle, where in a few weeks he would be Invested Prince of Wales. The two visitors were looking for lunch and they asked to see the menu of the day for they wanted nothing but normal and ordinary fare. Seeing on the list Welsh shepherds' pie, His Royal Highness asked Chris if it were a good dish, and Chris had pleasure in informing him that Welsh shepherds were usually very tender; so this meal was requested and apparently enjoyed.

Pen y Gwryd had not finished with Everest; in November 1972 Major Akluwaila stayed there as an honoured guest; he had reached the summit of Everest with the Indian team in 1965 and he says in the Locked Book merely 'I am delighted to be here'. Another member of the same Indian expedition who however did not reach the summit had been Major Harsh Bahuguna; but Major Bahuguna had unfortunately been killed when on the International Expedition of 1971; a tablet, carved in Welsh slate by the well-known Jonah Jones of Portmadoc, was placed in the Everest room in his memory. Major Akluwaila suffered the grave misfortune of being shot in the spine while serving his country in the Indian-Pakistan War, but although paralysed this does not prevent him from carrying out an important job in Delhi, and so it is just that his signature should be added to the ceiling list in the Everest Room.

Pen y Gwryd was lucky soon after the Everest expedition returned to this country in acquiring a bargain basement of oxygen cylinders, ice axes, boots, padded garments and other bits and pieces of equipment used on the climb; these have been well-displayed in an illuminated glass-fronted cabinet fitted into one of the walls in the Smoke Room and they attract the interest of many visitors.

The Twentieth Anniversary of the Everest conquest was well and truly commemorated in June 1973 when a large contingent of the team was present; unfortunately not Edmund Hillary as his wife Louise was suffering from a broken ankle in Darjeeling. Another absentee was Wilfrid Noyce; he had been killed at the age of 43 years on the Peak of Communism in the Pamirs in Russia while with the British Soviet Expedition; he was a great loss not only to mountaineering but also to the literature associated with it, for he was an accomplished writer. Unhappily Tom Bourdillon was another who was missing as he and Dick Viney had been killed in 1956 while climbing in the Alps.

Many trophies of every sort have decorated the walls at Pen y Gwryd at times, including photographs, shields and mementos of Service Units who have visited the Hotel or trained near to it; unhappily many of these have had to be removed before they were unofficially removed, as some have been, by some of those strange people who think that everything to be found in a hotel is public property.

It gives some idea of the many and various problems which assault this hotel to find that in 1968, fitted in between celebratory dinners and Himalayan visitors there was a State visit to Pen y Gwryd by His Highness the Sultan Hassanal Bolkian Mu'Izzuddin Waddualah, probably more often known in this country as the Sultan of Brunei. He travelled in company with his father and brother and with seven or eight of his Ministers, including the Chief Minister and the Financial Minister; also the Attorney General and the Royal Physician. With him were the Secretary of State for Wales and several of his Officers and the whole party had a State and no doubt a stately Luncheon which was attended by the Lord Lieutenant of the County, Sir Michael Duff.

A bunch of leaflets had already arrived from the Foreign Office to help the Hotel proprietors in the management of their distinguished visitors; a fascinating one was the 'Dietary Notes'. This points out that apart from the obvious religious rules the Sultan's tastes are very catholic but his father Sir Omar had rather different ideas; he would not eat curry or rice in any form; starch containing foods could be offered to him on the understanding that they would be politely refused; wines should also be offered but would not in any circumstances be accepted, and his only drink was soda water slightly chilled and poured out in his presence. It need hardly be said that Pen y Gwryd survived this royal visit with triumphant equanimity and ease and on leaving the Sultan expressed himself charmed with his entertainment.

But March 1973 was a very sad time for Chris and Jo and the whole staff at Pen y Gwryd, for Blodwen Griffiths died at the age of eighty-four years. She had been at the hotel since 1947 when the Briggs took over, and until an advanced age she did her full share of the normal labour of the hotel, being particularly active at tea time as she seemed to think that tea was a specially important meal, and she always served it in a way which made Blodwen a household word to the visitors. But above all, Chris, Jo and Jane were *her* people; they were her family and which of them she put first in her thoughts, it was impossible to tell, but all her Welsh thoughts were evidently for them and their requirements. Many visitors will remember her nightly visits to the Smoke Room at about half past ten or so, to see if the Briggs wanted anything further, and showing obvious reluctance to leave her family just in case there was no one available who could anticipate their wants; the idea of them having to look after themselves was abhorrent to her. And this care and affection was mutual for all the Briggs family loved her and tried to care for her in just the same way as she looked after them. The habitual visitors also had a great feeling of affection for her and without fail they would ask for her when they arrived and say good-bye to her when they left; although her English was reasonably adequate it was evident that she still thought in Welsh. Never seen but in her black dress and starched apron she was a lovely and much-loved character and certainly one of the outstanding features of Pen y Gwryd.

There are innumerable amusing stories connected with Blodwen; at the hotel one of the frequent visitors was a slightly eccentric professor from Cambridge, who among other fads preferred his bread ten days old. On one of his early visits Blodwen entered his bedroom with the morning tea, and could see no one in the bed or apparently in the room although it was not a big one; as she looked round in some concern a voice suddenly said "Put it on the table Blodwen", and there was the professor standing on his head behind the door, apparently doing some of his Yoga exercises; as a result poor Blodwen was so startled that she dropped the tray and fled for her life.

Taking morning tea was one of her favourite pastimes and accidents were practically unknown but there was one epic event. Until the last year or so under extreme pressure from the Automobile Association, Chris refused stalwartly to have locks on the bedroom doors as he said they had no stealing at Pen y Gwryd, and so far he had been right. However, one of the bedrooms, number six, had a slight step down into the room, and also some kind of a dud bolt which hardly worked; number six at this time was in use by a honeymoon couple who had apparently tried to bolt the door, but Blodwen did not believe in that and putting her shoulder to the door she gave a good shove, whereupon it gave way very suddenly and precipitated her into the room with such force that the tea tray sailed on through the open window. When telling this story with that quiet Welsh hiss of indrawn breath which Blodwen managed in such a masterly fashion, she said "They must have been up to no good".

A frequent visitor in the middle thirties was C.F. Holland, noted for his very direct approach to climbs and by the fact that he constantly tore his trouser knee when climbing. This was mended nearly every day for him by Blodwen, but finally even she became somewhat non-plussed; so she found a piece of old carpet and with that gave him a real knee patch, which did last him much longer!

Another tale of her unusual comments concerned a somewhat snobbish young man, whose engagement to a lady with a title had just appeared in the *Times*, and he pleasantly, rebuked Blodwen as she had not offered her congratulations, her only reply was "Oh, yes, sir, I did see your advertisement in the *Times*".

One of her greatest adventures was when she was taken to London: Chris and Jo had been invited to a Buckingham Palace Garden Party and as Blodwen was well on towards her eighties they thought to take her down to see the big City; her first comment was about the M1 Motorway which had only recently been opened and was the first of its kind in Great Britain, and all she could say was "Well you know they have stretched the road over the Llanberis Pass too". She was given a theatre entertainment where she expressed great surprise at getting tea in the interval and a late evening meal at the Savoy Grill, where she was pained not to get a good pudding, and showed great alarm at the size of the bill, which, however, she nobly offered to pay getting out her big black bag.

Blodwen has as her memorial in Llanberis Church two wrought iron flower stands bearing the following inscription:

In memory of Blodwen Griffiths — In her 60 years' service at Pen y Gwryd, she was a faithful friend to the mountaineers of the world. Presented in grateful appreciation by Mr & Mrs Christopher Briggs.

Christmas 1973.

And so as Pen y Gwryd continues on its way one other event of great note must be recorded for it is a happening which will have great significance on the future of the Inn, and it is the epic narrative of the wedding of Jane and Brian; for this surely deserves a more lengthy description than that of their old friend Emlyn Jones who commented "For the first time in its long history the Pass was choked with top hats".

It was not the first young man Jane had invited to Pen y Gwryd although she has refused the offer to include a full list in the Appendix. But this one, Brian Pullee had a small business in architectural interior decorating, but little knowledge or acquaintance with the mountains; it required but one visit to North Wales to start an affection for them growing in him; and so quite soon the wedding was fixed for January 25th 1975.

But disaster struck P.Y.G. at Christmas when Jo had the misfortune to trip over a cord helping with some clearing up, and suffered a very severe knee injury with a comminuted fracture of her patella. Although the winter weather had been far less severe than was customary in North Wales at that time of the year, there was a sprinkling of snow on the mountain tops. But the evening before the wedding a blizzard started, luckily without snow but with torrents of rain and sleet and gale force winds so that even in the well-built hotel water started to ooze through the cracks in places. Then at nine o'clock on the wedding morning the electric current failed because of the gale and the unfortunate staff trying to arrange for a reception were without electricity from that time until 3 o'clock in the afternoon. This did not help the bride and bridesmaids trying to make themselves even more beautiful than usual; it had been arranged that a hairdresser would be there all the morning and she arrived with full equipment but there was no electric light so vision was not easy and her considerable electric apparatus did not work. But things of this sort do not stop the Briggs in their tracks and a fire was lighted in the drawing-room, and the bride and bridesmaids lay in elegant attitudes in a half circle round it with their heads pointing towards the blaze, looking rather like some Druid pre-nuptial ceremony.

However finally all was ready, and the marriage service took place at St Padarns Church, Llanberis, conducted by the Rural Dean, the Rev Alun Jones, and some gleams of sun appeared at the right moment. Then everyone went back to Pen y Gwryd for a magnificent reception for about four hundred people from all parts of the globe.

Pen y Gwryd is lucky to have another Briggs preparing to give it care and attention. Jane after her early school life at a local Welsh School, where she picked up a good deal of the language, and acquired much of the Welsh love of music, went to Penrhos College. As this was a school created for the benefit of the daughters of Non-conformist clergymen, she was perhaps lucky to remain there after, at the age of about eight years when she was given in a botany class some myrrh to smell remarked loudly "It smells lovely, just like a gin and tonic". Later she found her bent as an air hostess in British Airways where she spent seven years flying round the world giving competent and cheerful service to all and sundry in the way which comes so naturally to her and she spent the last few years at the Heathrow Offices of British Airways. Jane had been wise enough to select the most useful and pleasant characteristics from each side of her exceptional family and to combine with those attributes quite a bit of Welsh genius. With the help of her husband Brian, who has already shown something of his talents in the complete reorganization of Hafod y Gwynt and in repairing the trout hatchery, there seems every likelihood that Pen y Gwryd will continue to be fortunate in the troublesome and tumultuous days ahead.

It may be of interest to add as a postscript to this chapter some ideas gleaned from Kevin Fitzgerald, author and notorious habitué of Pen y Gwryd, thus adding to some of the stories I have already stolen from him without acknowledgement. At least one of his exciting books uses Pen y Gwryd as its venue, while it is quite possible that some of the more unlikely adventures described in other of his books were real happenings at this unusual hotel. From the start Kevin Fitzgerald had no hesitation in describing Chris and Jo as unmatched as a pair of managers in this country.

He notes that at that time the hotel swarmed with climbers, and the Smoke Room after dinner was a scene of 'experimental dead lifts' traverses, stands on the head and other feats of strength and endurance while everyone was waiting for the refreshment always given during the evening — the world famous cheese and onion sandwiches. He has seen the pattern of guests change from that time when non-climbers were a comparative rarity and remained self-effacing in the corner while the climbing fraternity described their adventures with the normal Alpine Club understatement.

The visitors today are of more varied types, but Kevin still finds the same warm welcome, the same news of friends, albeit sometimes with just a morsel of not unfriendly scandal: although Chris is still capable of saying to an unwanted guest, as he was heard to say years ago "I don't want you in my hotel, ever. I don't want to see you here, ever. You will never be served here. Now, please get out and stay out." Yet he finds Chris and Jo still 'always ready to succour the afflicted, help a friend, just as they were thirty years ago'.

Among his stories Kevin Fitzgerald tells too of times when he thought he had cause to make some complaint: once he complained about the lack of a Sunday newspaper: going to bed at midnight he was awakened at 3 a.m. by an eerie knock, knock on the window, and calling "Who's there?" and getting up in some alarm the window was pushed open from outside to show Chris standing on a ladder saying "Your Sunday paper, sir, with the apologies of the management."

Quite recently Kevin wrote to reserve accommodation at

Pen y Gwryd adding to his letter 'as usual I require a small sitting room and a private bathroom'. He arrived to find the door of his usual room bearing a large poster 'Intensive Care Unit' while the inside of the room was divided across the middle by a large screen behind which was the washbasin and an enormous commode: the screen carried a picture of the Welsh Dragon and an inscription 'En suite arrangements'.

More recently he was invited as a guest to a Climbers' Club function and he found the table of the Smoke Room bore a large collecting box labelled 'Kevin Fitzgerald Fund', with a caption underneath 'Attempts are being made to restore this ancient ruin and contributions, however small, will be welcomed'. Kevin fails to tell us how much the box collected. But among his many stories is one of hearing with shock a loud voice in the hotel dining-room remarking "In my view all this climbing is a lot of bloody nonsense on the part of silly little extroverts in fancy dress". Perhaps it is as well that the comment was made by a female, and in those days women were among the protected species.

Unfortunately in recent years Pen y Gwryd has suffered a sad set back by reason of a legal dispute; the Briggs original purchase was of the Hotel only, the previous owner Arthur Lockwood retaining the house (Hafod y Gwynt) in which he continued to live, the lake which he had designed, and the petrol station on the opposite side of the road. The Briggs had always understood that the deed of purchase included a clause by which they had the first option to buy the house, lake and petrol station should Lockwood wish to sell; and also when he died. Because of the strange and abstruse legal language used in agreements of this sort intended to prevent disputes in the future, when Lockwood died, Mr R.E. Pritchard who for some years had held a lease to the petrol station put in his claim to the property. The result was a long lawsuit producing finally some forty pages of judgement finding in favour of the Briggs. This was followed by an Appeal at the end of which the three judges, in a judgement of seventy pages, found in favour of Mr Pritchard. It seems that everything hung on one or two very difficult and controversial points of law; innumerable previous cases were cited by both sides, and the whole business was doubtless fascinating to the barristers, but unintelligible to the layman. One of the Appeal judges did express considerable sympathy for the Briggs, whose opinion in their transaction had seemed eminently reasonable to the ordinary man, but apparently not to the law.

The loss of a house adjacent to the Hotel, and of a lovely lake providing some good fishing obviously caused considerable grief to the present owners, as it leaves the Hotel lacking what had once been its estate. But there is no cause for alarm – an Inn which for one hundred and fifty years has been one of a very small handful of the foundation stones of British climbing, and which throughout the world is well known to everyone who claims to be a mountaineer, is not in jeopardy. Pen y Gwryd will always remain.

CHAPTER 6

THE MOUNTAIN RESCUE SERVICE

The first glimpse of any kind of organization to deal with accidents on the mountains appears to have been when the Rucksack Club combined with the Fell and Rock Climbing Club to form a Stretcher Committee so called because one of their earliest tasks was to produce a suitable stretcher, in the design of which Eustace Thomas played a major part. Not until 1936 was a more permanent committee formed and this by stages has grown into the present competent and important Committee, the Mountain Rescue Committee. But in many places makeshift equipment was still used for some years, old Army stretchers, or Heath Robinson contraptions made from bits of signpost with branches or rope used as a mattress.

As far as Pen y Gwryd was concerned a small amount of rescue kit was available early in 1936, this having been provided by the Midland Association of Mountaineers, and it was in the charge of Arthur Lockwood. But in 1936 a small committee called the First Aid Committee based in Manchester was formed by the main climbing clubs and this provided some more reasonable equipment which enable a series of mountain rescue posts to be set up in different localities: these posts were merely depositories for the first aid equipment, and when an accident happened teams of proficient climbers and other helpers had to be collected by the main organizer of the post while numbers could be made up from quarrymen and local workers. There was no question of a team standing by ready for action, and, of course the number of accidents occurring did not warrant such procedure.

When Chris Briggs took over Pen y Gwryd in 1947 it had for some years been a Rescue Post, one of the four in the neighbourhood, but the arrangements were in many ways rudimentary and one of the many services which Chris Briggs has given to Snowdonia has been his steady guidance of the developing rescue service.

The chairman of the First Aid Committee in its early days was Wilson Hey, a Manchester surgeon with a world wide reputation for his surgical work and withal an enthusiastic climber. One day he was climbing with a couple of medical friends on the Glyders and high up on the mountain they came across a man who had broken his leg; naturally they had not taken any first aid equipment with them on their climb and so the party went down and collected a gate for use as a stretcher, and on this they placed the unfortunate man and took him back to the hotel.

During the journey down the mountain the victim suffered considerable agony for with only makeshift splinting available and in the absence of any pain killing drugs little could be done to help him until the ambulance arrived, and as no prior notice could be given the waiting time for this was long. Wilson Hey decided there and then that the Committee should try to improve the equipment for the Rescue Posts, and that a main ingredient of the first aid kit must certainly be morphia.

Owing to the very strict rules and the legal difficulties about supplying drugs in the absence of a doctor, Wilson Hey decided that the best way for a short term was to take over the issue of the morphia from his own personal stock to which he was entitled as a medical practitioner, recording the issues in his own dangerous drugs record book. But the number of mountain accidents tended to increase, and whoever succeeded him in the chairmanship of the committee was unlikely to be in a position to undertake an issue of drugs, or wish to do so, and so Wilson Hey felt that the time had come to arrange some legal way of getting rescue posts a regularized stock of morphia. He thereupon started negotiations by writing a letter to the Home Office stating the problem and letting them know of his temporary solution by using his own stock of drugs. The immediate reaction from the Home Office consisted in the arrival at his surgery of two large policemen wanting to examine his dangerous drugs book which, of course, they found not strictly in order as it should have included the precise details of the name and date of every dose of morphia. As a result of this investigation he was taken for trial at the local court, but with the help of several witnesses, including Chris Briggs he managed to avoid a prison sentence! However this stir up of trouble had in the end a beneficial effect, for it led to questions in the Houses of Parliament, and at the Home Office, and eventually permission was given to hold stocks of morphia in all first aid kits at Rescue Posts, given reasonable safeguards.

In addition to the morphia the first aid kit today consists of a stretcher, splints, bandages, needles and catgut for stitching wounds, and means of heating liquids to provide hot drinks and hot-water bottles for patients requiring them particularly on prolonged rescue attempts.

The stretcher is one specially designed for use on mountains and it was thought out by a climber-engineer named Eustace Thomas who ran an engineering firm in Manchester: it differs from the ordinary stretcher in having runners underneath for use not only in snow but also to help slide it over rocks; it also has extended handles in front and rear, giving a large gap between the stretcher and carrier so that the latter can see where he is putting his feet. Probably no one who has not tried this kind of work would have any idea of the immense difficulty of carrying a damaged person safely and with fair comfort over the kind of terrain used for climbing and mountain walking.

To begin with the only method of communication with the outside world provided to a rescue party was a Very pistol by which red and green rockets could be fired to let other searchers know that the place of the accident had been found. Later radio sets were provided in the rescue kit and this proved very helpful. The method by which Mountain Rescue Service works is worth recalling here as it is similar in all the posts which are distributed throughout Britain. Anyone who sees or find or knows of an accident telephones the nearest Mountain Rescue Post or the nearest Police Station who pass on the information, and the man responsible for that Post gets together a party of climbers to find the accident and to carry down the victim. This way works very well as it is not necessary to call people away from their work and they do not have to travel long distances; with luck a selection of fairly expert climbers may be easily available, maybe on a climb, or perhaps in their huts or tents or even in exceptional circumstances in the local pub with a beer mug at hand. Most of the year they can be gathered together relatively easily and they may be already caparisoned with climbing boots, anoraks, ropes and other climbing paraphernalia. That the team is now able to carry with it some morphia is a godsend for it alleviates shock, and relieves pain and so indeed it may help to save a life.

About twenty-five years ago the Royal Air Force, who already had in existence their own air rescue team, asked Chris if they could be included in the call out for mountain accidents for it would be invaluable experience for them to see the experts at work on the hills as so many aircraft crashed in hilly areas. This was agreed and the Royal Air Force headquarters at Valley, Anglesea, was contacted when an accident call was received but after the phone call it took sometimes over an hour for the Air Force Team to get to the scene and they would often arrive when the rescue was over. They had their own landrovers and full first aid equipment and even if they were late they thought it worth while, but in order to improve things further they started a scheme for weekend camping in the mountains for their rescue teams and this cut down the time taken for their arrival to ten or twenty minutes and then they really could see what happened. In this way they became steadily more and more involved in civilian rescue work, and quite soon they started to bring helicopters into the picture and this of course revolutionized the rescuing of accidents, the casualties could be found much more readily if it were daylight; and they could be picked up and taken for treatment quickly and easily. The helicopters now deal with seventy to eighty per cent of all accidents; many are minor ones such as fractures or strains occurring in places easy to get to by helicopter, and where the patient can be lifted off without too much difficulty. Any tourist or traveller in North Wales will be familiar with the lorries and landrovers frequently seen on the local roads bearing the sign R.A.F. Mountain Rescue Service. With their manpower and radio and other equipment they can take over a considerable part of this hazardous task, and so take a load off the climbers. But climbers, and expert climbers, cannot be dispensed with; mists, winds and blizzards together with the remote and often very difficult terrain in which accidents may happen means that there are times when the final approach can be made only on foot. Happily this is one of the few places in modern life where unpaid voluntary service is not looked on as a form of 'exploitation' and it is always willingly given.

A great boon which the R.A.F. brought to the Rescue Service was their excellent radio set, a tremendous advantage when there may be ten or more parties scouring different parts of the surrounding country looking for the accident. For often the only knowledge of a possible catastrophe is that a walker or climber does not return, and someone may or may not know where he was going on his expedition. The original radio sets were heavy and bulky to carry, and suffered a good deal from blackout areas in the hills and valleys. The arrival of the transistor improved things a lot, and the Rescue Posts eventually got commercial sets instead of Service type sets. The Mountain Rescue Committee started buying these and they proved good for the job, but licence fees had to be paid, and repairs done, and worst of all they were told at a later date that wave lengths would have to be changed, and that this would cost about £30 or £40 per set, an amount the Committee would find almost impossible to produce.

As always Pen y Gwryd stepped into the breach as one of its guests happened to be the man in charge of all the radio sets used by the Police Force and Home Office communications services and given a slight nudge he started to cogitate about the new problem. His first thoughts were not particularly helpful for he wrote to say that he could arrange to have the Rescue Post radios serviced with the police ones at a charge of £200 per set! This was far too expensive even to be considered, and long negotiations started, and after some time Chris Briggs after consultation with the Committee agreed that the radio sets would be given to the police, so that all Mountain

Rescue Sets were the property of the Police Force and could be serviced by them for nothing; this was possible because the police had already agreed that the rescue squads were in fact doing work which the police would have to do and so in effect it was a police service.

This is the present position with regard to radios and has proved another step forward in the history of Mountain Rescue.

A further problem which the committee wanted to sort out was that of insurance as although the climbers volunteered willingly to help in rescue, Wilson Hey felt that sooner or later a rescuer might be killed or badly injured, and then they or their relatives might suffer hardship. Any private insurance firms approached asked for impossibly large premiums which could not be afforded; then for a time the Committee accumulated a reserve Emergency Fund from which some ex gratia payments could be made to hard cases, but this was small and usually inadequate. Naturally such cases were not expected often but inevitably one happened and in a bad accident in the Lake District when a boulder came away from the mountainside, a rescuer was killed and several injured and so the insurance problem had to be looked at again.

In 1951 there was a disaster on Snowdon while a man and his girl friend were on the P.Y.G. track; she fell and he in trying to save her was pulled down and both were badly injured. A Pen y Gwryd guest called Dr Woodruff and a friend were on the ridge on Crib y Ddysgyl and saw this happen, and started to cut steps in the snow to go to help the injured but during the attempt Woodruff slipped and was killed in the resulting fall. He was the first rescuer to be killed or injured during the Briggs era at Pen y Gwryd: his family was given some compensation from the Committee's Fund, but it was a mere gesture as it was so small.

The Home Secretary at that time was James Callaghan who, as this is written, has just become Prime Minister, and through his very good offices they established a system of insurance, again through the police service. It was accepted that the rescuers were temporarily doing police work and should have police insurance cover.

During his time as Home Secretary James Callaghan, having

had reason to have a number of discussions about the Rescue Service and other matters, became a visitor to Pen y Gwryd and a friend of the Briggs, so that in due course they were presented with a copy of his book; the title seemed unsuitable for a gift to this hotel so it may be hoped that *A House Divided* refers to the House of Parliament.

It may give some idea of the magnitude of the rescue expeditions to hear from Chris Briggs that on one big recent search by means of a few telephone calls and visits to camps and huts he got together more than four hundred volunteers at 6 o'clock in the morning to take part in a search. This was unusually large, and normally Chris tries to keep the areas sub-divided so as not to deplete every area in case another call should arrive to find no one available for an extra rescue team. He tries to get those climbing near to the accident for these suited his purpose best and could provide maximum effort with minimum loss of time.

Chris Briggs fully deserved the Certificate for Distinguished Services awarded to him by the Mountain Rescue Committee and he also is a valuable and experienced member of that Committee.

It is always easy to forget the ones left at home when talking about those in the firing line; while Chris Briggs and his team were out on a rescue attempt, often all night, Jo and Marjorie Crutwell or whoever was helping at the time, would never consider going to bed, but they would sit in the corner of the Smoke Room waiting for the telephone to ring, or going out on a clear night to look for the rockets from the Very pistol giving some good news. But rescuing, particularly at night was inevitably a dangerous business and the telephone call could so easily be one of bad news. Meanwhile Jo and her helper would be preparing hot soup and sandwiches ready for the sudden arrival of Chris and perhaps a dozen climbers who would come in cold, wet and hungry: how often sitting at home can be the worst part of the business.

This is no place to try and give a full list of all the mountain accidents, nor even to give a series of gruesome details; the daily press took on that role some years ago and carries it through with great eclat. But a mention of one or two specimens of rescue work may help to give those readers with little experience of mountains some idea of the work entailed, and this accompanying photograph should help to enhance their understanding of the difficulties as it shows a group of climbers with Chris. Briggs at the head, all obviously mentally and physically weary.

From the time that men first started to live in mountains there have been accidents and sometimes fatal ones to those such as miners, quarrymen, shepherds and others who had to travel the rough ways, and little is heard of these except for the occasional skeleton found in some remote part of the country. But the first fatal accident which is recorded in any of the hotel Visitors' Book is that of the Rev Starr killed on the mountains in 1846. The first accident to be found written up in the Locked Book took place on May 19th, 1888; the climbing party concerned consisted of E.J. Bedford of Nottingham, E. Kidson of Birmingham, W.E. Corlett of Liverpool and Alfred Evans of Manchester all mountaineers of ability who did much of the early pioneering work in the Snowdon area. They had already done a hard day's work but were trying to climb the face of Lliwedd: Corlett had managed to get off a difficult ledge and ascend the cliff face and was resting there when Evans tried to follow him, but failed after several attempts and after consultation he decided he was too exhausted to continue and that he would go back. Corlett and Bedford went on and reached the top at 7 o'clock but they felt a bit unhappy at having left half the party behind and hurried back to the hotel and it was not until they got there that they knew what had happened. Having been left by the two companions Kidson managed to get off the ledge via a huge outstanding butress with scanty footing or handholds and Evans was trying to follow by working his way along a five or six foot traverse, part of the time holding on to Kidson's ankle. But his foot slipped and 'his arms slowly came to their full stretch and with one quickly utter "Oh" he fell outwards, rolled down a steep grassy ledge and was deflected to fall two hundred feet on to the scree below; after his first exclamation he made no sound'. Kidson, although an expert climber could do nothing to save his friend and when he climbed down to reach him five minutes later he was already dead.

But the following account given by Chris Briggs gives an

excellent description of the problems besetting those who try to organize mountain rescue work in the present day. Chris had a telephone message to say that a climber had arrived at his lodging in the Llanwrst neighbourhood telling of how his companion had fallen during a climb on Craig y Ysfa and he had been unable to reach him without help. Having got together a party of five or six Chris went across to Llanwrst to interview the climber, who told them of how his friend had slipped and fallen and was lying at the apex of a patch of snow in a certain gully which he tried to identify for them. Chris tried to persuade him to join the search party to help them find the exact spot but the climber felt too exhausted: this was a pity for finding the position of an accident is often the most troublesome part of the venture, and so the party set off without his help. They climbed for many hours round Craig y Ysfa exploring many snow gullies in their search for one particular triangle of snow with a large rock at the top, which after all is a description which can be given to a multitude of gullies, but although spread out and calling repeatedly they had finally to give up the search. On their way back to Pen y Gwryd they called on the original climber and arranged for him to join the search party the next morning. So starting out with a fresh party they picked up their informant, but he thought he could find the way better if he took another path and met them on the other side of the mountain. However leaving the stretcher at the lower end of a likely route the main party fairly soon found the right place where they found the accident case who was already dead. He had made no effort to get anything out of his rucksack nor to make himself comfortable in any way suggesting that he either died at once or that he was much more seriously injured than his friend had realized, and was probably unconscious from the moment of the fall. His friend had not been able to make any effort to reach him when he fell, but had only seen him from above, and it had taken over two hours to get to a telephone to ask for help. In fact the friend took no part in the rescue search and gave the general impression that he was either very shocked at the occurrence or rather inadequate. These two climbers had in fact met only the night before the climb and so knew nothing of each others' climbing abilities.

Chris Briggs other anecdote of a rescue turned out much more happily and to the rather macabre minds of the climbing fraternity appeared amusing. It happened on the eve of a Climbers' Club Dinner at Pen y Gwryd when a message arrived that a party who had turned up for the dinner had met with an accident while climbing on Lliwedd; the party included the new President of the Club and one of the former Presidents and several experienced members. Chris and his rescue party reached a ledge at the bottom of a climb named the Matchstick during which it is at one stage necessary to climb between a huge block of stone and the cliff behind: having passed this rock the climber has to push himself off the face of it to reach the main cliff. Unhappily when one of the party on the original climb pushed off from the rock the whole thing came away and went rolling down the cliff face where it came to rest on Herbert Carr who was belaying the climbers from below. Herbert Carr, the co-author of *The Mountains of Snowdonia* and the writer of many of the early guide books on rock climbing was not only a very expert climber but also a very tough one. Even this would not have helped him but luckily he was standing where there was a slight hollow and the rock which fell rested across this as a bridge; so although he got a badly cracked shoulder and several other injuries none of them were too serious. But he was quite incapacitated and had to be lowered down the cliff on a stretcher in steps of one hundred feet at a time. All this took a very long time and it was not made easier as it was dark. So none of the climbing party or the rescuers were in time for the Dinner, but some of the successful diners went out to help the party on the way back over the scree. It is said that Herbert Carr so enjoyed his shot of morphia that he asked for more, but owing to short supply the request had to be refused!

As is well known as the years roll by, the number of accidents on the mountains does increase; this is inevitable as the numbers traversing the mountains also increases steadily. Bank holidays are notoriously bad spells, partly because the accidents do happen so often to those inexperienced in climbing and even in scrambling. But the better facilities provided by the Mountain Rescue Service and the Royal Air Force, the improvement in the equipment and in the first aid kit provided, and the very fast collection of accident cases, the quick first aid treatment and transfer to hospital when needed are all items which have gone far to save lives and to reduce pain and discomfort.

But it is vastly important that there should be no let up in the efforts to train and educate those who take their pleasure on the mountains for if they have even reasonable knowledge it will do much to reduce troubles.

CHAPTER 7

AN ESSAY ON CONSERVATION

How has kind heaven adorned the happy land,
and scattered blessings with a wasteful hand.
Joseph Addison. The Campaign. 1672-1719

This section is alas much too short for it is a subject which deserves many volumes to itself, but it introduces some of the thoughts of Jo Briggs who has spent a good deal of her time at Pen y Gwryd in contemplation of the beauties of Snowdonia and in considering how best they can be preserved. And in a day when the ravaging of the land is so extensive, ideas on how such grandeur as remains can be retained cannot be expressed too often.

The National Parks Act was passed in 1949 and it legalised the creation of several parks throughout the country with the main object that in those areas such beauty and wildness as remained should be preserved and enhanced, and for the accomplishment of this industrial and other development would have to be suitably contained. Unfortunately this main object is today only too often forgotten by the many and varied authorities concerned in planning and by the general public. Perhaps it might be helpful if some of the original wording of the Act were once more reiterated and became more widely known, and particularly the following paragraph: 'A National Park is an extensive area of beautiful and relatively wild country in which, for the Nation's benefit and by appropriate national decision and action (a) the characteristic landscape beauty is strictly preserved, (b) access and facilities for public open-air enjoyment are amply provided, (c) wild life and buildings and places of architectural and historic interest are suitably protected, while (d) effective farm use is effectively maintained'.

The recent National Park Review Committee after collecting opinions from many sources, including the Countryside Commission, and after due deliberation did in January 1976 produce their comment that 'Priority for conservation over all national park purposes in order that beauty and ecological qualities of the National Parks may be maintained' was the first priority. They further asked for the 'Adoption of environmental quality as the primary criterion in all matters, including roads and traffic management and the provision and management of tourist facilities'. The Committee also pointed out that there had been vast changes, particularly in the number of visitors, over the last twenty years resulting in two statutory purposes sometimes being in conflict in some areas; these two purposes being of course the maintainance of beauty and the provision of free access to the public. So the Committee very reasonably recommended that the statutory purposes should be amended to make it clear that public enjoyment of the parks must be such as 'will leave their natural beauty unimpaired for the enjoyment of this and future generations'.

On July 19th 1946 King George VI and Queen Elizabeth visited North Wales and they were escorted in the Pen y Gwryd region by Mr (now Sir) Clough Williams Ellis who was at that time Chairman of the Council for the Preservation of Rural Wales. The enclosed photograph shows Their Majesties standing outside the door of the hotel while they were being shown both on a relief map and over the beautiful countryside itself something of the two hundred square miles including the Snowdon massif which it was hoped and expected would soon become the Snowdonia National Park.

For Pen y Gwryd lies in the middle of this Park and the uninitiated visitor might get the impression that in Snowdonia there remain few problems on conservation matters: nothing could be further from the truth for as with freedom so also with preservation, the price to be paid is that of eternal vigilance. Members of the Park Committee and of other similar societies find themselves constantly assailed by plans and schemes which at first sight seem eminently reasonable, but which if allowed to go unchallenged would go far to spoil the beauty of the Park. In part this has been due to the fact that when once the National Parks Act was on the Statute Book no later Government has shown itself willing to reconsider the main objects for which the Parks were created: nor have they been willing to provide either the financial aid or the legal backing needed if controlling committees are to carry out their appointed tasks of preserving and enhancing the beauty of the area. So much could be done with a comparatively small sum of money, particularly if some of it could be given in compensation for those living in the Parks district whose livelihood might be diminished by some aspects of conservation.

All those interested in retaining unspoilt beauty may think themselves lucky that Pen y Gwryd fell into the hands of Chris and Jo Briggs and not of speculators whose aim was solely the improvement of the trade of the Inn regardless of scenery. All country lovers are very conscious of the slow whittling away of the loveliness of the land which uncontrolled development may produce, and they soon noticed the very frequent demands for more road widening, or more ugly petrol stations, and the recurrent requests for the erection of chalets or more cottages as holiday dwellings, often badly planned both in siting and constructions. Jo was very concerned with what she described as the harsh and insensitive smothering of many areas of Park land by the Forestry Commission who are exempt from any form of planning control and whose final aim is one of economics.

Very soon after their arrival at Pen y Gwryd Chris and Jo joined the Caernarfonshire Branch of the Council for the Preservation of Rural Wales and they now serve on many of its committees and give a lot of their valuable time to this work. One of their early tasks lay in founding the Friends of Snowdon; this started as a local group which afterwards acquired many additional members from all parts of the country. It came into being to form an opposition to the plan to create a pump storage scheme which would mean filling practically the whole of the Snowdon Horseshoe with an artificial lake, and boring an outlet tunnel through the foot of Lliwedd: happily this scheme was dropped partly because it was being considered at the time that nuclear power was all the rage. But unfortunately the conservation societies have recently lost the battle when they tried to stop or reduce the size of the huge pump storage scheme at present under way at the foot of the Llanberis pass, which will alter the whole landscape in the Nantperis neighbourhood, and which, with road 'improvements' and possibly pylons and power lines will disfigure this delightful bit of the valley.

A powerful industrial company put forward a suggestion for drilling for oil or minerals in the very lovely Mawddach estuary and on this the 'Friends' managed to raise such a loud public outcry that the idea was not pursued.

A good deal has been accomplished in the constant battle with planning authorities about widening roads and siting new ones, and about 'upgrading' some minor roads. And in a side line not always thought about by the uninitiated they have kept a close watch on the problem of ugly and frequently unnecessary 'road funiture' such as chain link fencing hanging on large concrete posts in lieu of the customary farmland wiring, and the erection of abnormally big direction signs of the motorway type.

There are two other causes of almost constant guerilla warfare: the first is the problem of the picnic site which the planners so often wish to put in places which will cause the maximum destruction to the very view that people go to see. It is frequently not too difficult to find a picnic site which is pleasant for those using it, and which with proper screening, is not directly in the line of vision of those who wish to contemplate the view; the Friends of Snowdon or the Preservation Council can often be helpful if given the opportunity.

The other almost inescapable trouble is that of the caravan. A leaflet produced by the Caernarfonshire Branch of the Council for the Preservation of Rural Wales expresses their opinion with fervour when it says 'We in Caernarfonshire face intensified exploitation of the County with its unique character and long coastline by powerful caravan and chalet interests which ruthlessly degrade the character of the landscape and the heritage of centuries'. Here again the conservationists are not trying to take away the pleasures of some of the people, they are trying to enhance the pleasure of all the people; their intention is not to eliminate caravans but simply to keep the numbers within a reasonable limit, to confine them to well-serviced parking areas designed to stop them being offensively obtrusive, and with proper site selection and adequate screening this can be done. Many members have for years urged the control of the colour of caravans, for if white and blue and other glaring colour schemes could be avoided caravans would be much more acceptable.

Another controversial challenge confronting the conservationist is the relationship with the farming community. Farmers often claim to be strict conservationists and it need not be emphasised that many of them show great interest in maintaining the beauty of the landscape: but in their tiresome and exhausting job of dealing with the waywardness of nature on one hand and the capriciousness of the market on the other, considerations of pure economics must play a big part. This may sometimes give them the bias of thinking that good, well-cultivated farm land is one of the most beautiful sights that anyone can wish to see, and that the provision of a barn or farm building, provided it is convenient to the farmer just adds to the beauty of the scenery. Whereas many of those who are interested in looking at lovely country, while agreeing that good farm land is a most attractive sight, point out that Great Britain can show thousands of square miles of such country, and it can be seen within a few miles of any town and it needs no National Park for its appreciation. What is wanted in addition to attractive farm land is country which looks different and which is different, and particularly country which can be crossed by the walker without his having to wend his way along statutory footpaths skirting growing crops. Again, although farm buildings are obviously essential to farming far too many are needlessly unpleasant to look at, and often a slightly different position or the provision of some screening would help to prevent disfigurement of the landscape. Hence many conservationists feel that farmers should come under planning rules, as do all the rest of the community, and while good planning need not, and should not, handicap the farmers' difficult job, it may preserve the loveliness of the views. This is a troublesome and very controversial problem but it should be solved and it certainly could be solved given some give and take on both sides.

Another of Jo's time-consuming tasks is in serving on the panel of judges assessing the entries for the annual competition for the best kept village in the County organized by the Caernarfonshire Branch; the County is, of course, now that of Gwynedd. Besides giving her the chance of travelling round the area and watching local developments this gives Jo the opportunity of attending study conferences on a variety of matters closely allied to the care of the country. Such for example, as the consideration of water conservation, of forestry, and of the land use of Wales all of which come within her far ranging interest. From such talks there may arise ways and means of preventing possible damage to otherwise pleasant land which may arise from some so called progressive schemes put forward by a modern and largely urban population. This is hard but always rewarding work. For all this important and unending labour and those who undertake it, deserve much credit for it is only through such work and enterprise that the children and grandchildren of this present generation will have the chance of enjoying the full beauty of this very lovely land.

CHAPTER 8

THE NORTH WALES WANDERERS

The great source of pleasure is variety.
Samuel Johnson.

Many pages have been spent in considering the foundations of this Inn and in thinking about the architects and craftsmen who produced not merely the structure but the spiritual cornerstones and the intangible walls which make Pen y Gwryd a home. Now perhaps a mention should be made of those for whom it exists, that is the guests. To those who stopped only for a night's visit while passing through, to those who went to climb or walk or fish, or just to look at the birds and animals: to those who went to rest and relax and enjoy the superb scenery and thereby return home refreshed; for the advantage of this remote and lovely mountain haunt is that it can cater for all country pursuits and for each and every taste.

In the formative days of Pen y Gwryd in the early years of the nineteenth century some went there to fish or to botanize, but many of the guests were walkers, staying there to wander round the local valleys and to look at the lakes and rivers. Some were exceptional walkers and of these George Borrow was surely the champion covering an astonishing amount of ground, surveying the country and looking at the buildings. Many walkers get additional pleasure in talking to the folk they meet in their travels, although few, alas, can follow Borrow's example and surprise the locals by talking in their own Welsh language; and probably few would be willing to carry on such lengthy and intimate discussions with those met on their travels. It is a tragedy that in his long and circuitous tramps round the Principality he missed looking in at Pen y Gwryd for had he done so we should know far more about the Inn in mid-Victorian times than we do. But Borrow tended to keep to the roads and highways and to progress from town to town, whereas the walkers who did so much to create the Inn were the natural explorers and somewhat more venturesome; often the ones who wanted to reach places where no foot had trod before and to see new and exciting things.

The men who obtained their greatest satisfaction from some sense of achievement and where better can that be found by the ordinary man, than in mountain walking, scrambling or climbing.

It was by reason of its wide field of adventure, coupled with that quiet loneliness which mountain regions can supply so well, that the Inn was selected by certain species of visitor. During the second half of the nineteenth century, Pen y Gwryd was infested by staff and students from Oxford and Cambridge, and by masters and senior boys from the public schools. Of course many were also from other universities but they were in lesser numbers, although in this century the younger universities have come into their own and have provided swarms of visitors; probably the Scottish Universities have always sent fewer students than most places, but with their own magnificent mountains close at hand why should they go elsewhere.

An interesting thesis could be written comparing the reasons why some professions took their holidays in Snowdonia, and what caused the variation in numbers. If the Visitors' Books tell the truth, and there is no reason to doubt their accuracy, the Church easily led the field, followed by medicine and the law in almost equal proportions. The Anglican Church is well ahead of all other denominations, with comparatively few from the Roman Catholic Church and a mere handful from Non-conformist ranks. The reasons for this could give rise to a whole book full of fascinating surmises, some kind and some rather offensive: did the Anglicans maybe have more time to spare, or were they less conscientious in their work than their colleagues in the chapels? Were they the wealthiest among the priesthoods and so could better afford to travel, and better afford to pay curates to do their labours for them? Or was it that they usually worked with such constant intensity that a period of peaceful thought combined with a little physical activity was essential to their well-being, enabling them to return to the fray after ten days or so, rested and with greater zest for battle with the devil? Or was it simply because such a large proportion had been educated at the two older Universities and had learnt bad habits there? Were the Non-conformist clergy of England in such constant struggle with the underworld that they dare not leave their parishioners even for short holidays; or did they maybe feel a bit apprehensive at the idea of meeting some of the wizards of the Welsh Chapels? Had they known it this risk was a small one for there were surprisingly few visiting ministers even from nearby towns.

But it is hardly safe to pursue these contemplations further, but to suffice it to say that the clergy were great supporters of Pen y Gwryd; it has been stated on authority that at any rate until recent years every bishop of the Church of England had at some time spent a holiday at this Inn, and it may be that in the dark mysteries which surround the election of bishops it will be found that a certain length of time spent at Pen y Gwryd is an essential qualification.

The chapters which follow are an effort to reap the fields of the Visitors' Book and in particular of the Locked Book: and to assemble the facts and fantasies so gleaned under suitable headings, so that whatever the reader's enjoyments he or she may find something of special interest and by studying the whole may get a better idea of what happens in Snowdonia.

CHAPTER 9

THE AMBLERS

> The skipping King, he ambled up and down
> Shakespeare. Henry IV. Act III. Sc. II.

In medieval days the amble was sometimes considered to be the favourite pace for horse riders and it was certainly the fastest pace for women who travelled or rode but seldom. On the rare occasions when an abbess moved house she apparently always went on an ambling palfrey. It is not easy to understand why this strange gait became popular but it may have been easier for the occasional and relatively inexperienced rider who had not learnt to rise to the trot and who wished to avoid the unhappy bumping on a tender seat. But the odd swaying motion resulting from a horse using together both legs on the same side must have been not unlike travelling in a dinghy in a cross swell. Nor was the amble an easy pace to teach the horse as several instructions show. It could be done 'by the help of a new plowde field' or more commonly by the use of 'trammels' which strapped together the two legs on the same side.

Fortunately for human beings such troublesome training is not required as ambling seems to be the natural gait for many of us, and it is one which becomes increasingly common with advancing years. According to the Oxford Dictionary the human ambler became the human rambler sometime in the first half of the seventeenth century – at least that was the first time the word rambler was used. It was not until the first decade of the nineteenth century that the ugly 'hike' replaced the more musical 'ramble'.

It is with the amble that this chapter is concerned. In our younger days my wife and I were addicted to mountain walking: although we never attempted any genuine climbing we were not averse to a bit of mild scrambling and that is so often needed on the best ridge walks. But in the tours described here we were perhaps beginning to show the first signs of decay. At least we had reached that stage when it seemed less hurtful to the pride to pause for a few moments looking round a church or an ancient monument and in taking plenty of time to read the inscriptions rather than to admit that the muscles were feeling a bit weak or the breath coming rather short. In this way the more expensive method of providing delaying action by taking numerous photographs could be kept for use on the more strenuous mountain climbs.

When wandering round the villages of North Wales and talking to the many friendly folk there, one wonders whether more could be learnt about the people and the countryside if one had been able to speak Welsh. George Borrow thought he gained much by knowing the language and he was always delighted when he surprised the natives by launching into their own tongue but it is possible that he did sometimes get less information because he roused suspicion. Certainly we have never had any conversational difficulties by sticking to English which has always produced an excellent response. This is quite unlike the story told by Sir John Wynn of Queen Catherine, daughter of the King of France and widow of our own Henry V. For when she later married Owain Tudur he proudly took her to see some of his famous and titled relatives in North Wales and he introduced her to five or six (including such well known characters as Jevan ap Meredydd and Howell ap Llewelyn ap Howell) who are described by John Wynn as men of 'goodly stature and personage'. No doubt Catherine had advanced a little in the English language since Shakespeare gave her the first lessons and she tried these honoured guests in English but without result, and then in French her native language but this again was not understood; she probably tried yet again in Latin as a common tongue for educated men but to all her efforts she got no reply. So trying to cheer up a somewhat despondent Owain she turned to him and said that 'they were the goodliest dumb creatures that ever she saw'. There may possibly have been other times when the Welsh have been described as 'goodly' but this must be the only occasion when they have been considered 'dumb'.

The natural reaction when waking up to fine weather on the first day of a visit to North Wales and on looking out of the window to see Snowdon sublime and lovely in the early morning sun is to start without delay for the summit. Who knows but that the morrow will see the mountain obscured by cloud or lashed with rain so the urge to go up is almost overwhelming. But for the true ambler this urge must be resisted at all costs. The approach to Snowdon should be made decorously and by slow degrees by anyone not already in full training lest too strenuous efforts at this early stage lead to the amble degenerating into a crawl for the next few days or one may even have to descend to fishing. Or the result may be even worse. Some years ago we were clambering up the interesting and not too difficult tourist route to the top of Tryfan accompanied by a charming Austrian lass who was temporarily working at Pen y Gwryd. Halfway up the ascent she confided to my wife that the last time she had climbed a mountain had been in company with a middle-aged gentleman (looking at me rather speculatively) and as they neared the top her companion had dropped down dead. I refused to slow up, but wondered if the frightening moral of this story might not have the very effect I was wishing to avoid.

We decided that a good start for the first day would be the Crafnant-Gierionedd tour which some years ago we had christened the wet weather walk because it was just slightly less exposed to the worst of the mountain storms. So we took the car to Capel Curig and going into the climbing gear shop for a small bit of equipment we had a great stroke of luck. For there sitting talking to those serving was Ifan Roberts the discoverer of Lloydia serotina in the confines of Twll Du, and later a Snowdon Warden: much more is written of him in another part of this book. Still wearing his Warden's badge and carrying his walking stick, Ifan Roberts is unhappily now almost blind but he retains his full enthusiasm and his zest for life in a way which should encourage us all. He was delighted to have just been told that a specimen of saxifraga caespitosa or the tufted saxifrage had just been found in one of the high Snowdon valleys. The name of the exact site was not to be breathed abroad for this is a very rare specimen of saxifrage belonging to high northern and Arctic latitudes and found but very rarely in this country and then only in the mountains of Scotland, Ireland and Wales. What could be a better start to a day than to meet and chat with this grand man and to hear him talk at length on botanical discoveries and mountain explorations?

Leaving him reluctantly we started up the footpath on the opposite side of the road to the Capel Curig post office and carried on up the well-marked and gentle slope leading through Clogwyn Mawr and very soon meeting the other limb of the path which begins behind the garage on the Betws-y-Coed road. This track wanders along the slightly marshy and rock strewn land where stepping stones are lavishly used for crossing the wettest parts, and it leads round the shoulder of the mountain into an attractive and wide depression filled with little streams and tussocky grass. With luck that most delightful of birds the green plover or peewit can be seen here although luck was not with us this day. However the raven was there and also we saw flying at a good height and in a very purposeful manner one of the hawk family which must almost certainly have been a kestrel.

It takes little less than an hour to reach the col in the hills from where well down below the lovely prospect of Crafnant Llyn appears, with its farmhouse and farm buildings at one end and the few houses and cottages dotted along the road running beside it.

At the south-west end of Llyn Crafnant there is a flat tract of field and rocky moorland which looks as though it had been left behind when the water of the lake receded for it is so flat and level. In this area there can be seen (although a diligent search is needed) several scattered prehistoric earthworks of the kind which housed the earliest village people; and there are also a few of the tumulus or burial mound type. The larger earthworks can easily be mistaken for sheepfolds and indeed it is probable that some have been used for this purpose from time to time. Genuine archaelogical monuments seem sadly few and far between in North Wales and in the rough, rocky and arduous country they are too well-hidden.

Close by one of these mounds seemed an excellent place for lunch and while we were resting on a rock, sipping sherry from the hip flask, a well-accoutred young horseman came by on a shaggy Welsh pony. The offer of a sip of sherry was welcomed and in the chat which accompanied the drink — for surely this is just what ambling is all about — it turned out that he was the editor of an Southern English county newspaper and that most of his riding was done in the New Forest but he often took holidays in a riding establishment near by Trefriw.

We continued on our way along the narrow road bordering Llyn Crafnant until we reached the small township of Trefriw. This was well-known as a summer resort in Victorian times and those from neighbouring towns used not only to spend their holidays but also used to take the waters in that form of spa treatment common in the overeating and overdrinking days of the nineteenth century. A.H. Bradley in his book *Highways and Byeways in North Wales,* makes some rather uncomplimentary remarks about some of the frequenters of the spas, thinking particularly little of the dissenting minister. He comments that the English Parson when on holiday will be found walking in the hills or energetically riding his bicycle round the roads of Wales whereas the non-conformist minister seems to prefer taking the waters of the local spas. He rather rudely remarks 'It may seem strange that men who lead temperate, well-nourished, well-occupied, but not laborious lives, amid the fresh breezes of the Welsh hills, should be so fond of filling their insides from the nauseous fountains'. He later becomes even more offensive (and one hopes inaccurate) when he says 'One is given to regard these places as the haunts of jaded Sybarites from cities, whose livers are oppressed with burdens too great to bear and joints racked with the penalties of too great indulgence. But the simple preacher from the Welsh hills would drink one of these men under the table in the matter of sulphur or alum, and go on his way rejoicing. If anyone doubts my words, let him spend a week at Llandrindod Wells, and note the feats performed there at the pump rooms in the morning by Methodist and Baptist experts'. But we may take heart from the fact that some at least of his observations seem inaccurate or else times have greatly changed for later he states 'Violent exercise and games of a robust sort are wholly against Welsh non-conformist tradition'. Had he watched any of the superb Welsh rugger sides in action at any time over the last sixty or seventy years he would realize that either non-conformist teaching has changed dramatically in recent years or else the Welsh ministers have lost their grip entirely on the male population of the Principality.

We started our trip round Trefriw with a visit to the Vale of Conway Woollen Mills. Standing on the bank of the Crafnant river this mill started as a water-driven washing and fulling mill, or 'pandy', which dealt with the spinning and weaving carried out as a local cottage industry in the early years of last century. This 'pandy' was bought by Thomas Williams in 1859 when it had been working as a full woollen mill for thirty years and the original building is still in use as a warehouse.

Moreover the 'Trefriw Woollen Mills' are still being managed by descendants of the same family. Up to the beginning of the last war one of its tasks was to spin and weave into cloth and blankets the fleeces taken in by local farmers who then used the material themselves; but one of the 'improvements' since 1939 has been a change in the law so that this can no longer be done, but the law decrees that all the wool used in the mill has to be bought from real wool merchants.

We tried to shut our ears as well as we could to the astonishing clatter in which the large staff of women work in the spinning, weaving and warping departments. In some cases the women were wearing the ear muffs provided but often they did not trouble as this inhibited communication between the workers. The building in which they work seems surprisingly aged and one would have thought, hence less efficient than it should be for its purpose, but the workers seem completely happy and full of interest in their work. We then visited the showrooms where the vast number of garments, coverings and ornaments made from the grand Welsh wool was indeed surprising and so we found it difficult to keep our purchases small. Another surprising item of information which we picked up was that the river at Trefriw which drains both the Crafnant and Geirioneed lakes was at one time navigable right up to the town which had a thriving boat building industry.

It was but a short step to the church which was originally

built in 1230 by Llewelyn the Great apparently for the benefit of his princess 'who before was obliged to go on foot to Llanrhychwyn' which certainly is quite a long trek. But there is little left of that church as it was rebuilt in the 16th century and again completely restored in the middle of the 18th century. So apart from an old pulpit and some parts of the altar, the church on the whole is pleasant but ordinary.

From the town the road climbs steeply through some lovely woodland which opens out later to give a truly magnificent view over the whole plain of the Conwy valley and the flatter lands around Llanwrst. Near the top of the hill peering over its high surrounding stone wall is one of the real gems of North Wales the 12th and 13th century church of Llanrhychwyn. The very old lych gate carries the inscription IT ID OT 1462. W.D. which to us was without meaning nor could we find anyone to give us an interpretation. But some experts such as Harold Hughes and Herbert North say without hesitation that the date has been altered and should read 1762.

The key of the church, for unhappily even remote churches have to be kept locked these days, was kept by a recently retired farmer who lived in an adjacent cottage. A true specimen of Wales he had that erudition and knowledge not only of the church he cared for and in which he was overwhelmingly interested, but also in a considerable number of local historical facts; and he was delighted to find others to whom he could pass on his knowledge. He was also rejoiced to let us know that they were having a wedding at the church in the near future, the first one for many years. As the roads to the church are extremely narrow and the church itself is almost surrounded by sloping fields it is not clear how a wedding party's transport could be parked. It may be that they intended to follow the example of many country funerals where the coffin is carried immense distances by stalwart bearers. If so, one can but hope that neither bride nor groom were of too ample proportions! Entering the church by the narrow doorway which is less than three feet wide we were in the older south aisle, itself but fourteen feet wide and most of which, including the roof is early 13th century work. The north aisle is rather wider being about fifteen feet across and also a little later bring probably a 16th century addition put in by Meredydd ap Ieuan who built the church at Dolwyddelan. This aisle contains the fine old oak pulpit dated 1691, with a reading pew of the same age and material. The windows have no true stained-glass in them but the pictures are made of a brown and yellow stain. Perhaps the most interesting objects are a circular collecting bowl and a very decayed iron tipped wooden spade, both of the 17th century; a font of the earliest design being a square stone one only 1 foot 9 inches square and 1 foot 8 inches high, standing on two stone steps. Also they are very proud of the bell which is decorated by a number of fleur-de-lys and is probably 14th century and may have started life in Maenan Abbey. We were sorry to leave this beautiful little specimen which not only shows exactly what some early church work looked like but also which has not had a number of later additions so that it gives one better than most the true spirit of the age at which it was built.

A very short walk now took us to Llyn Geirionedd which is an unusually enclosed stretch of water surrounded by quite high hills giving it a slightly gloomy appearance on a dull day; an appearance not improved as the Forestry Commission have planted almost the whole of one side of the lake with their beloved conifers. But luck was with us, for at the moment the conservationists are leading in the battle for the preservation of the peace of Geirionedd. The lake has been taken over several times by large parties of water skiers who fill the whole valley and much of the surrounding country with not only parked motor cars, but also with the truly appalling noise which accompanies this sport. Of course the country walker is a very biased man but unless the walkers get into the countryside in very large hordes as unhappily is happening in some specially beautiful places, he does little damage and does not upset his fellow men. But a form of sport which needs a motorized accompaniment and takes place in an enclosed area produces a degree of noise almost up to the standard of the jumbo jet and is very disturbing to human and animal life over a large area. It is difficult not to feel that such particularly noisy sports should be limited to the open spaces of parts of the sea coast, and certainly not allowed in hitherto peaceful places such as Geirionedd. Long may the conservationists succeed here!

Leaving Geirionedd it is soon possible to hit on one of the

numerous tracks which wander round the countryside leading from one mine to another or from one quarry to another for both lead and copper were found here in some quantities during the last century. Many of the mine workings and towers are far from beautiful and fortunately some of the unsightly towers are now being removed.

There are so many criss-crossing tracks round here that it is essential to keep one's wits well-sharpened and to use to the full a sense of direction, but by doing so we arrived at the Betws-y-Coed road where it crosses the river and alongside the so called Ugly House. Indeed a pleasant and most interesting day. A reasonable training run for the next day's expedition seemed to be a region about which we knew surprisingly little, although it loomed large in Welsh history and although we had visited Snowdonia on many holidays, never before had we been to the Dolwyddelan area. We started along the Betws-y-Coed road passing the two hotels and noting outside one of them the well-preserved sample of a Victorian stage coach. About a mile further on we crossed the river Llugwy by the Pont Cyfang and this led us on a good track to a chapel where a sharp turn right and a climb up a rather steep hill brought us to some pleasant open country. Although the surrounding ground is wet the track itself is good and we enjoyed first class views of Moel Siabod which appears very close and more distant views of the Carneddi spread out along the horizon. There are reputed to be several prehistoric graves by the side of this path but with so many earthy banks and so many rocky outcrops we failed to find anything which we could confidentially pronounce to be prehistoric. Two miles walking took us to a fence and a gate leading into some Forestry Commission land where as always the paths are wide and well-kept but where as always there are no waymarks · or signposts. There are so many side issues of well-kept roads that route finding is exceedingly difficult. In this tightly planted conifer country which some folk find rather claustrophobic there is no view to guide one on the way and if this land is to be used for rambling a few not too conspicuous waymarks would be of great service. However after a few blunders we came finally to the stream crossing we were searching for and where a short side path leads to a small series of tiny waterfalls. Then we hit the side road taking us to the main road alongside 'Elen's Castle Hotel'.

The name Dolwyddelan means the Castle of the Valley of Helen's Way and this hotel stands by the side of the Sarn Helen which was the Roman causeway leading to the coast and the construction of which was, it is said ordered by Helena the mother of Constantine the Great. Others consider that this road and the castle were built in about A.D. 500 by the Britons on their first retreat into Wales. As so often in ancient history you can take your pick.

Having walked four or five miles we thought our first port of call should be the church of St Gwyddelan and so we duly turned left. Gwyddelan was one of the Irish missionaries who came to this country after the Romans had left, for the purpose of encouraging or restoring Christianity and he arrived in Wales in aboutA.D. 600. Then a very small wooden church was built on a hill top about 300 yards from the present church, and in the early 12th century this was replaced by one of stone on the same site. Madog up Meredydd, Prince of Powis who had lived for some years in Dolwyddelan Castle built for himself a new house in Penamen which he considered the best ground in Dolwyddelan and when he had moved there he then rebuilt the church on its present site in about A.D. 1500. His building consisted of the existing nave and chancel while the south chapel was added in the 16th century by his descendant Robert Wynn. There is an old farmhouse at Bryn y Bedd very adjacent to the site of the original church which still carried the name of Bod y Groes meaning the abode of the cross thus perpetuating the memory of Gwyddelan and his first stance for preaching the gospel.

When we went into the church we were greeted by two elderly ladies who were only anxious to help us to see and know about all that could be seen. These were only two of a group of nearly twenty women of the village who voluntarily give up their time to watch over their loved church partly so that it does not have to be locked, for even in remote parts of Wales vandalism has its sway, but also to ensure that everyone who enters it will know of its history. And what is there to see? A fine old screen mainly 15th century, although it has been suggested that parts of it may have been taken from the older church. An interesting poor box carved out of one of the oak pillars which has three locks and three drawers inside. Also one of the oldest beams on the north side holding up the barrel vault of the chancel is carved the Dolwyddelan Dragon which has the advantage of having a head at both ends. It is one of the things which might easily pass unnoticed but for the helpful ladies. Here again is a square bowled font only 1 foot 8 inches across by 11 inches deep. But their greatest treasure is the Cloch Wyddelan an old bell of Celtic type which may date from the 7th century. It was dug up on the Bryn y Bedd site in the middle of the nineteenth century, and shows its age by being very rough and torn and serrated at the edges. For a long time this exceptional relic was kept for safety at Bangor but since the church is now well-guarded it is temporarily back at home. Also at present on view are two unusual and very old brasses, so well-worn that they need a glass cover; these commemorate the builder and the English translation of the Welsh insecription reads 'Pray for the souls of Meredith ap Ivan ap Robt. Esq and Alice his wife who died the 18th day of March 1525 on whose souls God have mercy. Amen.' The pews are replacements put in at about 1710 and they have some most interesting aspects. One of the front ones bears the carving 'Maingc i'r dyla' i Clyw' meaning 'a bench for the hard of hearing'. Also all the pews are connected in an odd way at the foot for a single oak beam of about five inches in thickness runs the length of five or six pews, and at the entrance to each pew a semi-circular scallop is cut out to allow one to get into the pew by lifting one's feet by nine or ten inches. Its an odd design that I have never seen before.

On the good advice of the ladies in the church we decided to have a short deviation in our walk and we went up the road soon turning into a footpath running up the valley between Fron Goch and Rhiw Goch. This proved to be a beautiful little valley with fascinating rapids and waterfalls from time to time. Our object was to find what was a possibly prehistoric burial mound about which, however, the experts are in some doubt as it might be a natural phenomenon or it might be a much later artifact. But as it seems that investigation would have to start with a full bulldozer dig for which neither money, nor enthusiasm are at present available, we are likely to remain in ignorance for some time yet. But it is a footpath to be highly recommended, and for those who wish, it is a fairly straightforward and easy way to Betws-y-Coed.

However, we had other work to do and retreating we headed for the castle. Before reaching it we had a glimpse of another of Dolwyddelan's prize possessions a 16th century farmhouse, which although it has been completely modernized inside still has most of the original outside work remaining. Near by is the foundation of a 15th century dwelling said to have been occupied at one time by Meredydd ap ieuan.

The castle stands high up above the road and must have been quite spectacular before it fell into ruin; and it must also have been well-situated to protect the river valley from the incursions of the English foes. No wonder that poets have found this a valley to love and that Southey speaks of one of his Welsh heroes finding time to: 'Linger gazing as the eve grew dim, from Dolwyddelan's tower'.

But the castle's great claim to fame is as the birthplace of Llewelyn the Great and history runs thus. Gruffuth ap Conan, Prince of Wales (the true Prince of Wales not the later English substitute arranged by Edward I) died in 1137 leaving the Principality to his son Owain Gwynedd who reigned until 1169 and who married firstly Gwladys by whom he produced a son called Yorworth; he later married Christian and she gave him another son David. Now as the eldest son Yorworth should have succeeded his father but strangely enough he was not considered worthy to hold the title because he had a broken nose! Could it be that the Welsh had been influenced by the teaching of the good Beaumanoir who thought that a man might be allowed to beat his wife but only reasonably and certainly should not break her nose for 'the nose is the fairest member that man or woman hath, and sitteth in the middle of the visage'. Or was it maybe that womens' rights had already started to raise their head even in that early age in Wales. For only about a century later we find that most exceptionally four abbesses were bidden to join the Great Council which dealt with the knighting of the Prince of Wales. Could it be that women had already started in Wales to play some public part in the affairs of state and not merely the normal underground part which they have exerted in great affairs since the days of Eve?

Whatever the reason, the title of Prince passed to the other son David, but his son did not inherit. Yorworth married Marged daughter of Madog ap Meredydd Prince of Powis and they produced Llewelyn the Great who in turn became Prince of North Wales in 1194 and later Prince of All Wales. Whether the title passed peacefully to Llewelyn or whether he had to scuffle a bit with his uncle David is not clear. To complete the tale Llewelyn died in 1240 and was succeeded by his son by one wife called David, who in turn was succeeded by Llewelyn, son by another wife called Llewelyn ap Cruffydd. He was slain in the battle of Buellt and was the last real Prince of Wales.

To return from our excursion into history and to get back to the castle we came to see. It is well described by Thomas Pennant as 'Seated in a rocky valley, sprinkled over with stunted trees, and watered by the Lledr. The bounderies are rude and barren mountains and among others the great bending mountain Siabod, often conspicuous from the most distance places'. He continues 'the castle is placed on high rock, precipitous on one side, and insulated: it consists of two square towers: one forty feet by twenty five: the other thirty-one by twenty. Each had formerly three floors. The materials of this fortress are the shattery stone of the country; yet well squared, the masonry good, and the mortar hard. The castle yard lay between the towers'. It is quite a hard climb up to the castle and a circuitous one with a pleasant trickle of water running down most of the way from the top of the mound on which it stands. One tower or keep is still in good condition but of the other tower and of the yard only the foundations remain. The keep was re-roofed in the nineteenth century. Looking across the road and the river Lledr it is just possible to see a rough mound of earth on which stands a flourishing copse of trees. This is all that is left of a still earlier castle built to defend the valley, but there is so little to see of it that in our laziness we did not bother to pay a closer visit.

After several generations Dolwyddelan castle passed into the hands of Meredydd ap Jevan an ancestor of the Wynn family whose influence covered so large an area round about. He moved from his house in Evionedd for he said 'I had rather fight with outlaws and thieves then with my own blood and kindred; if I live in my own house in Evionedd, I must either kill mine own kinsmen or be killed by them'. So he established a troop of 'seven score tall bowmen, every one arrayed in a jacket or armolet coat, a good steel cap, a short sword and dagger, together with his bow and arrows. Many of them also had horses and chasing slaves which were ready to answer the cry on all occasions'. So with these good Welsh bowmen, the founders of the real winners of the famous fights at Crecy and Agincourt the local bandits probably had a poor time.

We had intended to complete our round by going up the Lledr valley – and where will one find a lovelier valley anywhere in the world than that of the Lledr river throughout its whole length – and then striking out across the rough and desolate moorland at the foot of the Moel Saabod to find one of the footpaths which would take us either to the very doorstep of Pen y Gwryd, or another one which finished just above the head of Llyn Gwynant. Our change of mind was not merely laziness or the desire not to tackle the more desolate and rocky moor further down the valley, but it was because we felt we still had time to visit yet another castle. So back we went through the Forestry land and across the moorland which followed.

Quite close to the Pont Cyfang the river Llugwy makes a large loop and sweeps in almost to the old road, and there, only fifty yards away lie the remains of the fort of Bryn-y-Gefeiliau which guarded the Roman road running between Gaerhun in the north and Tomen-y-Mur in the south. Unfortunately very little now remains but the relics of some earth walls some with stone facing still visible, and some foundations evidently circling larger areas. The whole site is now overgrown with trees which were possibly planted partly to prevent the farmer destroying what is left of the fortress by ploughing more of the field as this site does occupy the middle of one of the fields. In 1920 the remains were fully excavated and a number of sherds and Roman coins were found and this enabled the archaelogists to date the fort as about A.D. 90.By its shape it was thought suitable for a camp for a small infantry unit or perhaps even a small cavalry unit.

After this round which proved as good as any we have ever had we returned once more to Pen y Gwryd. And so – if not to bed at least to an excellent tea.

Two days of genuine ambling should have put us into the right trim for something more venturesome and as the next day looked as though with luck it might avoid that steady unending rain which takes most of the joy out of any walking and all the joy out of mountain walking. So obviously the time had come to attempt once again the Snowdon peaks and if so the first decision to make was which route to follow. Should it be the Miners' Path which is so level and easy at the beginning as to be almost a motorway. After such quiet walking we would pass the lovely twin lakes of Llydaw and Glaslyn not gasping for breath but in a condition to appreciate to the full the beauty of these gems. From there the way does get a bit steeper but not unduly so and the occasional rocks are easily negotiated. But then with that dramatic suddenness with which things happen in the mountains one is faced with a truly terrifying scree slope which appears to rise at an angle of about eighty degrees and which relents not until the gate of heaven is reached within a few yards of the summit hotel. The thought of a drink at the top is about the only factor which stimulates one to manage the final effort. Then what about the Pig Track (or Pyg Track if you prefer it that way). A higher path and a much more interesting and exciting one with good views all the way, but again that brings you to the same horrible scree slope for the final push.

It is always possible to start at Llanberis and to toil safely, steadily and with little pleasure up the railway track, but this way has not much to offer. Or why not go to the other end of Llyn Gwynant and take the truly delightful Watkin Path which is probably the most attractive way for three quarters of its distance as it goes up beside the stream with its coloured pools and grand waterfalls. But this too is fine until it gets to the ridge between Snowdon and Lliwedd and then another scree slope appears, less steep than the Miners' Path but one in which one fries rapidly should the weather be hot. Or we could go further still and try the prehistoric tourist route from the 'Snowdon Ranger Hotel'. But that was on the bill of fare for another day.

Surely there is only one way up Snowdon — the Horseshoe. This gives that extra excitement of providing several stretches of genuine scrambling with just a touch of exposure so that one needs a good head and these bits are coupled with longer stretches of safe and easy walking where it is possible to enjoy the first class views. Anyway we could start that way and should the weather change or our courage fail it was easy to switch to the Pig Track when the first col was reached.

So off we went from the Pen y Pass car park starting on the horizontal but slightly boggy first part. Quite soon the very good hand and foot scramble begins and being a mere amateur this is the sort of scrambling that I most enjoy. It provides interest as it requires full muscular activity combined with the need to find good hand and footholds, but it is all done without risk. The worst that could happen in event of a slip would be a badly grazed shin. Stopping for a breather at the saddle we began the climb of Crib Goch. This is indeed a text book mountain and it always reminds me of an article in an older paper called *The Graphic* published in 1886 in which a gentleman who signs himself C.N.W. gets to the top of Snowdon at daybreak. He thinks Snowdon well proportioned but it is Crib Goch which really thrills him and as he climbs it on his way back his comments are 'Imagine a serrated edge mainly horizontal, but broken here and there by pinnacles like those shown in the engraving with sides plunging down almost vertically for more than a thousand feet. A top so narrow that almost everywhere it may be bestrode . . . it is a terrific place; to be carefully shunned by those with weak heads. The passage of Crib Goch is probably the finest piece of legitimate mountaineering which the British Isles can offer'. While his descriptions may well be thought exaggerated Crib Goch is a very fine mountain.

C.N.W. must have been a fairly accomplished mountaineer for his time for when he left at four o'clock in the morning in order to reach the top of Snowdon by sunrise he was seen off in state by Harry Owen with a lantern. But he suffered some disappointment when daybreak came as far too many people came creeping out of the hut at the summit where they had all spent the night! This is only one of many times when one is surprised at the considerable numbers to be found at the summit of Snowdon.

The route up Crib Goch is plain to see for it is well-cairned and as the years go by the scratches of many feet make the course of travel more and more obvious. No doubt for the expert the cairns are a perfect guide but for the less experienced they sometimes appear to direct one in several ways at once and although there should be little danger on this mountain, to lose the correct path might give rise to considerable apprehension. Even when going the right way there are places that make one feel like a fly on the wall and only real climbers enjoy that feeling. But although there are many peaks in this country for which the guide book can give a simple and safe tourist route for the scrambler however inexperienced Crib Goch is one of the few for which some reasonable scrambling experience is wanted.

Pausing in triumph at the top to admire the view which is almost perfect; the cloud is high but the day is dull and for perfection a day with bright sun and plenty of rolling cloud is required. After a rest we progressed on to the particularly narrow and hence for some particularly frightening saddle which looks like a fragile bridge of earth laid between two separate mountains and one which one feels rather as a builder must feel when he nonchalantly and almost jauntily strolls across a girder in space. For me it gives an irresistible urge to drop a leg over each side and to cover the distance after the manner of an agile young crawler! However it is soon over and next we face the problem of the pinnacles. Should they be climbed or should they be circumvented by toiling among the gravestones about their feet. It is not done in the best circles to avoid tackling them and if one goes round them one feels a failure. Perhaps they are best left to the whim of the moment and the hope that — as in this case — nobody will ever divulge either one's success or failure.

From the pinnacles the way is surprisingly straight and easy and it is not much more than a stroll after the rigours of Crib Goch while the way to the top of Crib y Ddysgyl seems child's play. It was not a full summer weekend but there were plenty of walkers and climbers about even if not quite the steady crocodile often found in the best weather. No wonder the conservationists are getting worried and wondering if these and other popular mountains are being worn down to sea level. Then we reached the summit cairn of Snowdon and found the crowds even worse and it had a Piccadilly Circus appearance because a train had just arrived. But what can be done? Surely everyone who wishes to must be allowed to climb to the top. And how unfair it would be to remove the railway and so stop the less athletic or the infirm from enjoying the extreme pleasure of the views from the top. One of the many questions to which there is no answer. Again would it be better to do away with the hotel up there? No doubt it would have been better had it never been built and also no doubt when the toiling scrambler is nearing the end of his journey and he thinks of the thirst quenching drink just above him he is much revived.

We had our refreshment and carried on along the simple track to Llwyedd which mountain although it fails by fifty feet or so to achieve the three thousand feet mark is a most attractive mountain. It has also that fearsome wall on the inner side which forms an unrivalled precipice.

The rest of the way is all downhill, thank goodness, but with its uneven and scree like steps is trying to the knees and ankles at the end of the day. But in due course the level ground is reached and by skirting the side of Llyn Llydaw there is the Miners' Path and then one has merely to trudge, rather wearily homeward. But is there anywhere in this country or elsewhere a more superb round than that offered by the Horseshoe or one guaranteed to make one realize what a remarkable meal tea can be.

But for those new to mountain country it cannot be emphasized too often that for mountain walking good weather and the correct equipment are essential. Even the more simple looking scrambles should be undertaken by the inexperienced only after full consultation with the expert or with an experienced local. A mistaken path or a little mist or low cloud can bring near disaster with surprising speed. Snowdon has a first class Mountain Rescue Service but it is not the object of this book to provide the Service with more experience — they get quite enough as it is.

And even the simple things of life can go astray. My wife and I have visited North Wales with unfailing regularity for twenty five years or so and we have, like all good amblers always spurned the idea of getting to the summit of Snowdon by using the mountain railway. In this we were soon taken to task by Jo

Briggs who told us at length what wonderful views of the mountain we were missing, views that could be seen only from the Railway track and which could be appreciated only when they were not obscured by the sweat running into one's eyes. So it was organized that we should do the trip up Snowdon by train and to save our pride we should then come down via the scree slope and the Miners' Path. Jo also assured us that lunch sandwiches were entirely unnecessary as her great friend who ran the hotel at the summit would produce a magnificent lunch of as many courses as we wanted and doubtless with champagne if required and all free of charge.

So we went down to the Mountain Railway station at Llanberis where begins the only rack railway in the British Isles. Running on a narrow gauge track of 800 millimetres (2 feet 7½ inches) it rises from a height of about 350 feet above sea level to one of just under 3500 feet; this is done at a speed a little less than 5 miles per hour taking in its stride a variety of gradients which in a couple of places reached 1 in 5½. And all the time winding round and round first this way and then that. It is open from Easter to early October but even during this period it is not infrequently closed for snow or high winds which make the going dangerous. It is reckoned that up to 175,000 people may be taken up to enjoy the top of Snowdon in most years. When the narrow gauge Festiniog railway proved successful in the eighteen sixties for carrying both passengers and slate from the quarries the work for the railway was given to Richard Cammell & Co. and started in December 1894. Despite many hold-ups because of weather and the fact that everything had to be dragged up the steep mountainside by manual work or horse drawn sledges, the task was fully completed in 72 working days and the track was finished by January, 1896. After the necessary preliminaries of testing and inspection and provision of rolling stock the first journey for the public was made at Easter, April 6th 1896. This first attempt with a locomotive and one coach was safely completed, but the second train which had two coaches left the track on the way down. The engine plunged down many hundred feet and was entirely wrecked, but fortunately the coaches which are not coupled but run behind the engine remained on the line and their handbrakes were automatically applied. The driver and fireman jumped from the engine as it went over and were undamaged but two passengers got themselves into a needless panic and jumped out of the coaches before these finally stopped. One of these died of his injuries. The accident was found to have been caused by subsidence of the track resulting from severe frost. Since then this railway has run without accident or injury to its thousands of passengers.

The train was nearly full when we arrived but the three of us managed to squeeze ourselves into a coach. The journey started and was enlivened for the travellers by Jo Briggs who kept them alternatively enthralled and quaking with terror by her descriptions of the countryside to be seen from the window followed by lurid accounts of the early accident which in her story had carried all the coaches down many hundreds of feet so that few of the passengers had escaped death or serious injury. One thing in which she was entirely accurate was in the remarkable views which can be seen from the train on this route. One can see aspects of the Snowdon massif which cannot be found in any other way and one can appreciate them to the full. But despite this wonderful panorama when the summit station was reached many of the passengers alighted white faced and weak kneed but greatly relieved; how many then decided to walk down I do not know.

But it was there that for our party disaster struck. The hotel was closed and neither meat nor drink were available. Naturally Jo Briggs was very dejected at her lack of organization as she had not thought to find out beforehand if the hotel would be opened. My wife and I also were somewhat daunted at the idea of the walk back with empty bellies but we had underrated Jo Briggs. In one of the most remarkable spectacles I have ever seen she went from party to party taking in every family on her rounds and begging a sandwich here and a biscuit there. We did not hear her pleas and persuasion, and indeed we were a bit embarrassed about it all but there is little doubt that according to her the aged and decrepit friends with her had only just left hospital after treatment for some near fatal disease and so would be unlikely to survive without food. Their deaths would be greatly on her conscience! Finally with the addition of a small box of chocolates intended as a present for our hostess at the hotel we had a spread in front of us rather better than we usually carried when out walking and certainly a much more varied one. A truly remarkable achievement!

And so refreshed we were able to go down the hill at a canter very different from the normal amble and we arrived at the end of the long trek home in first class condition.

A quiet day for rest and recuperation had been well-earned and how better could it be spent than in exploring the environs of Llanwrst where so much of interest could be seen. This small township was at one time the centre of the wool market in North Wales although in the eyes of Sir John Wynn it did not rank with some of the larger towns. For speaking of Caernarfon he comments 'Civility and learning flourished in that town so as they were called the lawyers of Caernarfon, the merchants of Beawmares, and the gentlemen of Conway'. But it was a flourishing place and doubtless much helped and governed by the Wynn family.

We started with a visit to the parish church of St Grwst who was a missionary of about the sixth century. Although the town is one busy with traffic, the church is in a surprisingly secluded place close to the river and has an air of peace about it. Tradition has it that the first church was built in the early 12th century on a piece of land given for the purpose by Dwnant (the murderer of Idwal) in atonement for his sin. The present building is mainly 15th and 16th century work which replaced the first church devastated during the Wars of the Roses. It is an interesting and pleasant church as are so many and it does contain several relics taken from Maenan Abbey when that suffered dissolution at the hands of Henry VIII, and when he removed most of the stone and solid timber from the Abbey for use to repair Caernarfon Castle. But happily the carved music gallery and the pulpit were of no use for this purpose and they were acquired for the parish church.

But the real gem of this building is the Mortuary Chapel attached to the south side of the main church. This was built by the Wynn family who owned Gwydir Castle on the other side of the Conwy, and it is possible that the suggestion that it was designed by Inigo Jones is a reliable one in this case. A claim has been put forward that Inigo Jones was born in

Llanwrst but this seems without foundation and it has usually been accepted that he was born in London in 1578. This distinguished chapel has as lovely a carved screen as one could wish to see, reputed to be the work of the monks of Aberconway Abbey, and it contains many monuments and memorial brasses recording the Wynn family who built and cared for it.

But its prize possession is the enormous stone coffin of Llewelyn the Great who when he died in 1240 was first buried in Aberconway Abbey. Edward 1st wanted the site of this Abbey for town and castle building (this has a rather modern ring) and he gave land and financial assistance to replace the Abbey at Maenan. Llewelyn's coffin was taken by river to this new Abbey. At the dissolution of the monastries he was again disturbed and apparently dumped at Llanwrst church from where the coffin was later rescued and transferred to Gwydir Chapel where it now remains. It is an impressive sight large enough to take any ordinary giant from fairyland, but still in good repair after its several journeys. Beside it lies the large stone effigy of Howel Coytmor said to be the natural son of David Prince of Wales and hence the grandson of Llewelyn the Great. It was this Howel Coytmor who led a hundred archers at the battle of Poitiers. The effigy is clad in the armour of the 14th century and the inscription reads 'Hic Jacet Howel Coytmor ap Gruffyd Vychan ap Davyd Gam'. His English companions preferred to call him Sir Howel Poleaxe and it has been claimed that he was responsible for the capture of the King of France at Poitiers and he accomplished this feat by striking off the head of the King's horse with one blow of the famous axe. This — as is delightfully said in the records — caused the King to dismount and he was taken prisoner. But needless to say there is much controversy about this story and there are many claimants to the capture of the French King. But there does seem no doubt that it was this Howel who sold Gwydir Castle to Jevan ap Meredydd the ancestor of the Wynns.

Leaving the chapel reluctantly we had a look round the market place, unfortunately cluttered up with cars as so common in the ancient towns of all countries. We might almost have preferred to see it after the ravages of the Wars of the Roses, when 'Greene grasse grew in the market place in Llanwrst, called Bryn y botten, and the deer fled into the churchyard as it is reported'.

Close by the church is a small well-built row of almshouses put there by Sir John Wynne in 1610 for 11 old men and one woman to act as their bedmaker. He also gave £5 a year for each of them; a living wage for those days. It is well-worth while pausing for some minutes to admire the most attractive high arched 18th century bridge which spans the Conwy here, and which still stands up to the constant passage of modern traffic. Its durability makes it doubtful that the recordings of some eighteenth century travellers were correct when they said that if they stood in the middle of the top of the arch and struck the bridge sharply with a stout stick the whole bridge would shiver. Although Inigo Jones has been claimed as the designer this at least is very doubtful, but one must remember how often at that time the architect or designer whether of bridges or cathedrals gave but brief instructions, and it was the builder and the mason who did the real work and adjusted the modifications as he thought necessary.

Across the bridge to the west side we paused yet again, and this time for a cup of coffee which we took in the Tu Hwnt i'r Bont the 15th century court house now the property of the National Trust and used as a restaurant. It is pleasantly and suitably furnished and serves its purpose very well.

Turning to the left across the bridge along the Betws-y-Coed road we came almost immediately to the Gwydir Castle entrance gate. Above this gateway is the inscription 1555 and this is a small part of the original house much of which was destroyed by a disastrous fire in 1924. Included in this old gatehouse is the gloomy chamber which was referred to by Sir John Wynn in a letter which he wrote in 1608 to his new chaplain and which shows that in those days the aristocracy knew well how to keep their clergy under control. Some extracts from this letter run as follows: 'First, you shall have the chamber, I shewed you in my gate, private to yourself, with lock and key, and all necessaried. In the morning I expect you should rise, and say prayers in my hall, to my household below, before they go to work, and when the come in at nygt — that you call before you all the workmen, specially the yowth, and take accompt of them of their belief, and of what Sir Meredith taught them. I beg you to continue for the more part in the lower house: You are to have onlys what is done there, that you may informe me of any disorder there. There is a baylyf of husbandry, and a porter, who will be commanded by you.

'The mornings after you be up, and have said prayers, I wo'd you to bewstowe in study, or any commendable exercis of your body.

'Before dinner you are to come up and attend grace, or prayers, if there by any publicke: and to set up if there be not greater strangers, above the children — who you are to teach in your own chamber.

'When the table, from half downwards, is taken up, then you are to rise and walk in the alleys near at hand, until grace time: and to come in then for that purpose.

'After dinner, if I be busy, you may go to bowles, shuffel bord, or any other honest decent recreation, until I go abroad. If you see me void of business, you shall commande a geldinge to be made ready by the groom of the stable, and to go with me. If I go to bowles or shuffel bord, I shall lyke your company, if the place be not made up with strangers.

'I would have you go every Sunday in the year to some church hereabouts to preache, giving warnynge to the parish to bring the yowths at afternoon to the church to be catekysed; in which poynt is my greatest care that you be paynfull and dylygent.

'Avoyd the Alehowse, to sytt and keep drunkards company there being the greatest discredit your function can have'.

It seems evident that in Wales at any rate the power of the layman increased dramatically when once the grip of the Pope of Rome had been loosened. For surely few schoolboys have been given more closely guarded instructions as to their behaviour.

Looking through the gateway at the fascinating grounds in the forefront of which is a low hedged ornamentation which has the appearance of an effort at making a maze, but which seen from the windows above shows that it is modelled on a Tudor rose. The other most striking sight is the immense flock of peacocks and hens, and spring must be in the air for most of them are in full display with their unbelievable tails fully extended. In the grounds at the back of the house is a still stranger sight, for there are several white peacocks and a fully spread white peacock tail is an exceptional sight. Not to be overlooked is a large blood red parrot strutting backwards and forwards along his perch, but not very talkative until we left when he deigned to say good-bye.

There is reputed to have been a fortress on this site as early as the 6th century and this was enlarged and a watch tower added by Howell Coytmor in the 14th century. The building of the present castle was started by Meredydd ap Jevan the ancestor of the Wynne, and when he died in 1525 it passed to John Wynn who continued enlarging the house. It is thought that Meredydd built the banqueting hall and the smaller tower (an incidentally also had time to have twenty-six children) and John Wynn added most of the rest. When the whole building was destroyed by fire in 1924 only the walls were left; Arthur Clegg bought the ruins in 1944 and he was responsible for the superb repair work done with such taste and ability that one could easily be deceived into thinking it was the original house. Moreover he spent much time and money in searching out furniture which fitted into the period of the house, and in fact managed to get hold of a few pieces of the original furniture which had been sold away by earlier owners. A number of original oak beams buried under a later ceiling were brought to light and unexpected old fireplaces were found concealed in later stone work.

The next day was set aside for a tour which barely deserved even the title of an amble as it would be better described as a potter. We thought we would have a look round Nantperis and Llanberis to see what of interest could be found there. How often on holiday one leaves aside towns and villages (often those which one flashes through in a car when going somewhere that seems more important) only to find that one is neglecting the treasures on one's own doorstep. Many times we had passed through Llanberis on our way to Caernarfon but we had seldom stopped there except maybe for a quick call to a shop. So we took the car down the long winding road from Llanberis Pass which goes steadily down through some of the most dramatic scenery in Snowdonia and visited the Nantperis church. The main part of this interesting church is of the original 14th century work and the church itself is dedicated to Peris of whom little is known. It was not the custom to give the title of saint to those worthy Celtic men until the 15th century, and it was after that date that many of them were so christened for the first time. This church does show a somewhat unusual plan for although the nave is of the normal 14th century design as far as the Sanctuary from there starts a remarkable addition dated probably early 16th century where three aisles have replaced the more usual chancel and there are valleys between them thus looking like three chancels and three high altars, a form of construction thought to be unique in North Wales. It may have been when this change was made that the oak screen was moved to a new position just behind the entrance door at the west end; there it stands looking in some ways odd and out of place but for this very reason rather attractive. At the top of the screen are two wooden candle holders and one of the sills is hollowed out to form an alms box. There are two special fittings of which the incumbent and congregation are particularly proud, one is the very melodious bell dated 1610 and the other the small stone font placed on a pedestal approached by three steps. Mr G.J. Bennet who was often looking for some striking if slightly cynical remark for his tourist guide commented that this font looked rather like a washing tub and fortunately for himself he was out of the neighbourhood when the guide was published or he might have suffered a well-deserved lynching by the whole congregation of Nantperis.

A few hundred yards away from the church is the Ffynon y Sant, a small square well, surrounded by a wall and a seat all round it. The well is square in shape and only about three feet across and one foot six inches deep and it was erected in the 18th century. About every fifty years two trout are dropped into this well and when one dies the other sacred fish is left until he or she departs this life naturally when two more are supplied. It proved difficulty to get any reasonable explanation for this odd custom, but I was told that it used to be the habit for lovers to look into the well and if they could see even one fish then the omens for their future were indeed good. It was also said that it was not unknown for the young man before taking his girl to perform this ceremony, to slip up and drop in a fish which he had just caught so as to be certain that one would be visible.

Moving on, the Llanberis church there is dedicated to St Padarn about whom again not much is known except that the ruins of his original chapel were visible before the railway station and the Victoria hotel were built over them. This is a large and spacious church as a parish church for a village of the size and on entry seems like a small cathedral. It is a pleasant but fairly normal parish church of the 19th century kind.

The lake here carries the name of the same saint as it is Llyn Padarn and at its southerly end stands the castle of Dolbadarn which was built in the 12th century by one of the princes of Gwynedd as a method of guarding the Llanberis Pass and so stopping the English invaders reaching the coast. Some fairly extensive foundations are left covering a good deal of the high rocky mound on which the castle stands but the only large part of the fort which remains is the forty foot tower so often seen in these Welsh castles of about this date. To reach the mound we had to work our way through four or five long horned goats which must have been wild ones imported by the National Trust which owns the site from the mountains. At least the goats had no visible signs of belonging to any of the nearby inhabitants.

We managed to work our way up the winding staircase which gets steadily narrower and narrower until the top is reached. From there the view should be one of sheer beauty with the whole range of mountains behind and the long stretch of Llyn Padarn in front. But alas looking out one realizes that Llanberis has jumped, or in the matter of the next few summer months, will jump into the twenty first century, for spread out over an area of many acres are hundreds of parked motor cars, scores of lorries of every size and shape and a multitude of bulldozers and forms of earth moving equipment representing every type of earth-quaking apparatus which has ever been invented. For one is looking over the proscenium of the Dinorwic Pumped Storage scheme of which more will be said in a moment. Coming down the stairs we look to see where the other two main towers of Dolbadarn castle had stood, and we remember that according to legend, it was here that Owain

Goch was kept prisoner for twenty years by his brother Llewelyn the Great. The castle was, of course, used as one of the state prisons.

Chatting to the learned locals of Llanberis we were given some details of the Llanberis annual carnival which has been going (albeit a little sporadically) for many years and which has followed the pattern usual for such village festivals and in which the well-known Llanberis Silver Band plays a full part. Over the last two years an addition has been made by the inclusion of the Snowdon race. The originator and present secretary is Ken Jones and the object is to get to the top of Snowdon and back in the shortest time. An exception is made for junior teams who are given a shorter distance. It is both an individual and a team event, the teams coming not only from local inhabitants but from a variety of other athletic clubs. There are events for men, women, local juniors and veterans, but unfortunately the number of women candidates is small. To give some idea of the time taken, a sample of last year shows that the best time was three seconds under 45 minutes to the summit for the best with a total of just over one hour twelve minutes for the journey there and back. The tail enders can can take up to about two hours and a half. The two age grouped junior teams go only to a halfway house and not to the top and so their times are not comparable. Unfortunately the local best times are well behind the outsiders, but perhaps they are already looking for a better candidate for next year. For the veterans there seems to be no age limit either above or below so presumably they must be judged on grey hair and general appearance. For the remainder everything is well classified according to Amateur Athletic Association standards including birth certificates for juniors. Despite the apparent absence of rules for veterans they have put up a brave show one at least having got to the top in 59 minutes and done the whole journey in one hour twenty three minutes. But so far no funeral arrangements have had to be laid on for the veterans.

Now we must take ourselves however reluctantly into the next century and spend a few moments talking about making electricity. For many years now the Central Electricity Board of the British Isles have been looking with envy at the great lakes of Wales which often lie high up in the mountain terrain, and thinking that if only they could be fully harnessed by hydro-electric schemes they would provide a lovely amount of electricity for the whole of the United Kingdom. But not all of them are large enough or high enough to provide the head of water for a real hydro-electric generator and so the experts have thought up a new plan by which the water runs down from the lake above to the lake below making electricity as it does so. It is then pumped back (by electricity) to the lake above and once again runs back again turning the generator. A deadly combination of top ranking electrical engineers and exceptionally expert economists have calculated that by driving the water up with cheap electricity made by nuclear fuel or coal one is not in fact losing money by this fairy tale method even though in the case of the new scheme at Dinorwic it will take four units of current to pump the water up and in coming down it will produce three units of current. It is persuasively explained that this conjuring trick is accomplished by pumping up with off-peak electricity and in this way evening up the load on generators generally, for one of the great problems of making electricity is that the requirements vary tremendously and there is of course no good method of storing current.

The engineers and administrators are very anxious to deny that the Dinorwic scheme was started to avoid the New York unhappy event. For there was a time when New York was entirely without electricity for twenty four hours because of an extreme power failure and the result (or one of the results) was a short but alarming increase in the birth rate. It is strenuously denied that Parliament even considered this aspect when they agreed to the Dinorwic plan.

In fact the Central Electricity Generating Board has had such a plan in mind for some years and it must now be over twenty years ago when they wanted to start one in the very bosom of the Snowdon massif. The lakes Llydaw and Glaslyn were to be used as the top reservoir and a tunnel was to be bored through the base of Lliwedd to connect with a lake below. Happily this plan was delayed for some time by the efforts of those who had no wish to see this special region devastated and luckily the nuclear power ideas came to the fore, and it was probably that, rather than individual efforts

which saved that area.

On this plan Llyn Marchlyn Mawr, resting in the arms of Elider Fawr and of Mynydd Perfedd, is to be the upper reservoir and on this Llyn a dam will be built to raise the water level 120 feet higher than at present. The water will drain through a vast tunnel system at a rate of eighty five thousand gallons every second into the Llyn Peris. The generating and other machines will be housed in an underground cavern thought to be one of the largest in the world. It will be twice as long and half as wide as a soccer pitch and higher than a sixteen storey building. It should be said that this cavern was part of the Dinorwic slate quarry and even when it was a quarry it was considered to be one of the world's largest holes in the ground. Llyn Peris has been enlarged and deepened to take the full supply and the engineers in control of the task are regretful that they are not allowed immediately to deepen the Llyn still further and so increase the amount of water used for pumped storage. In their view it would be more economical to do this at this moment and they are quite convinced that so successful will the whole scheme be that they will get instructions to increase the size at some later date.

The Board have made many concessions to keep the amenities; for example the dam built in the Marchlyn Mawr will be of stone and also they will not have any pylons or power lines running through the Llanberis valley. There is no doubt that they are anxious to do the mimimum amount of damage to the surrounding countryside and when the scheme is complete which it is anticipated will be in about 1982 they hope that the beauty of the valley will be unimpaired. The Board have honourably carried out their promises to emply as much local labour as possible and about 75% of the two thousand men employed come from the neighbourhood. But when the station is working only about ninety people will be required.

It does indeed seem possible that when the plan is finally finished and vegetation has had some years to regrow, apart from several more wide roads the general scenic effect will be reasonably good, and undoubtedly the Board is making every effort to make it so. They are even taking special steps in conjunction with the Welsh Water Authority to study the fish as Llyn Peris contains an exceptional species of char unchanged since the last ice age and efforts are being made to establish those elsewhere.

But as always one is frightened; not so much for this scheme but because already there have been many investigations in many valleys in North Wales where some form of hydro-electric plant might be established and we shall be fortunate if a new start is not made elsewhere as soon as Dinorwic is functioning. Even the nearby and particularly beautiful Dolwyddelan valley is thought to be under threat and in many other places the inhabitants feel themselves filled with foreboding. This apparently circumscribed expedition had proved to be a lengthy one as the Dinorwic workings cannot be considered at a short glance. And so feeling filled with facts both pleasant and unpleasant we once more ambled our way back to Pen y Gwryd.

Any mid-Victorian who tried ambling had to be tough. There were no cars to take you well on the way and most travel had to be on two legs or four. And should the weather be wet, (as it can be in Welsh mountains) there were no nice plastic waterproofs as light as a feather but guaranteed to keep out the rain, for protection was afforded by something not unlike a bell tent carried round the shoulders. And then if one wished to go to the top of Snowdon there were to all intents only two ways unless one had Alpine experience. The path from Llanberis following what is now the railway track which was safe but rather a trudge, although it was not difficult to hire a pony to go either halfway or even right to the top if desired. And the other way was from the 'Snowdon Ranger' cottage hotel, sited on the banks of Llyn Cwellyn which was a more interesting route and here again ponies could be hired. This building which became a hotel acquired its name from Evan Roberts who lived in a cottage there and who very early turned himself into a guide and who was probably the best Snowdon guide in North Wales. He was christened, or christened himself the 'Snowdon Ranger' and then when the cottage turned into a hotel this name was given to it and remained with it up to the present day. The 'Snowdon Ranger' is now one of the many youth hostels and gets its good contingent of young visitors every year. Borrow visited the Ranger in 1854.

We thought it was time we visited the 'Snowdon Ranger' and so we took the car to the large car park opposite to it, and we ambled round Llyn Cwellyn a remote and isolated place but a delightful lake. We also had a look at Llyn y Gadair round which Thomas Pennant had a good walk. Just south of the Ranger Pennant found Llyn Dywarchen or the Lake of the Sod which is the one where Giraldus first noticed what he called the 'wandering islands' which travelled round the lake and sometimes took animals with them, and which we now know are floating reed beds. This is a pleasant but less spectacular side of Snowdon and one which is probably visited by fewer tourists than any other as the general route seems either the Llanberis Pass or through Beddgelert to the coast.

We then thought to visit Beddgelert which in some strange way we had tended to avoid because of the very banal and probably quite untrue fable which is always associated with it, although Gelert's lonely grave in the middle of a field still attracts many visitors. We started at the Pont Aber Glaslyn where the Nantmor turning starts across the river and took the fairly new track which used to carry the narrow gauge railway and which is now a recognized footpath. The beginning was not too easy as recent bad weather had carried away some of the hillside and the path below, and the temporary crossing provided, was more suitable for a mountain goat than for a couple of amblers. However having once got going it is a wide and easy way and one in which one can appreciate to the fully the glory of the Afon Glaslyn, that turbulent torrent so good to look at and equally so as a fisherman's river. About a mile and a half takes one to Beddgelert and it also gives one time to think about the railway that this track used to carry. Following the success of the Festiniog Railway (a success incidently which it still has as it carries hundreds of passengers every year through some of the best country side in North Wales) a company was formed called the North Wales Narrow Gauge Railway Company which had an ambitious programme. For they meant to start several rail links of 1 foot 11½ inches gauge, and the one which concerns us here should have run from Portmadoc to Caernarfon.

Strangely enough the link between Partmadoc and Pont Aber Glaslyn was in some ways less important because before the Portmadoc embankment was built it was possible to get barges and other small boats up to Pont Aber Glaslyn. The first part of this railway was opened in 1877 to carry both passengers and, of course, slate from the quarries and it went from Dinas junction about three miles south of Caernarfon to Rhydd-Dhu a point about a mile beyond the southern end of Llyn Cwellyn this station being later called the South Snowdon station. The whole of this section was complete by 1881. Financial troubles held up the continuation for some time and it was not until 1900 that a start was made on the extension to Beddgelert. The work continued in a desultory way through the first twenty years of this century with a natural hold-up during the 1914-1918 War and it was not until about 1922 that the section was opened which gave stations among other places to Croesor, Nantmor and Beddgelert. There were times when a passenger service to Beddgelert were completed merely by post chaises. At its heyday during the summer of 1923 there were four trains a day on this route but by 1933 this had been reduced to one a day. The speed of the trains was a leisurely 10 miles an hour or so – thus providing the perfect speed to enable the passengers to enjoy the beauty of the country through which they were passing. The railway finally ground to a halt sometime about the middle of the thirties, although even in quite recent years there have been suggestions that it might be reopened. As the Beddgelert part of the track is now such a popular way for walkers it seems very unlikely that any change will be made, but again the great success of the Festiniog railway in carrying tourists may stimulate some speculators.

Thus on to Beddgelert of which Pennant said 'Its situation was the finest in the world to inspire religious meditation, amidst lofty mountains, woods and murmuring streams'. Also he said 'The church is small yet the loftiest in Snowdon'. Dedicated to St Mary it belonged to the Priory of St Augustine. To quote the invaluable Thomas Pennant yet again 'There is reason to suppose they might have been of that class which was called Gilbertines, and consisted of both men and women, who lived under the same roof but strictly separated from each other by a wall'. He gets this idea because there is a bit of ground near the church called 'the Meadow of the Nun'. The

Prior owned for his support several pieces of local property including plough land and share in swarms of bees. He had also an allowance of fifty cows and twenty two sheep, but it was thought that he needed all this as the house was an expensive one being on the great road from England into North Wales and from Ireland to England. In the strange way that things happened in those days in 1535 Henry VIII bestowed the abbey on the abbey of Chertsey in Surrey and in 1537 both were given to Bisham in Berkshire.

Having reached Beddgelert after enjoying the mile and a half along the bank of the Afon Glaslyn we next paid a visit to the Church. It was built on the foundations of the old priory abbey a 12th century edifice, but that was destroyed soon after it was built. The next attempt was in the 16th century but little of this one is left, and most of the church is 19th century work. The early remaining work includes some of the east end including the triple window which has been considered one of the finest specimens of stained-glass in Snowdonia. The font is curious being a hollowed out stone and so small it may at one time have been a holy water stoup. The inscription round the font is modern and is the Doxology in Old Welsh and the name of one of the rectors.

If one is feeling very full of energy when back at Pont Aberglaslyn a very good walk can be found by going through Nantmor, where there is a pottery to be seen and the local crafts are often exciting. A mile of rough track will take you on to a very poor road which goes through most desolate country and finally gets back to the main Pen y Gwryd — Beddgelert road just between Llyn Dinas and Llyn Gwynant. It is quite a long way and as happens so often when walking one is in grave need of a driver to meet you at the other end. Good circular walks are not easy to find and they are apt to be very lengthy. I often think that the ideal way to take a walking holiday would be to have a car and driver always at one's beck and call so that it would be possible to walk in a straight line in any direction with the certainty that there will be a car at the right meeting place.

Next day we were ready — almost ready — for another day in the mountains and so where should we go? The Carnedd range is second only to the Horseshoe as a ridge walk but it has the slight disadvantage that it is laid out rather after the pattern of the three legs of the Isle of Man, so that to do things properly and to cover all the three thousand foot peaks it is necessary to walk immense distances and often then to walk back again. So that although the views are unrivalled and a good deal of new lakes and country can be seen from various points on the ridge you have to be at your strongest to enjoy the trip.

Then there was our old friend Cnicht not very far from where we were yesterday at Beddgelert; a pleasant and not too demanding climb and an interesting one because after travelling up what seems to be a very ordinary mountain, quite suddenly you come out on the prow of a ship as the ground drops away in front and on either side giving a quite unexpected feeling of exposure. For it is another mountain like Moel Siabod that goes up slowly and gradually to a final peak and then there is nothing. In the case of Moel Siabod the best and precipitous side tends to be covered by forest formation and is less evident than in the case of Cnicht in which it stands out in plain view for all to see.

In the end we decided that this was a day for the fascinating walking and exploration round the Glyder ridge, taking in maybe Tryfan or Llyn Idwal or even the Devil's Kitchen. It's a long hard slog to Glyder Fach and we thought we would cover more exciting ground by taking the car to Ogwen Cottage and start from there. Ogwen Cottage is in fact no longer a cottage since an education authority got its hands on it, but it is now one of the Welsh valley tower blocks which seem to be springing up in various places.

We started along the well-marked if slightly wettish path which as it leads not only to Llyn Idwal but also to the climbing nursery of the Idwal slabs is now practically a three way highway. Llyn Idwal seems to have a slightly sinister appearance except on the sunniest day and it may be this that has been responsible for its sad traditional story. For the young prince Idwal is said to have been murdered by being thrown down Twll Du by the man who was supposed to be looking after him. Or to quote the inescapable Thomas Pennant writing about Llyn Idwal 'Infamous for the murder of a young prince of that name, son of Owen Gwynedd, by Dunawt, son of

Nefydd Hardd, one of the fifteen tribes of North Wales, to whom Owen had entrusted the youth, to be fostered according to the custom of the country. It was a fit place to inspire murderous thoughts, environed with horrible precipices, shading a lake, lodged in its bottom. The shepherds' fable, that it is the haunt of demons: and that no bird dare fly over its damned waters, fatal as that of Avernus'. Other stories say that the wails of the murdered victim can often be heard resounding through Cwm Idwal in bad weather, while others declare that since the deed there have been no fish in the Llyn, but how it is that some folk have managed to catch a few trout there is not explained — no doubt put in there by the Devil for his special favourites.

We passed round the left hand side of Llyn Idwal following its top and clambering up the rocks to have a long look at Twll Du or the Devil's kitchen from below where it is indeed an impressive sight. This narrow knife cut in the mountain side with the rapid stream running deep inside and the sinister black rocks rising sharply on either side is a sight to frighten anyone. Behind you at the foot of this strange slit in the rocks is a magnificent view across the lake with the rugged head of Pen yr Ole Wen looming above Llyn Ogwen and with Carnedd Llewelyn and his impressive brothers forming a grand ridge of mountains in the background.

The Scramblers' Path up the left side of Twll Du is steep and hard going although the cairn at the top gave us hope for the future, and so puffing and panting we arrived at the plateau above. The chance to see Twll Du from above should not be missed for it looks different but still dramatic and it is a unique feature even for the mountains of North Wales. Moreover the little plateau is isolated and surprisingly empty of people and the walk round tiny Llyn Cwn and the twisting scree slope climb to the summit of Glyder Fawr is well-worth the effort involved.

The ridge walk from Glyder Fawr to Glyder Fach is exceptional by any standard. Masses of rock of immense size are scattered in a haphazard way all along the route as though some particularly large giant had spilt them from the hod he was carrying while on his way to build himself another bigger and better castle. And all the while the view on all sides are wonderful, but you must be prepared, for often the wind blows cold on the Gylder ridge. There is very little vegetation there for the rocks are bare and wind swept and collect no water so that even moss is sparse. But going down a bit on the eastern side the heather and bilberries are growing well and a few animal species are to be seen. Sheep as always are there in numbers and with luck foxes and even badgers can sometimes be seen. So can the wild goat and we have in the past come across one there, although on this holiday the only ones we came across were the half wild ones at Dolbadarn. The wild goat dislikes human company and is clever enough to know how to avoid it. The bird life on this ridge is better than on the Snowdon Horseshoe with members of the hawk family, particularly buzzards frequent, and crows and ravens not uncommon. People have claimed to have seen some grouse here, and most nature books will tell you that small flocks of choughs can be sighted at the right times. When we reached Glyder Fach we decided that Bristly Ridge was not for us and could better be left to real climbers and we took the easy way down over the saddle and past Llyn Bochlwyd and by easy stages back to Ogwen Cottage.

From the col above Llyn Bochlwyd it was very tempting to try and take Tryfan in our stride, but with our muscles muttering a few complaints we thought it better left for another day. The climb up Tryfan is always worth a special journey for there are few routes to a mountain top more entertaining to the scrambler. It needs a fair gymnastic agility going from rock to rock but you are always going upwards and there are no straightforward slogs along dull paths, as all the time you can find numerous side tracks and different methods of approach and each one has to be separately chosen and so if available a little brain work is desirable. But nowhere is there any feeling of frightening exposure even for the least experienced. And then although it can claim only ten feet above the needed three thousand, what mountain top is more exciting to stand on than Tryfan? It seems so isolated and on every side the rocky faces drop away sharply to the level of the A5 motor road and this gives a great impression of height. And what other mountain has the two square stony blocks of Adam and Eve perched on top and standing close enough together to be ready for the enthusiast to leap gracefully from one to the other with only a few hundred feet of space to fall down should the foot slip. It makes you very glad when you can claim to be too old even to try the jump!

On one occasion we had enough vicarious excitement while resting on the summit for on that small restricted space there were two children aged about three and five years who were running at large to the complete unconcern of their parents. It appeared that these parents had made a vow to take themselves and their offspring to the top of each of the North Wales Three Thousands and had already accomplished several. As children of this age had often to be carried up steep and difficult places it seemed an unusual method of parent battering, but no doubt they found it a satisfying experience and the children undoubtedly enjoyed it, even though they probably failed to understand the true purpose of the exercise. Children may have a strange absence of the fear of heights and be quite careless of risks, but for the onlooker it was a terrifying experience and all the half dozen or so there evidently felt as we did, unwilling to stand this alarming sight any longer and very quickly we all turned and started on the downhill.

But surely there can be few mountains so compact or rising so sharply and suddenly from the surrounding countryside and having such easy and interesting access to the non-climber. And so surely no other mountain could provide such a fitting end to a visit to Snowdonia and we ambled home happily and with great content.

But we cannot claim quite the same feelings when we packed up and went back to London the following day, for how much more there was to see and how much more there was to do. How fortunate were the Thomas Pennants and the George Borrows of this world who had the time and the money to wander at large round the glorious countryside of Britain and who also had the great ability to describe what they saw in words which can still thrill much later generations. It is indeed difficult to claim that all men are born equal.

CHAPTER 10

THE ANGLERS

The pleasant'st angling is to see the fish
cut with her golden oars the silver stream,
and greedily devour the treacherous bait.
Shakespeare. 'Much ado about nothing' Act III. Sc. I.

In considering the country pursuits for which visitors go to Snowdonia, fishing should be high on the list even though in numbers they are fewer than those who go to walk or climb: for this region lures those who are looking for pleasant surroundings in addition to their sport: the Gwryd river was not very productive until Lockwood dammed it and stocked the lake; Cwm Ffynon and Llyn Llydaw are fairly good and within easy reach, but some of the better rivers such as the Glaslyn are more easily reached from Beddgelert, while the excellent Conwy is nearer to Betws-y-Coed. This often meant that fishermen staying at Pen y Gwryd had to go further afield for their sport either to the bigger centres such as Gwynant, Dinas or the Ogwen lake, or they had to make for the small remote lakes and streams found in the high hills, and these journeys have often provided some descriptive prose, so that even if Pen y Gwryd did not always attract the greatest fishing addicts it certainly attracted fishermen who were adventurous and willing to cover the countryside.

The angler commonly seems to have been a fertile writer; is this because the sport allows plenty of time for thought, or because it is the thoughtful man who takes up fishing? In either case there is no doubt that many anglers have left behind some delightful tales of exploit and adventure, which are still most readable. But maybe ardent anglers should avoid Thomas Pennant's *Journey to Snowdon* for the angler might not agree with the ideas on sports and games expressed in that book. Pennant lists, in order of merit four 'Manly games' which are Archery, Playing with sword and buckler, Playing with two-handed sword, Playing with two-ended staff: then follow (again in order of merit) the 'juvenile games' and these are Coursing with the greyhound, Fishing and Fowling. So here fishing is only just above the 'Domestic games' of Poetical competition, playing upon the harp, Reading Welsh, Singing with music, Singing with four accents (this is presumably singing in harmony), Drawing a coat of Arms and Heraldry.

The chalk streams of England and the salmon rivers of Scotland may have attracted the elite among the fishing folk but few writers about the sport would be quite as offensive as the dandy of late Regency times who is quoted by Thomas Medwin as having said 'Who would read a book about angling, and poor angling too, in that terra incognita of goats and barbarians – Wales?'

Although rather before the time-span of this book it has already been seen that friend Giraldus Cambrensis has much to say about the habits of fish even if his one-eyed fish are now apparently extinct; but John Henry Cliffe wrote at length and in superb style on angling in North Wales, starting his recollections about it in 1840.

A good deal of his time was spent with Beddgelert as his centre. As an angling site he does not rate Pen y Gwryd in the top flight, but he thinks that for anyone prepared to rough it in the country, it provides a fair sport, although with the time honoured and unending complaint of fishermen everywhere he dilates at length on the ravages of poachers. His full and comprehensive account of Pen y Gwryd, if somewhat unhappy, gives one of the earliest reasoned accounts of the Inn and how it progressed, and it is an account untrammelled by the exaggeration and flourishes often employed by the novelists who wrote of it. 'Barren, solitary, dignified Nature in her ruder aspects, is aptly portrayed in the desolate Nanty Gwryd. The gigantic mountains around, stern and full of dread lift above it their bare and rugged heads, and fold it, as it were, in their embrace; and the wanderer as he slowly travels on his way towards the Pass of Llanberis — a scene of still wilder grandeur and sublimity, may call to mind the cold and selfish world he had left for a brief space, to enjoy that quiet and tranquillity, that freedom from carking cares and anxieties of human existence, amidst the solitudes of mountainous wilderness we now propose to explore. In the midst of this solitudinous region formerly stood a wretched roadside alehouse, known as Pen y Gwryd Inn. Occasionally a weary benighted tourist, after a toilsome ascent of the Pass of Llanberis, would direct his steps to it, glad to receive such shelter and entertainment as the slender resources of the place afforded. In the process of time, however, and in accordance with the march of improvement, which is gradually spreading over the nooks and byeways of Wales, the humble roadside pothouse becomes transformed into a very comfortable inn; where not only the wayfarer meets with civility and attention, but even in the culinary department he will have no reason to complain. The enterprise of the landlord, Harry Owen, has in a great measure accomplished this desirable result; and, in a few years more, we confidently predict that Pen y Gwryd Inn will occupy a still more important position amongst the hotels of Snowdonia. The Inn is happily situated at the junction of three roads, severally leading to Beddgelert, Llanberis and Capel Curig. It is literally an oasis in the wilderness, a palm tree in the desert, a solitary spot of verdure, snatched by the industry of man from the wreck of Nature; and notwithstanding its elevation — for it is oft-times in the clouds — and its exposure to the frosts and snows of winter, you will observe several kinds of garden flowers and vegtables flourishing luxuriantly; and hereafter, we have little doubt that human industry will still further improve the outdoor character of the place. Behold us, then, reader, comfortably installed in a neat parlour at Pen y Gwryd Inn which, though small, is sufficient for our wants, discussing with a zest and appetite unknown to any, save a mountain wanderer, the savoury viands prepared by the hands of Mrs Pritchard, our host's mother-in-law — an old dame who, in days of yore, was a domestic in the service of Thomas Pennant, Esq., of Downing; whose fame, at the close of the last century, as an antiquary and topographer, is so well-known and appreciated.' His repast incidentally was 'a leg of mountain mutton' which he found gratifying after the eight mile walk from Beddgelert. His inspired prophecy as to the future of Pen y Gwryd is interesting but it is a pity that a man whose observation was so good did not include in his praises Ann Owen and perhaps a little more praise of her mother; Henry provided the most marked civility and attention, but so did they and they also provided the culinary excellence.

In his talk about how much Owen did to reorganize Pen y Gwryd, Cliffe does give an idea about dates when he says 'Our first sojourn at Pen y Gwryd was in 1849 before the Inn was partly rebuilt and enlarged. Accommodation then was a small rudely furnished room and two or three bedrooms of the same character. But then few anglers or tourists visited it, merely calling for a glass of cwrw or some bara-a-caws'. In case the reader should happen to wish to call for refreshment at Pen y Gwryd or other Welsh Inn, it should be said that 'cwrw' means beer or ale, while 'bara-a-caws' means bread and cheese. For correct pronunciation he should apply to a real Welshman. Later he became so attached to its improved style that he specially noted that it was only two and a half miles from Llyn Gwynant, the better of the fishing lakes and that the old road which ran lower in the valley than the new turnpike was slightly shorter.

Cliffe also gives a further lead about the contributions made to fishing by Harry Owen pointing out that he provided one of the boats on Gwynant for use by the fishermen staying at Pen y Gwryd. He also gives quite a long account of a fishing expedition made with Harry to Llyn Edno, a rugged five mile walk from the hotel led and cheered by Owen, and in due course they caught six handsome trout of one pound each; Harry Owen said they should think themselves very fortunate as catches on Llyn Edno were far from common.

Cliffe also gave a lot of advice to those who went in for the local fishing; for example, he advocated fishing Welsh waters only with flies made in Wales, presumably to prevent the fish having language difficulty. Also he was in favour of a short rod for boat fishing suggesting one about twelve and a half feet long, while for shore fishing he thought that a thirteen to fourteen foot rod would be about right; some of today's anglers might find those a bit on the long side! However, to cheer up the angler of Victorian times he pointed out that the twelve foot rod would cost about thirty shillings (which is £1.50 in present day money) while the fourteen footer would have set the buyer back by about two pounds five shillings and to this should be added the cost of the boat and boatman, reckoned at approximately five shillings a day.

Following the best angler's example, Cliffe gave a number of very good reasons why the catch at any one time did not come up to expectations; but then the rabid fisherman has always been weak on the law of averages, and usually thinks that his maximum catch should be caught every day. In his book a good deal of the blame for lack of fish was laid on the poisonous water flowing from the lead and copper mines further up the hill, while poachers were very largely responsible for the small number of fish about. He seemed slightly unfair as he admitted that the landlord of at least one hotel netted the lakes at least twice a week, while the gentleman living in Plas Gwynant beat everybody by having a special net made which gave him about 1500 trout per season with just a few casts!

On the subject of poaching as an undesirable side of the fishing industry, another author writing in 1862 produced some interesting information. The Rev George Tugwell was irritated because he thought that Cwm Ffynon had recently been 'latched'. The latch, which was later improved and modernized and given the name of the 'Otter board', was a device used by poachers, hoteliers and other wicked people, and it consisted of a large flat board, fitted with some sort of small sail, and trailing several long lines on each of which were hanging hooks decorated with different kinds of flies; the latch was dragged across the lake on ropes and apparently guaranteed a good catch. The more modern otter board works on the same general principle of a flat board floating with one edge above the water and with many lines of flies attached to it; unfortunately when dragged across the water not only does it catch a lot of fish, but it also pricks and frightens many more that are not caught, thus disturbing the fish for some time and annoying the fishermen for much longer. An article in

INCLUDING
Thos. Halliday · *Frank Berril* · *Rev J.N. Burrows*
M. Black · *Roderick Williams* · *M.K. Smith*
H.F. Bowring · *C.Stewart*

INCLUDING
Thos. Halliday *Frank Berril* *Rev J.N. Burrows*
M. Black *Roderick Williams* *M.K. Smith*
H.F. Bowring *C. Stewart*

THE KANCHENGUNGA PARTY
Tony Streather, Norman Hardie, George Band, John Clegg, Tom Mackinson
Neil Mather, John Jackson, Charles Evans, Joe Brown

THE MOUNTAIN RESCUE PARTY
Led by Chris Briggs

NANTPERIS
In the 18th Century

SUMMIT OF THE GLYDERS

SUMMIT OF THE GLYDERS

THE FIRST CAIRN ON SNOWDON!

Country Life in October 1975 gave a number of details of the present day otter board, and the author was sure that even if a Welshman did not invent this fiendish device, he has certainly played a large part in preserving its use. Some poachers have even gone so far as to design a folding otter board which can be carried in the pocket.

John Henry Cliffe is a mine of good stories and he gives an interesting account of an adventure which befell him while fishing on Llyn Lldaw from a boat when they were pursued by a three months old colt which was so persistent in following them that they finally felt impelled to turn back and rescue it. With the help of Harry Owen they managed to drag it into the boat, in itself no mean feat with a colt of that age; they ferried it to the shore where they were very lucky to find the mare for which it had been searching and so they could hand it back to mother: there must be few fishermen who can claim to have caught a young horse! Still although Cliffe kept his eyes open he admits that he could see no sign of any one-eyed fish either in Llydaw or elsewhere.

G.J. Bennett published a book in 1837 which he entitled *A Pedestrian's Guide to North Wales*, but this name should not put the angler off, for Bennett was a keen fisherman and told some fascinating stories of fishing exploits. He was staying briefly at Pen y Gwryd while he rested and repaired a damaged rod, and while there he tried his luck on Cwm Ffynon 'a large oval lake on which the black and sterile rocks which form inaccessible ramparts on one side are reflected in its generally unruffled surface; the scene is wild and desolate such as despair herself would select for her abode'. This description is of the kind not uncommon in Victorian times for what would now be considered beautiful country. He agreed that there were plenty of fish in the lake, although they were, as they still are, small and shy. He was far too experienced a fisherman to let anyone know how big was his catch, and one cannot tell if it was excitement or disappointment which gave him the nightmare lobster described earlier in this book.

The Visitors' Books of Pen y Gwryd are really rather disappointing about entries on angling subjects. Anglers seem very self-effacing compared with climbers, and they appear to fall into two categories: the expert who always sidesteps the direct question except for a laugh about the one which got away, and the inexperienced or less fortunate angler whose main anxiety is that no one should know how few fish he caught in how long. But John Hope Clerke of Cheshire, making an entry in 1860 remarked that because of the drought the stream was shallow (strange how for climbers and walkers it always rains all the time and for the anglers it never rains at all) and the banks of the stream were very slippery, but a few pools were well-stocked. Three rods in his party caught six fish, but how big they were and how many days work it cost is not mentioned so it is not as helpful a comment as it might be. He does add that most unusual remark for a fisherman that it was bad weather for fishing!

It might be expected that Charles Kingsley would not be able to help giving a lecture about angling; when writing to Tom Hughes inviting him to join the party at Pen y Gwryd he asks him 'Pray bring a couple of dozen moderate lake-sized hooks, to tie flies on, for I am out of hooks, except the very biggest size, salmon-peel size — in fact'. Then after a discourse on his successful fishing expedition on Lady Mildmay's water at Warnborough he continues 'Mind and don't get those flies too small. A size larger than what I said would be no harm, but I don't mind small hooks, if a big fly be tied thereon — see what a difference a wise man and a pool may make. (Here followed a sketch of a wise man's fly and a cockney maiden's fly). Why do fish take your caperer, in spite of his ugliness, but because he looks the fattest one they ever saw yet? Think over these things'.The caperer is apparently the name given to the caddis fly in the mid nineteenth century.

Kingsley does not tell us much about his fishing fortune and what there is, suggests misfortune. They tried the Llyn Edno — 'So there we got, and ate our hard-boiled eggs and drank our beer, and then set to, and caught nothing. The fish always sulky and capricious, would not stir'. One would think that a clergyman would not be too upset at having toiled all night and caught nothing but one of his bad verses in the three man poem suggest otherwise:

"I came to Pen y Gwryd in frantic hopes of slaying
Grilse, Salmon, 3 lb. red-fleshed Trout, and what else there's no saying:

But bitter cold and lashing rain, and black north-eastern
skies, sir,
Drove me from fish to botany, a sadder man and wiser".

When one gets nearer to the present day one finds, unhappily as far as the Pen y Gwryd Visitors' Books are concerned, that the fisherman is strangely silent; admittedly fishing claims to be and is a silent sport but surely only until the angler has completed the last cast of the day and starts to leave the river for then his spate of words begins and it continues for a length of time that only the golfer can beat. Let us hope that those who fish in North Wales are all engaged in adding to the great literature which angling has produced in the past.

But even if the angler cannot compete with the climber in Visitors' Book essays they are not entirely immune from accident; Sir Francis Dyke Acland while he was Under Secretary for Foreign Affairs had the misfortune to dislocate an elbow joint, and it is reputed that this accident happened when he was following his Parliamentary bent and fishing for one-eyed trout.

Nor should one forget the possibility that some poor angler has been lost without trace, after having fallen in a river in spate and been carried out to sea; the Visitors' Books have no record of any such tragedy, but to anyone who knows many of the sections of the Welsh Salmon rivers would agree that this would not be impossible.

The fishing lower down the valley, such for example as that on the Aberglaslyn, was usually better than that on the Gwryd and this was some disadvantage for Pen y Gwryd. It is not always easy to remember that in the days before the motor car when the anglers' transport was a pony and trap or shank's pony the siting of the Inn was of great importance. However, despite the lure of the lower river one honest gentleman in 1867 was prepared to say 'Better a dry morsel at Pen y Gwryd than a stalled ox at the Goat'; the Goat being a long established and normally considered an excellent hotel at Beddgelert.

Undoubtedly the most ardent and rabid fisherman anytime or anywhere in the Pen y Gwryd area was one of the local general practitioners; one who was always called in for any medical trouble which might occur in the hotel. He was probably the only doctor in this country, or perhaps in any other country, who had a telephone installed on a tree beside his stretch of fishing, so that he could spend the maximum of his time on the river, and not be out of touch with either angling or medical practice. It is easy to see how the patients could be trained to wait until the particular fish had been landed, but not so easy to understand how the fish was trained to wait on his line while the patient was on the telephone describing the symptoms at length.

The next hundred years show very, very few entries about fishing in the Visitors' Books. It may be that the expert angler tended to stay at the hotels further down the valleys where there were wider streams, bigger lakes and better fishing chances, but it is possible that the anglers were still shy of putting their simple, and some would think almost dull, remarks alongside those of the danglers who spent their time clambering round rocky slopes. How can talk about catching five or six trout compare with dissertations on dangerous scrambles with details of chimneys, toe-holds and glissades in the snow, and still less with the account of a difficult first ascent. Many a good, tough long distance ridge walker has at times felt out of place at Pen y Gwryd when surrounded by a covey of courageous climbers!

Although Harry Owen and the others who followed him were always helpful to anglers and in a position to give them good advice, the first landlord who took fishing as a serious adjunct to the Inn and ranked it almost on an equal level with climbing, was that ardent angler Arthur Lockwood. Even before he owned the place he had suggested to the proprietor William Hampson that the marshy, boggy area in front of the hotel fed by the Gwryd river, had great potentialities if turned into a lake and that conversion would be cheap and easy and as soon as he took over the hotel he started moving on this scheme. And yet despite his evident love of fishing and although he has made many entries in the Locked Book on all sorts of subjects, all written in his beautiful handwriting which is as legible as typescript, and although he has many details of weather and climate which would be worth further study, he hardly mentions fishing. But as was usual with him he went in for action rather than words, and Lockwood's lake and Lockwood's trout hatchery did more for the local anglers than many pages of remarks. Descriptions of the construction of both lake and hatchery are given in the Lockwood chapter and this shows that his contribution to fishing at Pen y Gwryd was very considerable.

Lockwood and the fishermen had a stroke of luck when G.C. Carlisle presented the hotel with a twenty foot punt for their use; it was built to his own design by Salters of Oxford, and was christened Georgina with all due ceremony and with the drinking of healths. In April 1928 Lockwood tested the fishing himself and was delighted to get ten trout of an average length of 7½ inches and by July 1929 some of the trout had grown to 17 ounces and many had spawned; this encouraged him to make some spawning beds.

Naturalists were interested to hear that one result of making the lake was a large increase in bird life, a fact that would of course be expected today. In April 1930 he sighted four pairs of moorhens, three pairs of mallard, two teal and many snipe and sandpipers nesting, and a whole variety of smaller birds. At one time Lockwood got worried because he saw what he called a water ousel, which is probably what is more usually called a dipper and he thought it might be devouring the fish spawn; but fortunately he read Buckland's book on birds and this persuaded him that the bird was an innocent one, and so the dipper was spared from being shot.

But then luckily Arthur Lockwood was interested in birds and naturally kind to them: on one occasion he rescued a cuckoo with a broken leg and nursed it back to health when it became quite a pet for him as the picture will show. Could it be the ghost of this cuckoo which still sometimes haunts Pen y Gwryd and keeps the guests awake?

Lockwood had already been given a special notice in the *Fishing Gazette* of July 1929 which had included the following paragraph: 'Another lake not on the Ordnance map is Lockwood's Llyn, as it is called locally. This is a nine acre lake made by Mr Lockwood who as he told us is altering the scenery somewhat. About four years ago he made a dam just below the hotel and is still engaged in enlarging the lake which resulted. This lake has been well-stocked with brown and Loch Leven trout, and is available for visitors and the fish are free risers.

The hatchery is to be Mr Lockwood's next undertaking and his enterprise deserves success'.

It was about this time that he started noticing the floating islands, and next year he was dismayed to find that many of the trout were dead and dying: he put the blame on the floating islands as these were made mainly of sphagnum moss entangled with the roots and leaves of water weeds, and in his view the trout took shelter in the bright and sunny weather under the edges of the islands. As the decomposition of the weed gave off marsh gas it seemed likely to him that the trout became stupefied by methane, or that they suffered from lack of oxygen in these places. It was for this reason that he started the energetic splitting up of the islands in the manner described elsewhere, and whether for this reason or not the death rate certainly fell.

Lockwood worked very hard to keep the lake well-stocked with fish, importing trout from Loch Leven and also some American rainbow trout from the Chirk Fisheries; but he was rather disappointed with some of the results, as apparently the fish did not always take kindly to North Wales mountain water, and the cost of importation was considerable; so this started him on the new venture, the hatchery.

The new lake stimulated the interest in fishing round Pen y Gwryd, and brought many more anglers to the Inn. Everything went very well until about 1944 when the number of salmon and trout caught in the surrounding rivers and lakes dropped alarmingly; this may have been due to the importation of too many fishermen, or to lack of realistic stocking for the numbers of fishermen involved, but the anglers, both local and visiting, grumbled loudly and the River Board was called in for prolonged discussion of the problem. Stocking was expensive, and the Board's first move was to send a small deputation to have a look at an unused hatchery at Black Pool on the river Conwy near its tributary the river Nug. It had become very derelict and would need a lot of rehabilitation and Lockwood suggested that rather than spend so much money on that inconveniently placed hatchery he should be given a grant to build a new one at his house Hafod y Gwynt, where it would be easy for him to look after it. This idea was accepted and he was given a grant of £50 on the understanding that he would guarantee to have it completed by 1946 and ready to take 50,000 ova; so Arthur Lockwood promptly set to work once more. As always he was offered a good deal of free help; slate slabs for the troughs were given by Mr Owen from the Rhos Quarry at Capel Curig, and some control gear for the sluice came from Mr A.L. Bird of the Cambridge University Engineering Department. His only delay was one common for those post-war days and it was in getting a permit for two rolls of wire netting, which however finally came from Llanwrst! As always he gave a very full account of all his work, meticulously written in a small book: the smooth slate of the troughs was covered with a layer of clean granite chippings from the Pengwry Quarry and as a lid for the troughs he used roofing felt, and bits of old carpets from the hotel kitchen, and within the stated time 50,000 eyed ova bought from James McNicol & Sons of Ross and Cromarty were well installed in their new darkened home. There were no labour costs for this enterprise, the troughs cost in all about £12 but the ova were expensive even in those days and they cost £62. But as can be seen the whole scheme was surprisingly cheap and the attention afterwards was free as it was given by Lockwood himself.

There is little purpose in going in length into the details of the many meetings, discussions and considerations about this hatchery which continued for some years; suffice it to say that although lack of experience, trouble with frosts and other poor weather conditions, gave rise to difficulties early in its career, and floods sometimes caused real havoc, this hatchery could claim real success and well-fulfilled its function in providing trout for the lake and for several neighbouring rivers. It was not until an ageing Lockwood found it impossible to give it as much time as it needed, and the River Board started providing bigger and better facilities elsewhere, that this hatchery started to fall into decay.

A considerable amount of the installation remains intact, and much of the rest can be restored; fortunately Chris Briggs has already started to superintend the rehabilitation work, and following the Lockwood tradition he has found a suitably strong and hard working tramp, in the person of his son-in-law Brian Pullee, and it is quite safe to assume that in a matter of months the trout hatchery will again be in excellent condition, so that it could be used as required.

An article in the *Liverpool Daily Post* of April 6th 1950 went far to sum up the local fishing industry and the contribution Lockwood had made to it as follows: 'Hafod y Gwynt perched on Pen y Gwryd in Caernarfonshire is a house almost entirely surrounded by fish. Fat trout inhabit the man-made lake outside the front door, and thousands of young salmon and trout teem in the concrete troughs of a hatchery in the back garden.

'This betrays the main life interest of Major A. Lockwood the man who lives there. As chairman of the Conway Fishery Board he conceived the idea of having a hatchery from which the Board's fishing preserves are stocked each year. Its a hatchery which is run almost entirely from voluntary effort.

'Trout and salmon ova are brought here from the Dee and from Scotland to the troughs at the back of the house, here they remain until the fish fry are of a size to be transferred to the river. The experiment began in 1946.

'Naturalists say that it takes four years for a salmon to take its mysterious course to the sea and to return to home waters. This season fish are being caught in the Conway which bear peculiar characteristics. The experts believe that they are the ones who were hatched at Pen y Gwryd four years ago. Instinct has brought them home'.

It is interesting that the fishermen follow the example of the fish they catch, although they may have been hatched in many and various parts of the British Isles, the instinct of multitudes of anglers bring them home to Pen y Gwryd each year; this instinct teaches them that there they will find good food, good fishing and good companionship, and they need search no further.

CHAPTER 11

THE WRANGLERS OR THE FLORA FOLLOWERS

Surely no nobler theme the poet chants
than the soft science of the blooming plants.
Stephen Leacock. The Faculty of Arts.

Fishing is one of the most ancient of pastimes; for as with all other ways of hunting it provided food, and often cheap food at that, even before the days of Government subsidies. Strangely enough the lords who owned the land seldom put so much violent effort in trying to stop the serfs from catching fish as they did into preventing the hunting of the four footed animals, mainly no doubt because his Lordship did not get the same enjoyment in fishing as he did in hunting stags or boars which could be followed on horseback. The Church added to the incentive by instituting fast days on which only fish could be eaten, unless of course one happened to be in close communication with a Pope in which case a dispensation was not too difficult to obtain. But the reasons that took man in search of plants and persuaded him to go in for botanical wanderings and observation is not quite as easy to understand; for although only in recent years has gardening become such a universal hobby, the search for botanical specimens has been going on for much longer. Probably it was originally a search for new drugs and medicines, and with a public almost as gullible as it is nowadays, to find a new herb which could be advertised as a certain cure for most ailments could lead on to fortune even in the hands of the ordinary man. The real expert, of course, went about looking for the 'Adder's fork and blind worm's sting, lizard's leg and howlet's wing' but for the simple countryman it was much easier to get hold of 'Root of hemlock, Digg'd i' the dark' or perhaps 'slips of yew' than to undertake the more major operation of excising the 'gall of goat or liver of blaspheming Jew'. Happily in recent years botanical exploration has become a well-known and pleasantly inoffensive leisure occupation for a vast horde of people.

The first recorded botanical wanderer in the Snowdon regions seems to have been Thomas Johnson who in about 1630 went on a journey to the top of Y Wyddfa for the express purpose of collecting plants. Doubtless, a potion extracted from a plant found at the top of Snowdon, and advertised as having been planted by Merlin would fetch a better price in the drug market of the day. His only trouble was that in his view the most important finds were growing very near to precipices or overhanging edges of cliff and could only be reached with help from his guide; while on Carnedd Llewellyn the guide would not even let him get near some of the precipices for fear of attack by eagles.

Of course, the remarkable Thomas Pennant has a good deal to say about the plant life of North Wales, among other things remarking that his favourite Glyder Fawr is a place of great note among botanists; for there can be found not only Saxifraga Nivalis and Bulbocodium, but most important of all the 'Lichen Ifelandicus; this last is of singular use to the Icelanders, a powerful cathartic and yet when dried changes its quality, and if grinded into powder is a common food either made into bread or boiled with milk. Haller also mentions its use in Vienna in coughs and consumptions made into broth or gruel.'

It would need someone very skilled in the wiles of botany to sort out the question of Bulbocodium; Pennant admits that it was later called Anthericum serotinum, and he complains that the reverend author of *Botanical Researches* had converted the name into Bulbocodium vernum, a plant which he pretended to discover on the Glyders but which in fact is not found wild either in England or Wales. More recent work shows that Saxifraga Nivalis is not very common in North Wales although it is quite often seen in the mountains of Scotland and of

Northern and Arctic Europe.

He has also followed up the folklore about the Gale or Bog Myrtle which he says abounds on the Glyders and perfumes the air with its spicy smell; it is also called the Bwrli or the Emerald Plant, and it has been known as Gwyrdd ling or the green plant. The countrymen use it as a yellow dye, or sometimes they lay branches of it under their beds to keep off fleas and moths; also some make it into a powder or infusion and apply it to the abdomen as a vermifuge; so it is a herb of multiple uses!

The remarkable Pennant also gives a long list of plants rare to him which can be found on the road to Llanberis; for the benefit of the interested botanist these include such specimens as Lobelia Dortmanna, Subularia Aquatica, Juncus Trifidus, Hieracium Alpinus, Rubus Saxatilis, Solidago Cambrica and a number of other. The last three are fairly common plants in Wales, and the Subularia Aquatica otherwise the Awlwort, is interesting as it grows under water and is rare in both Wales and Scotland in the hills. Much of the spelling is that of Pennant himself and its present day accuracy cannot be vouched for.

Pennant did not stop merely at wild flowers as he dealt with reeds, mosses and varying kinds of grasses also. Above Cwm Brwynog he found Juncus Squarrosus, the moss rush, Schoenus nigricans, the black bog rush; also Agrostis capillaris and turfy hair grass, or Aira caespitosa; the sheeps fescue grass Festuca ovina, and the Alpine meadow grass, Poa Alpina.

These facts are included here to show once again what a remarkably wide knowledge of many things Pennant had, for his facts on folklore and history are every bit as encyclopaedic.

Another man guaranteed to write at length on any subject is Charles Kingsley, but even if the weather was very bad and drove him to botany he did not produce much which added to the knowledge of plants in Snowdonia. In a gleeful letter of invitation to friend Tom Hughes he describes one place where 'The crowberry and desolate Alpine plants grow thereby, and we will sleep among them, like love among the roses, Thomas'. But he did do rather better than that for having tried fishing on the Ogwen river and found it in spate he looked round to see 'the parsley fern growing between each rock and the beech fern too, but that was poor'. And he picked his first Saxifraga Stellaris, sparganium natans and water lobelia, none of them uncommon; in his other travels while not fishing he claims to have found grass of Parnassus, Alpine Club Moss, Ladies' Mantle, Ivy-leaf Companula, beech fern and sweet fern and he specially commented on the great Butterwort and the Globe flower with its shiny yellow green starts of leaves in every bog.

The Visitors' Books soon start to bear out some of the findings of Pennant for in 1862 Peter Inchbold produced a list of over twenty fairly unusual plants which he came across on his way up Snowdon, including several ferns, four kinds of Lycopodium specimens, and assortment of Saxifrages ending triumphantly in the discovery of Saxifraga Nivalis found by him on the very top of the mountain. He also reinforces the idea that Glyder Fawr is something of a botanist's paradise as he gives a list of forty specimens which he found on the way up; this list is included in the Appendix.

H.B. Biden, one of Pen y Gwryd's most constant supporters was a better mountaineer than a botanist, but in 1878 he remarks on the masses of Sundew open in Cwm Glas and on the way to Capel Curig he noticed Parnassus grass and bog pimpernel.

In 1885 H.B. Carlyon did much better than that with a list of twenty six types of fern found in the immediate neighbourhood of Pen y Gwryd, a list also included in the Appendix. While not to be outdone, John W. Hawkins in 1890 adds two more to this list — such is the botanist's competition. That year E.W.S. talks of Bog Bean, and Silene Acaulis (Lychnis) or Moss Campion which is not commonly found, but he is impressed with the Milkwort which is white all over Lliwydd. Not to be outdone by the botanists in 1891, someone too shy to give his name reserves a whole page in the Locked Book for a list of thirteen coleoptera, giving the site at which each one is found. So that anyone interested can read such pleasant items as the Pterosticlus Aethiopos found under a stone on Crib y Ddysgyl, or Aphodius Lapponium to be seen on some sheep dung on the Glyders; only initials are given by this self-effacing gentleman.

But quite early the travellers were already complaining loudly that many of the exotic plants were being rapidly removed from view because of the unrestrained ravages of other botanists; this may have been one of the first signs of the spreading of the gardening hobby through the country for it is well known that the really keen gardener has few morals about other people's property when collecting their own stock or when looking for unusual specimens!

As the number of those writing about botany increased so did the wrangling; in 1892 Max A. Wright of Bolton ventured to mention two or three plants which he considered rare saying where he had found them, only to have written under his entry 'These plants are very common in this district'. Signed B.F. This is only the first of several quarrels among the experts.

Right at the end of the century W. Griffiths was happy to find some dwarf Juniper growing on the Crib Goch and Lliwedd, and he is anxious to know if there is much of it in other parts of the region; unhappily he had to wait for an answer until 1917 when Lockwood gave a reply that there was plenty of large juniper on the west slopes of Moel Mierch. In fact in Britain the dwarf juniper seems to grow only in Scotland, Westmoreland and North Wales.

But the botanists were quieter for a year or two after this, except for one who had been told that the Llanberis Pass was a particularly good area for the botanist by reason of the large number of rare plants, and who said gruffly 'made rarer because of the incessant researches of the botanists.'

One of the guides from the 'Victoria Hotel' at Llanberis was in great demand by the botanical experts for not only was he considered to be a very civil and intelligent man, but was supposed to know the habitat of every plant in the surrounding mountains. Botanists who met him at Pen y Gwryd obtained a lot of valuable information from him on many of the rarer species of plants, although it was he that complained most bitterly about the ravages of the botanists. It was not until about 1905 that W. Griffiths found some Asplenium Septentrionale (a fern called spleen-wort in English), which he thought very rare, but the experts again did not agree.

Then in 1907 a whole page of the Locked Book is entirely given over to three, still very well-preserved, leaves of Polystichum Lonchitis, perhaps better known as the Holly Fern; the first of these leaves was found quite near to Pen y

Gwryd and the other two were added later in June 1953 by some wandering celebrant of the Everest success, but he does not say where exactly it was found and maybe he did not know. This is worth its place because according to the botanists' bible — that really magnificent compendium of Bentham and Hooker — it occurs only in great mountain areas from Italy to the Arctic, and in this country only in Scotland and North Wales.

But no discourse on botany concerning North Wales would be complete without some mention of Lloydia Serotina, which is a close relative of the Tulipa family and probably found only in the Snowdon range, and even there as a great rarity. It was found by a slate worker called Ifan Roberts.

And here is a story of early endeavour and final success which is worthy of the telling. Ifan Roberts was born in Capel Curig in 1906 and he went to the local school until at the age of fourteen he followed his father and grandfather to work in the slate quarry on Moel Siabod: he probably acquired his love of botany from the grandfather that he never knew, but who used to pick ferns and flowers on his way to and from work and give them to a quarryman living in Llanberis, who planted them in the little house where he lived and there they still thrive. Ifan used to eke out his wages by acting as part-time postboy during his weekends and holidays, earning one shilling and sixpence (old money) for taking a telegram to the hotels and sixpence for bringing the answer back: it is said that after the death of one lady with many friends at Pen y Gwryd he earned more in a day than his father earned at the quarry in a week!

He spent his lunch time wandering round the mountains botanising, and he found in the snow one flower that no one seemed to know, until a real botanist staying in Capel Curig not only told him about it but made him a present of three books of Griffiths *Flora of Caernarvon* which roused his enthusiasm still further, and for the next fifty years he listed all his finds.

Searching one day in the Hanging Garden Gully, a cleft to the right of Twll Du (the Devil's Kitchen) a remote and inaccessible place, he came across the Lloydia Serotina and produced a fine photograph of it. This and his many other researches and photographs made him well known and finally brought him a well justified reward of the post of Warden to the first Nature Reserve of the Nature Conservancy Authority. Later many honours crowded on him: he was given the honorary M. Sc. at Bangor in 1956, and awarded the M.B.E. by Sir Alec Douglas Home; and in the view of some of his greatest honour when he was created a member of the Gorsedd of Bards of Wales.

Late in life by the offices of his many friends he was taken to Switzerland to a first class welcome, and he was allowed to inspect their many rare Alpine plants; but sadly his eyesight is now waning and he can barely see the plants which he loves so much.

Another find which has caused some botanical wrangles was that of a herb called Primula Farinosa, which according to the text books can be found not only in the Snowdon area but in many mountain pastures in the north of England and south Scotland; but in the Locked Book one bonny fighter states categorically that it can be seen only in Flintshire at the mouth of the River Dee; so far no Soloman seems to have made judgement on this knotty problem.

A fitting end to the botanical section may be to record a slightly unusual contribution made to the hotel in 1898. Francis Jenkinson a Cambridge Librarian presented Pen y Gwryd with thirty-two Scotch Firs, three elms, two oaks, mainly given as seedlings, which all came from a nursery garden at Bagshot; when planted the tallest (one of the firs) measured seventeen inches from the ground. All were planted in the Hotel garden on the same day by Mrs Halliday the wife of one of the habituées who was a climber of world renown; her assistants in the planting task were Messrs T. Williams, E.R. Turner, C. Sayle, and the Rev J.N. Burrows. Few trees can have had such a start in life, being stamped in by the boots of so many well-known and expert rock climbers, but the climbing boot must be the wrong weapon for tree planting for of those planted it is sad to say that by September 1899 only two oaks and one fir tree were still alive; if these three trees are still in existence surely they deserve a plaque in their honour.

Strangely enough Pen y Gwryd never seems to have become a haven for the bird watcher. This now popular pastime is of fairly recent development and over these latter years the

Visitors' Books have been the normal dull routine ones found in every hotel; the Locked Book has been there, but unless Mine Host happened to be keen on bird study he is unlikely to have given bird watchers the opporunity to enter their finds in that bible. The best places for the keen watcher are the river estuaries and there unusual birds can be seen frequently, and, of course many waders, but this is quite a trip from Pen y Gwryd and the watcher is probably more likely to stay nearer the coast.

Thomas Pennant tells of seeing a wheatear and a rock ouzel both at Ffynnon Las, but he does not display the amount of interest in birds that he does in other natural phenomena.

In the last century many tourists were doomed to some disappointment as they went to Snowdon hoping to see the famous Eryri eagles which often appeared in the book, and which one text book described as noble in appearance but ignoble in habits. But very early last century the eagle became tired of the horde of tourists who went up Snowdon and round the Snowdon Horseshoe, and he has fled to the solitude of the Scottish mountains. He has been replaced in large numbers by the seagull: the seagull is a crafty bird and he knows that walkers often have untidy habits, and he is very good at spotting the common picnic places. So these are nearly all well-populated with this species, which does help to do a little clearing up, the summit cairn being exceptionally popular.

Talking of eagles it is interesting to note that on one occasion at least the suggestion was made that golden eagles could be introduced into Snowdonia. James Fisher the well-known naturalist was one of Pen y Gwryd's friends and frequent visitors, and he considered the idea of taking eggs from a golden eagle on the Duke of Sutherland's estate; the Royal Air Force were willing to fly them down to North Wales, presumably suitably warmly wrapped up, and then putting them under a local buzzard for hatching. The site had been selected, somewhere near Cwm Glas, and so had the buzzard, which doubtless had already been given some suitable training by Chris Briggs. This idea was never put into action as it was soon found that the Law did not allow any egg of a preserved species of bird to be removed from its usual site. It would have been grand to have more eagles on the Snowdon range, but in view of the large tourist traffic and almost complete absence of really quiet and peaceful situations it is very unlikely that the scheme would have worked satisfactorily.

But a few of the bird watchers are not shy of saying their piece in the Locked Book, and in 1958 a short essay by Hallpike, Huddy and Sherwood is devoted to four choughs seen in Cwm Glas neighbourhood at a height of 2300 feet and of some more which appeared over the Carnedds flying at 3000 feet; they were reasonably delighted at this sighting because fear has often been expressed that the chough is becoming extinct in this part of the country.

To encourage the watcher, and to show that if he is keen and knowledgeable there is plenty to see, H.L. Richardson has entered a list of over ninety different birds seen within a radius of five miles of Pen y Gwryd, and if the distance is extended to twenty miles — not too far in the motor car age — the list reaches one hundred and two; surely as good a yield as one can expect.

It has been said with one exception any bird which can be seen in the British Isles can be found in Wales: in the twelfth century Giraldus Cambrensis was in the party of gentle Baldwin, Archbishop of Canterbury touring the country hoping for recruits for the next Crusade. The Archbishop found the journey round Caernarfon and the surrounding hills very hard work and resting one day against an uprooted tree at the top of a particularly severe slope he invited one of his servants to whistle a tune to entertain him and this tune led to a discussion about birds, and the Archbishop was asked why it was that the nightingale never visited Wales, to which the Archbishop shook his head and replied merely 'A wise bird the nightingale'.

But if Pen y Gwryd has no nightingale it has its nocturnal oddities, the best of which unfortunately has no mention in the Locked Book. For several summers in the early 1960s Pen y Gwryd was haunted by a notorious Cuckoo; he or she started work with great regularity at twelve midnight having been completely silent all through the day and this miserable bird then shouted without cessation until about 5 a.m. Every possible effort was made to drive it away or silence it, both fright and total elimination being tried: some visitors threw boots and bricks at it, and others got to work with a shot gun regardless of the fact that it was a protected species, and still more regardless of the other guests, who were in greater danger than the bird and who were also supposed to be protected by law. But this trial by slaughter was of no avail and its noise was much more disturbing than that of the bird it was supposed to silence. But after about five years, whether by reason of old age, retirement or emigration to some more appreciative region, the cuckoo left and the hotel was once again peaceful at night so that even that rare specimen in a climbers' hotel, the sensitive sufferer from insomnia could sleep quietly at night. At least this was true for many years, but lo, in 1976 the nocturnal cuckoo has again returned, and can again be heard at all hours of the night; could it be a hired supporter of the Welsh National Party trying to drive the English invader from the Principality?

Sadly the Visitors' Books are all without any reference to the other local fauna; one might have expected some mention of the wild cat or the wild goat, both species found in Snowdonia in quite recent years, although they too seem to have departed as the human population has enlarged. But, of course the Locked Book is concerned mainly with that strange human animal which clambers oddly round the rock faces; this two legged hairy monster has always been common in mountain districts but only in very recent years has it been found in such numbers in towns and cities.

Perhaps the constant climb of heavily nailed climbing boots and the frightening apparition of the hirsute jowl in unexpected places drove away the rarer four legged animals and gave them time to go into hiding; maybe the change to the quieter Vibram boot will help to stop the elimination of the uncommon fauna.

CHAPTER 12

THE WANGLERS OR THE TRAIL AND TRIAL OF THE THREE THOUSANDS

To climb steep hills, requires slow pace at first
Shakespeare. Henry VIII. Act I Sc. I.

As a suitable link between the more stately pastimes of angling and botanising and the physical gymnastics of the rock climbers, it might be a reasonable lead across to talk about the long tale of the Three Thousands. To any of those folk who are stupid enough not to have visited North Wales this phrase may mean nothing, but to the visitors of Pen y Gwryd it ranks immediately after the Ten Commandments. The whole Snowdon range contains fourteen mountain peaks which reach a height of over three thousand feet and they are arranged in three groups: the Snowdon group consists of Crib Goch, Crib y Ddysgyl and Y Wyddfa (the hutted top of Snowdon itself); this group is separated by the Llanberis Pass from the next group of five peaks, Elidir Fawr, Y Garn, Glyder Fawr, Glyder Fach and Tryfan (this lovely little mountain being only ten feet above the three thousand limit, and should it get much more human traffic it is likely to fall below this height at any time now); then one has to drop down across the Holyhead road, the A.5., and climb the next group consisting of Pen yr Ole Wen, Carnedd Dafydd, Yr Elen, Carnedd Llewellyn, Foel Grach to end at Foel Fras.

For a crow flying from mountain top to mountain top and alighting on each one the distance would be about fifteen miles, but of course the normal crow doing the trip would have the sense to stay at about the same altitude thoughout. For the walker the distance is much greater as he climbs up and down over what is roughly estimated as twenty five miles, and he also climbs an estimated twelve thousand feet. When this competition started the competitors went from road level to road level at each end, but soon after the first few attempts the route was stabilized to start at the top of Snowdon, even reached by train if desired, and to finish at the top of Foel Fras. These details of the total distance covered and height climbed are very approximate, as real accuracy is impossible; there are so many ways of approach, so many different routes, many so called short cuts as each candidate can make his or her own way and the only stipulation is that the aspirant must appear on each summit and their time of appearance must be checked and vouched for by a neutral observer. So far tests for sex or stimulant drugs have not been introduced!

It is an interesting fact that there are in the world another fairly well-known fourteen mountain summits, for there are fourteen eight thousanders; that is to say there are fourteen peaks of a height of over eight thousand metres (26,250 feet), all in the Himalaya or the Karakoram ranges. So far no one has tried to complete all these but as the crowds begin to congregate on the top of Everest, no doubt some enthusiast will think of it soon.

In the beginning of the Three Thousand trail the attempts were many and varied in type, but it was not long before it took on the appearance of a competition with recognized judges and time keepers. In recent years the Army has adopted it as a yearly competitive exercise for several of its units who show great keenness to win the yearly bout; but there are still no bans on private ventures, although with some of the records that have been made by individuals the times are now so astonishingly good that only the very bold would consider trying to excel.

As far as can be seen from the Visitors' Book's records the first attempt was made in August, 1935, the journey being undertaken by Robert H. Phillips and A.T. Clay but their method seems strangely leisurely compared with the rushed ways of today. For they started from Nantgwynant at 5 a.m., crossed the Snowdon group and then went down to Pen y Gwryd for a pleasant and not too hurried breakfast which took them from 8.10 a.m. till 9.05 a.m. Such a happy approach would be frowned on in this day, and would be considered almost indecent! The pair went across Y Garn, the Glyders and Tryfan and got to Ogwen in time for tea at 3 p.m.; leaving after tea at 3.40 p.m. they finally reached the top of Foel Fras by 8.15 p.m. and then walked down the road to Aber. Their total time for the journey was 17 hours, with calculated walking time of 15 hours 35 minutes. The pair also estimated the total height that they climbed that day to be 11,977 feet; probably a reasonable estimate and near the present day one, but they did not explain how one could work out the climbing distance to the nearest foot on such an excursion.

It was two years before someone else thought about this exercise, and in 1937 J.P. Cooper and E. Marshall, being a very heroic couple, tried it in January; they left Pen y Gwryd at 1.15 a.m., reaching the top of Snowdon by 3.35 a.m. No further details of the expedition are given but they got back to the hotel by 8.45 p.m. giving their time as 19½ hours, which is poor compared with the previous effort.

One of the most interesting of all the three thousand efforts was made in September 1938. It was the first time the modern start, course and finish were used and it was the first time that so much thought and training were put in before the final attempt was made. Different parts of the journey were tried using varying routes and methods and exact timing was kept; every foot of the way was studied to find the best access and even various kinds of clothing and footwear were experimented with and as a result when the whole party finally started on their trial they had a clear idea of exactly how they would tackle each bit of the long round. With regard to the final round a short extract from the Locked Book itself gives a good picture: 'Two parties, one of Mrs Firbank accompanied by Mr Thomas Davies, the other of Mr Firbank, Mr R.M. Hamer and Mr W.E. Capel Cull did the Welsh Three Thousand in miserable weather. They went up Snowdon by freight train and the first party left the summit at 7.50 a.m. and the second at 8.30 a.m. The route was Y Wyddfa, Crib y Ddysgyl, Crib Goch, Elidir Fawr, Y Garn, Glyder Fawr, Glyder Fach,

Tryfan, Pen y Ole Wen, Carnedd Daffydd, Yr Elen, Carnedd Lleyellyn, Foel Grach, Foel Fras. Mrs Firbank's party finished at 5.19 p.m. thus completing the course in 9 hours 29 minutes, and the second party finished at 4.55 p.m. completing the course in 8 hours 15 minutes.'

These excellent times show that it is important to examine the course very well before taking off and this original study done by the Firbanks was of great use to many parties and individuals that came after them, and Thomas Firbank has written *The Welsh Three Thousand* in the series called *Footpath Guides*. For this reason, and for many others the Firbanks deserve a full account of themselves, and this would seem the best place to provide it.

During the first few months of the Second World War, nicknamed at the time the 'Phoney War' because although the great nations were officially at war nothing much happened for the first six months or so and the amount of fighting was negligible. In Britain nearly all entertainments had stopped, wireless was at the lowest level it had ever reached, families were often separated and the blackout handicapped travel as also did petrol rationing; so once more music and reading came back into their own. A very large number of folk found pleasure in reading a recently published book entitled *I bought a Mountain* written by Thomas Firbank: in it Firbank describes with sympathy and interest how he and his wife Esmé bought a rather run down farm, and the attached farmhouse also in not very good condition. The farmland consisted of three thousand acres of mountain and moorland, some of the hills going up to nearly the three thousand foot mark round the Glyders and Tryfan. Starting with little real experience of farming, by hard work and intelligent thought, they surprisingly rapidly turned it into a thriving sheep farm, and similarly in later years they have converted the farmhouse into a lovely country residence.

Esmé Firbank, now for many years Esmé Kirby, was the first woman to complete the circuit of the Three Thousands and she held the women's record until 1965; anyone who has walked the mountains of North Wales will know that to climb fourteen peaks of three thousand feet in a time of nine and a half hours is a level of performance that few could manage.

Esmé has continued to farm the difficult land with success up to the present day and still gathers her own sheep over this rough and hilly country.

Thomas Firbank was less lucky for he held his record only a short time; two years later Captain J.P. Rivas of the 60th Rifles, stationed at a battle camp at Capel Curig claimed a time for the route of 8 hours 7 minutes the time being guaranteed by three watches held by three battle course instructors; a reduction of the time by a mere 8 minutes does not seem very much, but on such an arduous journey over this difficult terrain it means a good deal.

Unlike the First War, the Second War reduced the number of visitors to Snowdonia to a trickle, and as Pen y Gwryd was housing refugee schoolboys it had none; so for six years any further attempts on this mountain course were out of the question. In fact the waiting time was even longer than expected and it was not until 1952 that the next record emerges. John Disley, later the Olympic steeplechaser, with Dr John Mawe as company put up the good time of 7 hours 24 minutes; Mawe became handicapped by a foot injury and he took an hour and a half longer. Sadly for John Disley this record only lasted for five months, for in September 1952 a team of four all beat this time. A.A. Robertson took 6 hours exactly, Eric Herbert took 6 hours 37 minutes, Chris Brasher (another Olympic champion) did the round in 6 hours 58 minutes, and John Mawe improved on his previous time with one of 7 hours exactly.

These were all exceptional times and it is not surprising that it was many years before they were bettered; but during the interim one effort must certainly be put on record. In an exercise of the Royal Welch Fusiliers, David Rowland returned a time of 9 hours 35 minutes: the reader may wonder why that apparently slow time should be brought in here, but the reason is that he was carrying the standard Army equipment of a full pack weighing 25 pounds and a Sten sub-machine gun of 7½ pounds; his time was checked and signed on each summit. This was the first of what later became a fairly common Army exercise, and considering that previous climbers had carried round only themselves, then Rowland's effort compares very favourably with the previous experts.

But the very best was still to come; there was a somewhat eccentric and exceptional character called Eric Beard, who christened himself the Wandering Hoboe, and who in 1962 completed the fourteen peaks in the astonishing time 5 hours 26 minutes. Not content with this he tried again four months later and reduced this to the exceptional time of 5 hours 20 minutes; all these times were fully certified and were accepted as the record until 1965 when Beard himself reduced his time still further to 5 hours 13 minutes: he well deserved the new title which he then adopted of King of the Hoboes! Not unexpectedly this record lasted for a number of years and it was not until June 17th 1973 that it was beaten by Joss Naylor, a farmer from Wasdale, who managed to complete the distance in 4 hours 46 minutes — how is this possible without either two wings or a pair of seven league boots? He was soon afterwards awarded the M.B.E., but that apparently was for his many other marked contributions to sport and not merely for breaking the record for the Three Thousands although, that one achievement should have been enough for an award! It is surely right that the present holder of the record should come from that other great nursery of climbing, and now all that remains is for a Welshman to show what he can do in his native land.

When Eric Beard first tried the course and when he made the early record attempt he was one of the instructors at the Physical Training Centre of Pas y Brenin, and while there he accomplished several similar performances making mountain walking records in various parts of the British Isles, travelling to the Lake District and Skye and other parts of Scotland on his itinerary. Unfortunately he was killed in a car crash in a friend's car while coming back from one of his expeditions; had he lived, there is little doubt that he would have continued to put up many more startling performances.

Women have always been less competitive in the way of running round mountains than have men, and many will think this one of their signs of greater wisdom. Comparatively few women seem to have attempted the Three Thousands; so Esmé Kirby's record lasted for nearly twenty years and it was not until 1965 that Jo Fuller, a very well-known member of the Pinnacle Club beat it in a magnificent time of 7 hours 51 minutes, and this should last for some time.

These records, both male and female, are now so exceptional that only a particularly expert mountain runner could consider trying to beat them; it would need a good deal of planning and practice, and impartial observers would have to be found for each mountain peak, but in view of what is happening in other sports it may be that we shall have to wait for a government subsidy. It may sound odd that so much control has to be exercised in such a sporting event, but it would not be difficult to miss out one of the peaks either intentionally or accidentally, particularly on such circuits as the Carnedds; if anyone thinks this kind of deception is unthinkable in a sportsman, or sportswoman they should be reminded that the English Channel was on one occasion swum by a lady doctor, and it was not until many months later and after many enquiries that it was discovered that she had swum half the distance sitting in the boat rowed by her trainer. Her excuse when found out was that she was trying to show how easy it was to carry out such a deception.

As a last extract on this subject from the Visitors' Books one more expedition is worth a mention; in 1962 a party of three boys of unknown ages, together with a master, all from Oundle School, tried the Three Thousand trip starting from Pen y Gwryd and also finishing there; they did their round in 16 hours 2 minutes, but this was far from the normal trail. By their own calculations they covered a distance of 32½ miles and a total ascent of 14,700 feet; if these are accurate readings their effort ranked well with any of the others, and they did even better the next year when they finished the same route in 35 minutes less; a good attempt.

Each year for some years now the Army has staged a full scale exercise in the Trail of the Three Thousands; many regiments send in a team and the whole is staged in a grand way in the presence of the local Commanding General, and complete with helicopter and a plethora of trucks and Landrovers. It is a team event rather than an individual one, but unfortunately the records for it over the years seem unobtainable; one need hardly say that the Gurkhas have shown up well on several occasions.

Needless to say this is not the only competition which has

proved popular in Snowdonia, although none of the others seem to have achieved the same glamour. One very common one is the time for the Snowdon Horseshoe; a route easy enough for any normal individual to try, and it must have been done without any ambition for a record time by many thousands of walkers, for it is a ridge walk which needs a moderate endurance, a willingness to indulge in a bit of scrambling and a lack of too much objection to some minor degrees of what the climbers call exposure; for there are one or two paths, particularly on Crib Goch and on the narrow way between that and Crib y Ddysgyl which make the inexperienced a bit unhappy; but for all that, it is a ridge walk without equal in this country for the mountain walker who makes no claim to be a climber. The start is from the car park at Pen y Pass, the climb of Crib Goch, Crib y Ddysgyl, Y Wyddfa, Lliwedd and the return to the starting place via Glaslyn and Llyn Llydaw and then home along the Miners' Path; if desired it can be done the other way round.

There have been very few serious endeavours to make records for this trip, but one is claimed, probably justly, by David Rowlands already mentioned; he in 1961 returned a phenomenal time, fully checked and quite authentic, of 1 hour 47 minutes for the round; for those who do not know this ridge walk it might be fair to say that the average mountain stroller would think five hours pretty fast going! It can be presumed that he was carrying some Army luggage although this is not specifically mentioned.

There are one or two other ventures of the Horseshoe which are undoubtedly unusual and may be unique; a delightful titbit is written in the locked book by Barbara Price in July 1948: having been given a perfect day for walking and this day happening to coincide with the eightieth birthday of Oswald Cox, she and some friends escorted him round the Snowdon Horseshoe, starting from Pen y Gwryd at 10.30 a.m. doing the complete circuit and getting back to the hotel at 8.30 p.m. She says that they achieved nothing but a prodigious thirst which was soon handsomely satisfied, but the rest of the community of this country would think this a grave understatement more worthy of the addresses on expeditions given in the Alpine Club meetings. Most fifty-year-olds would be very satisfied to do the round in six or seven hours, and think they were showing surprising fitness at an advanced old age; to do it at the age of eighty and in a time of about ten hours is worth calling a record.

There was still another unusual Horseshoe walk in July 1972, this one in no way attempting particularly fast times; the Locked Book entry describes it well and is best quoted in full:

> '39 July 1972. The Horseshoe walk by Christopher Briggs, Esq. Thomas Skyrme, Esq., Secretary of Commissions to the Lord Chancellor. David Owen, Esq., Private Secretary to Lord Chancellor. The Rt. Hon Lord Chancellor, The Lord Hailsham of Marylebone. Starting from Pen y Pass about 0900 hours, returned to Pen y Gwryd about 1800 hours. A number of police officers (not fully ascertained) ascended by the P.Y.G. track and covered the latter part of the Horseshoe.
>
> Misty weather above two thousand feet, otherwise dry.'
>
> Signed Hailsham of St Marylebone.
>
> Note by David Owen P/S to that intrepid gladiator Christopher Briggs, o/c logistics.
>
> 'Lost one stick on Crib Goch Ridge, but not a Lord Chancellor.'

Even allowing for the fact that this was not a particularly youthful party, the time taken of nine hours seems a bit long; it is difficult not to wonder how much of it was spent at the hotel on Y Wyddfa where refreshments of all kinds are obtainable.

There were two other types of record attempt involving Pen y Gwryd which were very popular at one stage, but maybe fortunately not often tried as they could sometimes be lethal. The first was to climb the three highest mountains in the British Isles in as short a time as possible, which meant dashing by car from Snowdon to Scafell Pike and then on to Ben Nevis. Documentary evidence in this competition has tended to be somewhat meagre, and for the earlier runs there were no definite rules about starting and stopping, nor about how far up the mountain the car could be driven, or even from what altitude the times should be taken. However Chris Briggs soon came into the picture and made some rules which all competitors now accept and abide by; they are very simple ones, for they have to start at sea level and finish at sea level. This means that the starting and finishing lines are Caernarfon and Fort William, according to taste, for to start at Scafell would be too great a handicap. The time which counts is the total time for the journey, including both the car and the climbing episodes; in other words the car can be driven as far up the mountain as anyone wishes, even to the top if it can be managed. This is a subtle rule for in fact the climbing part of the journey is faster taken on the feet than attempted in a car. These rules have proved popular and a number of people still attempt this journey.

One of the best and a fairly well written up schedule may be re-told; in it G. Rhodes and David Robinson climbed all three peaks in what they called a summit to summit time of 11 hours and a sea level to sea level time of 13 hours and 11 minutes. Travelling in a Mini Cooper they covered the total distance in 8 hours 4 minutes. What strange things people do for fun; there may be some who still try this hazardous expedition but no news leaks through.

Another undertaking which had a long spell of popularity, but did not require any expertness in climbing techniques was to reach Pen y Gwryd from the Marble Arch in London in the shortest possible time by car. As might be expected most of the attempts were done by night or in the early hours of summer mornings and to judge by some of the astonishing, and one would think, highly dangerous times clocked up, there was no thought of speed limits at any place. Of those recorded, the best, or should it be the worst, was accomplished in 1955 in a Jaguar XK 140 which performed the whole distance in 3 hours 20 minutes. The official AA distance between Pen y Gwryd and London is 224 miles, and some expert mathematician can easily work out the average speed. It may be one of the unrecognized advantages of the opening of the motorways that this endeavour now seems to have fallen into abeyance, or it is possible that some bright spirits are waiting for some motorway extensions before beginning a new series.

CHAPTER 13

THE DANGLERS
OR THE CLIMBERS AND MOUNTAINEERS

Fain would I climb yet fear I to fall.
Sir Walter Raleigh.

If thy heart fail thee, climb not at all
Added it is said by Queen Elizabeth I.

It is when, one reads the essays in the early Visitors' Books, or even more when one looks in the Locked Book at some of the entries made by those who climbed the mountains in Snowdonia over the last one hundred and fifty years or so, that it becomes evident what has been the greatest influence producing an exceptional hotel, the Pen y Gwryd of today. It is fascinating to read these extracts and to watch the steady change from the rough and arduous, but fairly simple walking and scrambling done by mountaineers of this country in the early nineteenth century and to see it turn into the advanced scientific and gymnastic climbing of the present day.

But those mountaineers who first explored the mountains and the ways to the top of them should not be underrated. No doubt they reached the summits by what would now be called the easy paths or the tourist routes, and which can now be followed by vast numbers of ordinary citizens with little knowledge of mountain walking: but it should be remembered that in those days all routes were uncharted; there were no maps or guide books to help them on their way, no cairns, no footpaths beaten down by many feet, or scratched rock faces showing where others had been before and they had to follow their noses and only their eyesight and their instincts told them where the dangers lay.

These gallant scramblers were on the hills in rain, wind and mist, snow and ice, and they had little equipment but a stout pair of boots and a stouter heart and should they get into difficulties or lose their way, they would not necessarily be missed soon, nor could they expect a Mountain Rescue Party searching for them in a matter of minutes. A small minority realized quite soon the advantages of rubber soled boots on dry rock, but these were not easy to buy, and the rock was seldom dry, and for some time the old-fashioned metal blakie or the hob-nail was common; the blakie must have felt rather like having a series of small skis on the soles on the boots.

One far-sighted pair of climbers mountaineering in the snow went to Bethesda and bought a small wood chopping axe, which was lashed to a broomstick, also bought for the purpose and this served them as an alpenstock in the snow and ice. In the years that followed ropes were often carried, but these were seldom used for climbing but for the purpose of rescuing anyone in trouble and there seems to be no record of who first had the intelligence to think that if a rope helped to extricate someone from a difficult situation it might be used to reach the goal in climbs, and to help get over hard places; it is said that the climbing rope was first used thus in the Lake District in 1885.

But these were men with the true mountaineering spirit, well prepared to undergo hardships and to run risks if they could not reach the summit; and by doing so they fulfilled their wish to accomplish something they had set out to do, or in the phrase which unfortunately may become rather hackneyed today, they climbed the mountain because it was there. But they satisfied other desires besides that of accomplishment, for they really enjoyed the physical exercise, and they also found more spiritual gifts; the gift of God's good air, the varied delights of the changeable weather and above all the gift of seeing all around them the superb beauty of the hills. It may be that in this way they had a wider view of the pleasures and satisfactions of mountain climbing than do some of the enthusiasts of today. But their greatest accomplishment lay in starting a new enterprise, in demonstrating the fun and excitement of climbing and in encouraging it so that it spread through the whole country and led the many thousands who followed them to learn of real enjoyment.

One of the oddest characters that wandered round the hills in those early days was a strange clergyman well-described by John Henry Cliffe in his book, although these days he would hardly merit the term odd. He was a clergyman of the Church of England with an abiding mania for ridge walking, so he may have some claim to have started a new cult which is still with us. Even in those days when the eccentric was fairly common he was considered to be somewhat grotesque as his description by Cliffe shows; 'Tall, about fifty years of age, wiry and spare of habit, slightly built, dressed in a pair of dingy slop trousers, a linen spencer of the same complexion, without hat or covering of any sort for the head (in 1850 this in itself was enough to indicate marked mental abnormality), no neck tie, shirt collar unbuttoned (Oh what a mad parson!) with an enormous alpenstock or climbing pole seven or eight feet in length in his hand'. It is some indication of how things have changed to see that except for the exceptionally long pole he would hardly be noticed in the normal crowd going to the mountains nowadays. This strange gentleman would quite commonly walk for twelve hours at a stretch, without stop for food or drink, but quenching his thirst by sucking a small pebble and he aimed in his travels to keep as far as possible on the skyline. When he arrived back at the hotel, while waiting for his dinner, he continued to take gentle exercise, staff in hand, while he cooled off, rather like the marathon runner deciding to finish with a lap of honour. He was a non-smoker and had the reputation of being very temperate, taking not more than two or three glasses of sherry at a time, and he was a pleasant and intellectual talker who mixed well with everyone. Seen today he would appear as a clergyman of a slightly advanced school, but over one hundred years ago he was more like a prophet of the Old Testament come out of due season. His name is still unknown, but he certainly was not the Rev Mr Starr who had the misfortune to be almost the first recorded death on the Visitors' Books. Despite the warnings of his guide he insisted on venturing on the mountains alone, lost his way in a mist and fell headlong over the precipices near Clogwyn-du'r-Arddu; this fatality happened in 1846 but it was not until the next year that his body was found, or rather his remains for it is said the body had been torn to pieces by wild cats.

Also about the middle of the century a church dignitary preached an extempore, and very eloquent and somewhat lengthy sermon on the summit of Snowdon; there is no information about the denomination to which he belonged, but this behaviour seems to fit very well with the spirit and keenness of the Welsh Non-conformist Church at that time, and it is surprising that no more is heard of the use of the top of Y Wyddfa as a pulpit.

Well before the middle of the century there were some who called themselves Guides to Snowdonia, many being local shepherds and miners who had explored the hills and who had a good knowledge of the straightforward walks to the tops of the most popular mountains. Robert, or Robin Hughes from Capel Curig had a considerable reputation as a guide, and as he aged, his place was largely taken over by Harry Owen. But Owen himself in his typically self-effacing way made no claims to be an experienced guide and preferred being looked upon as an ordinary shepherd who knew many ways about the mountains, as anyone, with a flock of sheep, needs must; he adopted no frills or special costume as did some guides.

It is surprising and unexpected to find that a local guide book was published in the mid-nineteenth century and it was called *Odd Corners in North Wales*. It even includes a paragraph on Harry Owen 'There was a straightforward cordiality about Owen which made all lovers of the mountain feel at once that in his house they had a home to which they could return again and again with renewed pleasure'. It says a lot for the several managements which have followed his at Pen y Gwryd that this phrase could be written about it today with equal truth and equal accuracy.

Round about 1830 a miner called Morris Williams who worked in the copper mine in Clogwyn Coch, if not a guide in the true sense of the word had a good, inbred business instinct and found another way to help hill walkers and himself. Having for some time watched many walkers passing near the mine on their tramp up to the top of Snowdon he decided to start a trade in refreshments providing tea, coffee or bread and cheese for any who were willing to buy it. His trade flourished so well that six or seven years later he built the first hut on the summit of Snowdon, and there the refreshments could be taken, and even a bed for the night was available; business proved so good that he was quite soon able to take on an assistant guide, one William Williams. Evidently Morris Williams was a believer in advertisement to enhance his trade still further; he took to wearing a special personally designed guide costume consisting of a goatskin coat and hat of the accepted Robinson Crusoe mode, but as he was quite unable to speak or to understand English maybe this method of attracting trade was essential.

J.H. Cliffe was most upset by all these changes and felt that the romance had quite gone out of Snowdon saying, 'The summit of the mountain is absolutely mobbed during the summer and autumn', and he suggested that those who are looking for peace and quiet should go by night. He also had some stringent remarks to make about the hutments, saying that they were rude huts selling tea, coffee, ale, porter, spirits and other refreshments, 'Where such a number of hungry and thirsty visitors are congregated, the demand is great, the prices are commensurate; and we have no doubt the guides have found it a good speculation, reaping a rich harvest during the season. You can also procure a bed if you are desirous of remaining on the mountain all night; but as there is only one bed in a very small rude apartment, as far as we know the great majority of visitors who arrive over or during the night are obliged to rough it the best way they can. The appearance of the hut is unsightly . . . the charge for bed and breakfast is 6/6'.

He gives us several other interesting items of information about going up Snowdon. Ponies cost 5/- to the summit if it was practicable to go all the way; if one went right over the top this price was doubled. From Llanberis the ponies could be ridden right to the top if desired and so they could from Lyn Cwellyn, but for Pen y Gwryd the rider had to dismount at Llyn Ffynon Las. From Beddgelert it was possible to get nearly to the top on a pony, but the narrow ridge from Clawdd-Coch was thought to be frightening although it was safe in daylight; few experienced horsemen would attempt it now and the ponies must have been singularly quiet and well-behaved!

In addition to paying for ponies the guides' fees from Beddgelert were about 7/- to the summit and from Llanberis 10/-, while a night ascent cost 10/-. The charge from Pen y Gwryd was only 5/-, but in all cases the guides expected free refreshments when they got to the top. It is to be hoped that the ghostly spirit of poor John Henry Cliffe has not noted the crowded railway trains and the large hotel which now crowns Y Wyddfa, for if it had he would undoubtedly haunt the mountain peak unceasingly, and with many very unhappy moans.

Profitable business is bound to draw competition, and very soon a rival appeared in the person of John Roberts (not the one who built the original Pen y Gwryd cottage), and he put up another hut; both these huts remained in use until the turn of the century when the mountain railway was completed and the Railway Company replaced them with the present hotel.

It is most surprising to read that at that time during the height of the season two or three hundred tourists and pleasure seekers would reach the top of Snowdon every day. But an important factor was that the ponies took the tourist all the way on some routes and most of the way on others, and it seems doubtful if so many would have had the energy to walk to the top; it is not surprising that the refreshment trade did well and perhaps Cliffe was right to call it a rich harvest. It is easy to get the idea that talk of conservation only started in recent years, but even in the 1850s the local inhabitants from the surrounding villages were getting very worried about the invasion of tourists and complained that in the summer the mountain was mobbed and so the romance of the ascent was a thing of the past; they, too, recommended an evening journey when it was possible to 'hold communion with the Queen of Night, view the stars, the poetry of Heaven flickering above the misty mountain peaks, and watch the effect of early sunrise, the solemn splendour of colouring, the chaotic prospect around, in stillness and in solitude'. But today in the height of the summer not even the hour of sunrise would give the climber stillness and solitude up there; in fact he might easily find a crowd of strangely garbed or ungarbed figures engaged in practising the very latest cult and accompanying themselves with the odd, unhappy sounds reminiscent of the unearthly moans and chain rattling commonly associated with ghosts.

These guides of Snowdonia did not reach anything approaching the level of attainment of their counterparts in the Alps and any such standard was unnecessary in the region in which they operated. Those walkers they took up the mountains mostly wanted only the straightforward way up without any risk while the more venturesome would look for new ways by themselves. So the guides merely had to have first class knowledge of a few recognized routes, but on these they had to be certain of getting there and back whatever the weather; any man of experience knows how easy it is to get lost in a mist even on simple routes, and how dangerous that can be.

But as already mentioned many of the tourists who climbed Snowdon made three-quarters of the journey on horseback, and there were staging posts at varying altitudes on the different paths where horses could be left while the rider continued the last part on foot; it is surprising what a short distance they had to walk on some of the most popular paths. We effete folk of today would probably find a good part of the horse borne section as terrifying as a simple roped climb, for even the expert horseman might find riding on some of the rough and precipitous tracks somewhat perturbing. But this, of course, was the age when the horse was the normal method of transport, and at least we can console ourselves with the thought that the man or woman would cheerfully ride three-quarters of the way up Snowdon without undue trepidation might require a lot of Dutch courage to travel at seventy miles an hour on a motorway and a double or triple dose before taking a trip in an aeroplane! For the Victorian lady it was almost essential that she should appear physically weak, except perhaps sometimes in the hunting field; but certainly she should pose as quite unable to reach the top of Snowdon on her feet, although quite strong enough and strong nerved enough to ride three-quarters of the way if well-escorted by a gallant male companion.

What is now called the Pig or Pyg Track was then considered to be one of the more difficult ascents. The mention of this track leads at once to a still lively controversy as to the origin of the name Pig or Pyg: many hold firmly to the view that it is the Pyg Track as it originated from the words Pen y Gwryd Track, or the Track from the head of the Gwryd River; from there it is only a short step to imply that it means from the P.Y.G. Inn, and certainly no owner of the hotel will budge one inch from that interpretation. For those who do not know Snowdonia it should at this stage be pointed out that this Hotel is always and for ever known by those who frequent it merely as P.Y.G. and nothing else.

There are however, others, particularly those with academic leanings, who will prove at least to their own satisfaction that there was, in days gone by, a well-marked track across the shoulder of Snowdon along which swine were often driven from Llanberis via Cwm Dyli to Beddgelert or vice versa; this in Welsh was the Bwlch Moch which literally translated means the Pass of the Pigs; it is suggested that part of this path became known as the Pig Track and it has no connection with the Gwryd River and certainly no connection with the historically speaking very recent Pen y Gwryd Inn.

In the second volume of the *Climbers' Club Journal*, published toward the end of the last century there is a delightful and lengthy series of letters on this subject, in which the arguments for and against the two interpretations of the name are carried very far. Quite soon the correspondence showed signs of becoming violent and the Editor had to call a halt, in case some of the writers might be in personal danger. But it is interesting to read the vehemence with which some well-known climbers such as Gotch and Dakyns supported the Bwlch Moch derivation, which they translated as the Pass of the Wild Boar or the Pig's Gap: maybe these very few words will start this argument all over again.

Denis Hoare writing in 1950 claims that the first recorded ascent of Snowdon was by Thomas Jackson in 1639; there is no need to doubt his accuracy that this was the first ascent which was actually recorded, but it is difficult to believe that the fighting Welshmen led by Owain Glyndwr and other great leaders did not on some occasions get to the top of their tallest mountain in order to spy out the doings of their enemy in the valleys below: surely in medieval guerilla warfare, which happened most of the year in this part of the world, such exploits would be taken for granted and not worth recording except perhaps by the bards trying to keep the gathering amused after dinner, who would extol the courage of their countrymen willing to invade the Eagles' Nest on Eryri, or to risk the wrath of Merlin sitting on top of Y Wyddfa.

Hoare gives the information that in 1820 a small stone hut was built on the summit of Y Wyddfa and that in 1827 by order of the Government of the day a large cairn with a wooden pole was erected there; this was an early effort in the Ordnance Survey and must have been welcomed as a landmark by the seamen in the Straights, who undoubtedly used to look out for Snowdon.

Hoare's writings are always interesting and amusing, even if his facts do not always tally with those of other writers; no doubt he is often right but there may be times when, as with all humorists, he tends to improve his tales a bit by some slight stretching of the facts. He suggests that the average number of visitors each day on the top of Snowdon was about twenty, but he does not say if his average is worked out for every day of the year; several authors tell of two or three hundred tourists on top, but this is in the summer months when the crowds are very large if George Borrow is to be believed. As always the statistics are unreliable and most will know how wrong one can be in an estimate of even a small crowd constantly on the move.

Hoare gives some delightful stories. One about a gentleman who he says arrived at the top of Snowdon in a shocking state apparently because he had ingested nothing on his way up, but two pounds of mutton chops and one pint of brandy; he does not say if he thinks this too much or too little, nor what is the correct and reasonable amount of food and drink to get one to the top of a mountain in the right frame of mind. Another so called gentleman reached the top of the mountain saying that he had 'Lost my wife halfway up in a violent storm and have not seen her since'. There is no indication as to what happened to the poor lady or if the loss was a temporary or permanent one.

It is to Hoare that we are indebted for the story that in 1849 Mr Bradshaw of railway timetable fame went to the top of Snowdon; fifty years in advance of the opening of a railway seems rather much, even for a keen type like Bradshaw, so it must be assumed that he went up for the pleasure of the ascent on his feet.

But of all the venturesome men who clambered round the mountains of North Wales and who coursed the tops without help from guides or even from knowledgeable local inhabitants, the pride of place must go to Thomas Pennant in his travels in the latter years of the eighteenth century, and he also deserves the palm for his account of these adventures.

On one occasion he left his horses at Pen y Gwryd (probably within the old Roman Marching Camp for it was otherwise a barren spot) giving instructions to his servants that they were to be taken through the Pass to Llanberis; this was not an easy road for the path went up behind the present site of the Pen y Pass Hotel and was notoriously rough and difficult. Then Pennant and his friends set out to climb the Glyders, a course which seems like child's play to the twentieth century climber, but at Pennant's time was a high quality exploration; there were no cairns and no well-trodden path and it was quite troublesome for them to find their own way. Most people would agree with him that the route was 'extremely long, steep and laborious, wet and slippery; and almost the whole way covered with loose fragments of rock beneath which was the continuous roar of waters, seeking their way to the bottom'. But as with the many hundred who have followed him he found the toil fully rewarding, with the fascinating and quite unusual area at the top covered with vast stones of ten to thirty feet long often balanced precariously the one on top of the other; he also found what he thought to be shells embedded in the rocks and what he called pieces of lava. He and his friends wended their way along the Glyder ridge and reached the summit of Tryfan, but sad to say he does not tell of their route.

A hundred years later G.O. Spencer described how he and a companion went up Glyder Fawr in the worst winter conditions; they had no ice axe and had to kick steps in the snow, battling against a bitter east wind until they reached the frozen crags of Glyder Fawr: 'all around us was snow and ice; not a rock was visible for all were thickly encased in their winter shroud. It was curious to notice how the wind and formed cornices and curtains of ice round these large stones, of arborescent or leafy form, presenting a most beautiful sight'.

G.J. Bennett made his 'Pedestrian Tour' in 1837 and he

always seemed slightly pessimistic; maybe he never recovered from the nocturnal lobster and the trouble with the brass bedstead dealt with in an earlier chapter; but he does give a rather more optimistic note when he says 'A good horsewoman (do not forget he was writing well before the 1975 Act of Parliament on Sex Discrimination and even before the day of Florence Nightingale) may venture into the dark defiles or climb the craggy heights upon ponies which are always in readiness at the inns for that purpose', but he shows considerable sympathy when he also remarks 'Between man and his steed there will most assuredly be a strong feeling created by the conviction the one is a most unnecessary burthen to the other'. Many will have had that feeling.

The start of really keen rock climbing as it is known today was about the middle of the nineteenth century, and it was about that time that Pen y Gwryd began getting visitors who went with the primary object of climbing rock faces as apart from just difficult walking. Many think that F.H. Bowring deserves the credit for doing a good deal of the pioneer work and he first stayed at the Inn in 1847. Then a year or so afterwards Baumgartner, who was born in Geneva in 1823, but who went to Rugby and to Oxford and who was a constant visitor to the Alps, carried on the good work, having been invited to Pen y Gwryd by Bowring or by one of his keen disciples.

But real fame came to Pen y Gwryd in 1854 with the first visit of Charles Edward Mathews; for him with both mountains and the inn it was a case of love at first sight and he started his visit by going to the top of Snowdon. Throughout his life Mathews spread his net widely and he climbed at practically all the centres in this country and many on the Continent or Europe; but he always returned to his original love and time after time he visited Pen y Gwryd until the turn of the century. His very well-known *Reminiscences of Pen y Gwryd* published in the *Climbers' Club Journal* in December 1901 did much to popularise the Inn and the surrounding country, for in that article he gives a delightful and succinct account of the early history of the inn, and with it a glowing account of the Owens who ran it, and it is to this account and to many of his other historical researches that many later histories, including this one, owe very much.

In fact Mathews did much more than write the inn's history for he gave it the biggest boost it ever had when in 1870 he, together with Frederick Morshead and Adams-Reilly founded the Society of Welsh Rabbits, the precursor of the Climbers' Club.

The first of the Pen y Gwryd Visitors' Books appeared in 1854, a good leather bound volume carrying the name of the hotel in gold lettering on the front. From them many snippets of the history of the place, of the progress of climbing, fishing and botany can be picked up, and also notes of the unusual guests that found their way to the inn. Unfortunately many visitors seemed unable to avoid some form of exhibitionism in their writing in the Visitors' Books, so that from the beginning the entries included a mass of scribbles and scrawls; many efforts at drawings of which few show any signs of possible success, and still more efforts at writing amusing poetry, one or two of which succeed but far more have no claim to be either poetry or humour.

It is common to think of the Victorians as addicts of courteous and gentlemanly behaviour and to copper-plate handwriting, but if the Visitors' Books are anything to go on this is one of the fables, for even some of the sensible entries are so badly written as to be illegible. Sad to say this unhappy state of affairs continued for thirty years, when Hugo Young in desperation presented Harry Owen with the famous Locked Book which instituted a dramatic change and from selected entries in this book most of the ensuing chapter has been written.

However the early Visitors' Books, which deserve much more prolonged investigation, do give many details of the climbs attempted and completed, and indicate the routes of many expeditions starting from the hotel. They show that most of the visitors at that time went for the straightforward clambers up Snowdon or its satellites, or attempted the ridge of the Glyders and the scramble up Tryfan. The entries also demonstrate how helpful Harry Owen was to his guests as an advisor or a guide if wanted: from the beginning the guests are loud in their praises of him, and perhaps louder in their praises of Ann Owen and her mother for their wonderful meals. The sincerely happy and cordial atmosphere which has been the striking feature of this Inn was already well in production.

When describing the walks, climbs and fishing trips of that time it is not easy to remember that it was often difficult to get to the right place even to start, as this age is so used to the idea of a fifteen or twenty minutes car journey to the foot of a climb or the bank of a lake, how can people realize that the journey say from Pen y Gwryd to the Carnedd meant finding some kind of horse drawn transport to cover the six or eight miles. Either that or it meant shank's pony the whole way with the troublesome thought of the same distance back again when the day's labour was over. It needed considerable forethought and enthusiasm, but that never seemed lacking.

In spite of the almost impossible task of sorting out the good from the bad essays in the Visitors' Book, and in wading through pages of faded or illegible writing which would need a lifetime of effort to do properly, there are some unusual characters, some interesting tours and some strange behaviour which may prove entertaining.

A very early visitor who was there in 1857 was J.R. Dakyns, who was a pioneer in climbing and who acquired a great reputation; unfortunately he was no writer and his descriptions of his climbs are very short. Another fact that emerges is that very soon Pen y Gwryd began to receive guests from overseas, a habit it has always retained. As far back as 1854, N.T.J. Cornelson and G.E. Schwabe from Hamburg, Germany, expressed themselves well-satisfied with the country and with their excellent entertainment at the hotel.

But the hotel was not infested with climbers only, as in April 1860 the Penrhyn Glee Club spent a night there on their way back from performing at the Beddgelert Eisteddfodd. Being Welsh singers, they needed little persuasion to provide some entertainment for the other lodgers including the singing of the glee 'Maying', which had been one of their turns when singing to the Queen on Her visit to Penrhyn Castle a month or two earlier.

In July 1862 a triad of parsons the Rev John Stevenson, the Rev Fred Stevenson and the Rev Martin climbed Tryfan and sat in thought and contemplation on the top. This expedition has special mention not because it was undertaken by a

Church of England trinity, but because 'They did not attempt the leap of the daring tourists nor the leap of the shepherd girl, which I believe to be mere myth'. It can be presumed that the tourists' leap is the now common jump from Adam to Eve, as the two large rocks on the very top have been christened, a jump which requires sound nerves as there is nothing but air to arrest progress should the foot slip, but in none of the literature, nor in the knowledge of the learned locals, nor of the informed climbing fraternity can any information be found about the shepherd girl's leap. There is one slight rumour of a suicide jump by a young woman, but it is very vague, and in any case there seems no reason why any of the incumbents would even contemplate such a leap; so maybe it is a myth.

This visit of the vicars was about six years after Pen y Gwryd had started to get fame by reason of the visit of Charles Kingsley, for he paid his first call there in 1856; his comments on the leap of the daring tourist are 'Some years before a gentleman performed the hazardous and foolhardy exploit of jumping from one stone to the other. If his foot had slipped or he had lost his balance he would have been dashed to pieces on the rocks below'. Kingsley also states that at one time there were three big stones on the top of the mountain hence its name Trifaen; if this is so what has become of the third one and should it not be found and put back into place by some conservationist?

For this first of many visits of Charles Kingsley he was with his very good friend Tom Hughes of *Tom Brown's Schooldays* fame and over the years which followed they paid many visits to the hotel, sometimes together and sometimes with different company. Kingsley's letter of invitation which he wrote to Hughes is copied in full in the Visitors' Book and deserves a quotation: 'My dear old lad, Froude cannot go with us; so are you willing to go Snowdon . . . . Buy two sheets of the Ordnance maps (I'll go share in the pence) . . . then send them on to me in the coat pocket of the Hughes Esq., from Saturday night to a Monday morning and we will talk it out'. Charles Kingsley then added some verses of poetry.

The Visitors' Books are crammed with poetry and it should all be published in a volume entitled 'Anthology of the Worst Poetry in the World'. A selection has been put into the

Appendix of this book so that the reader can judge for himself; sad to say Kingsley does not show at his best in his verses, but here is one which was sent to his wife:

There is no Inn in Snowdon which is not awfully dear,
Excepting Pen y Gwryd (you can't pronounce it dear),
Which standeth in the meeting of splendid valleys three,
One is the Vale of Gwynant, so well beloved by me:
One goes to Capel Curig, and I can't mind its name,
And one is Llanberis Pass, which all men know the same.

The surprise is not that a well-known novelist should not also be a good poet — why should he be — but that he should write such a verse in a public book for all to see.

Another friend joined the Kingsley party, Tom Taylor by name and this trio went looking for trout in Llyn Idwal, which truly is, as Kingsley said 'A fine lake embosomed in the silent hills'. But they had no luck with their fishing. Before they left Pen y Gwryd Harry Owen specially asked Charles Kingsley to write in the Visitors' Book, and all three co-operated in so doing; but in common with several entries which might at a later date bring a financial reward if offered to the right people these poems and the signatures were cut out and stolen from the book. Luckily another habitueé had taken a copy and these verses were printed privately, and they were published for all to see in the *Life and Letters of Charles Kingsley* edited and published by his widow.

Quite a long time afterwards when he paid another visit to the hotel Kingsley created a storm about the way in which his great writings had been stolen and the result was one of those strange essays to which he sometimes gave birth: 'Fifteen years ago Thomas Hughes, M.P. Tom Taylor and myself wrote some verses in this book for these dear good people, and they were cut out and stolen by some snob after ten pounds had been refused for them.

'Now such snobs are unfortunately of the human race, and will wed, and are therefore likely to produce little snobkins. Some such snobkins may visit Pen y Gwryd and be still too uncivilized to be weaned from their parents activities. Any such, I warn that he cannot well steal this bit of writing and shew it again unless he wish to expose his own shame. And yet I am not sure this plan will be successful, snobs being half of them fools likewise, he may steal this for the mere pleasure of boasting that he stole it'. No one would disagree that such behaviour is irritating to a high degree but it does seem as if Kingsley made very heavy weather of this crime; what would be his reaction to some of today's vandalism?

A close study of the Visitors' Books illustrates very well the slow but definite change which was taking place at this time; the walkers were turning into scramblers and the scramblers were becoming more like twentieth century climbers, while those who were already climbers to some degree were getting steadily more venturesome and were looking for more difficult ways of ascent. Of course many of the hotel guests still remained strollers and they went there to think and to look; but it is noteworthy that as these changes took place the new type climbers and the advanced walkers still had a marked academic and ecclesiastical flavour.

Observe, for example, the entry in December 1860 when Professor Tyndall, Professor Huxley and Mr Busk when exploring the mountains. Before starting their walk they bought a couple of rake handles in Bethesda for fourpence, and then persuaded the local blacksmith to fasten some spikes on them thus turning them into rudimentry alpenstocks, which they used on the snow covered parts of the mountains. What a pity that the grand name alpenstock has passed out of use even if this weapon is no longer carried; the name might have been transferred and used instead of the rather dull title 'Ice axe', a name that seems more akin to the American ice pick, commonly used apparently in the States for chopping cocktail ice, or slightly less often as a murder weapon; in either guise most unsuitable for Alpine adventure.

Just after Christmas these two professors with Robert Hughes from Capel Curig as their guide started to plough through deep snow on the Pyg Track way up Snowdon. Their exact route is not easy to follow from their description, for it appears as though they reached the Horseshoe Ridge somewhere between Crib Goch and Crib y Ddysgyl, which would seem a somewhat dangerous trip. But they reached the summit of Snowdon in safety and were rewarded by a glorious view being particularly impressed by the wonderful cloud effects on that icy afternoon, saying that in their opinion the Alps could produce nothing better. They do not say how much Alpine travel they had achieved, but in their opinion as to the view from Snowdon there are many who would agree with them.

Mathews was willing to confess his mistakes when he wrote in the Locked Book: he tells of one trip in the winter session during which he was tackling Snowdon in company with A.W. Moore and R.S. Macdonald, the latter a Colonial Officer. Both friends had brought their ice axes, but Mathews laughed them to scorn at the idea that such implements might be necessary in North Wales, but they soon found the ascent quite impossible and they had to go back to the hotel to collect their ice axes and then start again; he was duly apologetic.

About this time the new school of climbers began to arrive thick and fast, and there is not room to talk of more than a small section. They included such mountaineers as R.L. Nettleship of Balliol College, Oxford, later regrettably killed on Mont Blanc. But one great character is always reappearing, and he is H.B. Biden; this constant visitor at Pen y Gwryd has put more information into the Visitors' Books than anyone else and it is always information worth having. Arthur Lockwood was very keen on climate and temperature readings but well before his time Biden was taking maximum and minimum temperature readings very zealously, using a thermometer hidden away somewhere on the top of Glyder Fawr; this was his greatest hobby and he made no claim to being an expert climber, spending his time scrambling and exploring the hills and walking the mountain ridges; he survived all his adventures and he died in his bed in 1887.

Now to come back to the Welsh Rabbits and to a great day for Pen y Gwryd and for climbing in North Wales. Charles Edward Mathews was not only a frequent visitor, but he was the pioneer of winter visiting for he found the winter meant a quieter and more relaxed atmosphere, a much emptier hotel so that the climbers could bunch up and chat together in the Smoke Room. Moreover he enjoyed the thrill and excitement of walking round the mountain ranges in snow and frost when the going was difficult and not without risk. Staying at Pen y

Gwryd in January 1870 was Frederick Morshead who Mathews considered to be the ablest mountaineer of his day and Adams-Reilly from Belmont in Ireland and the three of them got together and decided to form a Society, which they later christened the Society of Welsh Rabbits. This was intended to gather together several climbers of similar tastes who preferred exploring Snowdonia in the winter, as near to Christmas as possible, when they could have the hotel almost to themselves. Adams-Reilly, who was something of an artist, designed a suitable coat-of-arms for the Society, and the shield he produced for some years adorned the dining room at Pen y Gwryd until, as happened surprisingly often even in those apparently civilized times it was stolen and never seen again.

There is no full record of the founder members of this Society, but some of the joiners included F.A. Walroth, Rawdon Levett, C.T. Dent, Osmond Airy and Horace Walker, names which to those who know the history of climbing will need no introduction. This Society may not have found full popularity as not all climbers liked the winter weather in that part of the world, but Mathews gathered round him many of his own particular friends. Moreover this Society bred fairly fast and turned quite naturally into the Climbers' Club which in turn spread through the length and breadth of Britain and which still keeps a strong attachment to its original birthplace the 'Pen y Gwryd Hotel'.

It might be as well to recall at this stage that the Alpine Club was founded in 1857 and this was a stimulus to British mountaineering although that was already in good fettle. Members of the Alpine Club went in large numbers to North Wales to increase their experience and they also went to one of Pen y Gwryd's rivals for the same reason; that was the Wasdale Inn in the Lake District whose part in improving the techniques of climbing on difficult rock faces was immense. A complete book could be written, and perhaps it should be written, concerning the rivalry between Wales and the Lake District in attracting the climbing fraternity, and in pushing forward their climbing ability so that they could then go with every confidence to tackle climbs in the Alps or the Dolomites. Most mountaineers used both Wales and the Lakes and it can be said with certainty that both regions played an outstanding part in forwarding climbing and mountaineering; fortunately it is no job of this book to decide between them, for that needs a Solomon, as the influence of both places was so great.

Many of those who joined the Welsh Rabbits were already members of the Alpine Club, and many also had demonstrated excellent first ascents and magnificent mountaineering skills in France and Switzerland. To give just a few examples, Adams-Reilly completed the Forbes Map of the Mont Blanc chain; A.W. Moore made the first ascent of the Brenva Ice Ridge in 1865; Macdonald made the first ascent of Pelvoux in company with the great Whymper, a name which unfortunately never appears in any of the Pen y Gwryd books. Morshead claimed the first solitary ascent of Mont Blanc, and also the first ascent and descent of that mountain in a single day, while Clinton Dent laid seige to the Dru until he was finally successful at the eighteenth attempt!

It is very easy when reading a book written in the Victorian era to get the impression that women went up the peaks only when well-escorted by members of the male sex, and that even then they were often taken at least half way up by a pony. This may be true of a number of them but in fact some women started walking the ridges quite early on; in 1872 Maria V.G. Havergal and Frances Havergal stayed at Pen y Gwryd for the purpose of mountain walking and they went on several ridge walks and undoubtedly reached the top of several three thousand footers. And what about the party of seven strong which went up Snowdon from the Llanberis approach — it consisted of two women, four boys aged about twelve years, and a grandfather of seventy two; there is no suggestion that grandfather was the leader, and it seems just as likely that he was hauled up by a couple of Amazons.

For the Victorian ladies dress was a considerable problem, skirts could be used for ridge walking although not always easy or seemly in wet and windy weather; but the real trouble started when women became keen on rock climbing for then skirts put both ability and decency at a premium. The advent of the knickerbocker helped enormously, but even before that came into use there were some advanced climbing women who did not hesitate to discard their skirts when the occasion warranted, although history does not reveal what was then revealed. It must have been a wonderful day for the woman who was keen on the mountain adventures when trousers or breeches were at last accepted.

Perhaps it was something to do with incorrect dress worn by the ladies which produced the tragedy so sadly written in the Visitors' Book in poetry form in 1817, under the title *The Legend of Snowdon*.

The evening sun was sinking low
 To seek his crimson bed,
When down Old Snowdon's rocky side
 Two happy lovers sped.
The rugged mountain far and near
 Was silent as a tomb
Save where the lovers' footfall pierced
 The ever deepening gloom.
The mist arose and hid the moon,
 The night came on apace,
And soon it was so dark they scarce
 Could see each other's face;
But what cared they that happy pair
 As long as they might wend
Their way through life's uncertain path
 Together to the end.
The mist grew thicker every step,
 Around them all was black,
Unable now to see their way
 They wandered from the track.
Alarmed they clasped each other's hand,
 And breathed a prayer on high
For help, if haply they might live
 For grace, if they must die.
Beneath their feet a chasm yawned
 A chasm dark and drear,
The entrance to an ancient mine
 Abandoned many a year;
One slipped and fell, the other tried
 Alas! in vain to save,
He slipped as well, and so they two
 Were hurried to their grave;

One single gasp, one shivering moan
  Ascended to the night,
And from the pit's deep bottom gleamed
  A ghastly sheen of white.
When morning dawned across the sky
  The mountainside was bare,
But lifeless in that chasm's depth
  They found the luckless pair.

It is perhaps just as well that only the visitor interested enough to turn back the pages of the book would see this sad story; had it been for general publication probably Pen y Gwryd would soon have had to close for lack of guests!

The splendour of the scenery brought many visitors to Pen y Gwryd who were not seeking physical activity but just wished to look and wonder, and sometimes these included well-known and important people, a habit which has continued ever since. In the 1870s Lord Coleridge, a nephew of Samuel Taylor of that ilk stayed at the Inn with his wife and family when he was a judge on the North Wales circuit. In 1878 the hotel was visited by Annie Besant; this is a name that is nearly unknown today but she was one of the very popular authors of her time and she was also very well-known for her reforming zeal, doing much, both in writing and in action to improve the way of life in what are now called the underdeveloped countries. She often wrote in conjunction with Charles Bradlaugh also an active social reformer, and so it is not surprising that her friends at the Inn were Alice and Hypatia Bradlaugh, who presumably were sisters or relatives of Charles.

Leaping to April 1914 one finds an annotation stating that a whole page of the Visitors' Book had been torn out for some unknown reason and that it contained a complete list of a large party of masters and boys from Winchester College which took over the whole hotel in 1871; many of the names listed were of men who either then or later acquired some fame in the climbing world for led by Morshead they also included George Richardson, E.J. Turner, J.T. Branston, C.H. Hawkins, Theodore Kensington, A.J. Toye and E.A. Mere. This was probably the beginning of a long period when Winchester showed an outstanding interest in climbing; for years they were great supporters of Pen y Gwryd and they are one of the schools that have produced for this country many expert mountaineers.

The invasion from abroad showed a steady increase in the late nineteenth and early twentieth century; visitors came not only from all the Commonwealth countries but also from the United States of America, and there are names of folk from New York, Nebraska, from Philadelphia, Canada, and from European countries. One who must not be forgotten is the Wandering Welshman returning to have another look at his native country, one W. ap Medoc from Utica.

Then there was Geo. F. Godfrey from Bangor, Maine U.S.A., the home of a popular ditty, who found it 'a pleasant and novel ride for a Yankee' and a short Armenian essay signed by P. Masditchian, S. Eliazarian, S. Manoukian and Y. Manoukian which is entered as 'An expression of testimony to the marvellous beauty of the Welsh Landscape and to the Greatness of English genius'. With this remark about English genius it is perhaps as well that the Welsh contingent was not about to manhandle these stupid Armenians!

Naturally all hotels will have those who decry them but it is to be hoped that the overseas visitors found the hotel better than at least some of those from England, for one of the British visitors complained that he could find nothing but a broken chair to sit on, while another was concerned that he had to pay for his light, although he was not allowed good wax candles. One guest wrote in the Visitors' Book just three words 'Fleas ad infinitum' and nearly as miserable was the one who said the hotel contained only one bed, two sofas and rats! Fortunately some of those who wrote such offensive remarks were well-chastised in later entries, as was Mr Radcliffe when he wrote that the ladies of North Wales were all very well in their way, but were not to be compared with those of the South of France. It is pleasing to report that he was thoroughly torn to shreds for this very unacceptable comment. But taking all in all, the complimentary comments far outnumber the dissatisfied ones, even if one caller thought the beer to be poor stuff but patted himself on the back with the remark that 'to the contented all things are bearable'.

It is necessary to read only a few pages of the Visitors' Books to realize that the weather has changed not at all during the last hundred years for here mountains remain always unpredictable; there are constant references to soaking walks and to the great pleasure of getting back to dryness and warmth. Strangely enough a bit of bad weather can be almost an advantage in running an Inn in mountain country; if it provides warmth, good baths, good food and drink, and above all first class drying facilities for wet clothes, the reputation of the Inn, like the persons of its visitors, is home and dry. The guest is so happy to be warm within and without that the psychological effect is immense and nothing else matters. But all this was not enough for one disgruntled cleric who after a week of rain announced in the book 'I'll go back to my pulpit; there at least I'll be dry enough'.

It is quite a change to find these books used for something other than descriptions of climbs and walks. In 1876 Thomas Bowen of Cambridge became very annoyed with a group of four men who in his view drove a horse and cart much too fast up the Llanberis Pass, thus putting the public in grave danger; they must have had a strong horse to get very fast up this slope, and probably they had, for he added a little philosophy to his rather modern view on traffic when he thought that perhaps 'they were getting exhilaration from doing the thing'. Is this, perchance, the first glimpse of that modern and unhappy phrase about 'doing your own thing' which has had such a markedly harmful effect on modern life?

There was very little the visitor could do about getting transported around Snowdonia, for Rawson Owen at Pen y Pass was about the only owner of horses and carriages for miles. He was always willing to take parties about but the cost was not small, about 1/- a mile was a common charge and this was a fairly heavy sum at that age. But there were some keen business men who were thinking seriously about transport; in 1876 Henry Martin Morrison of Longsight stayed at Pen y Gwryd for several days with Thomas Parton and some members of the staff of an engineering firm while they were exploring the possibility of putting up what they termed an Aerial Tramway to the summit of Snowdon. After prospecting they appeared very confident that they could manage this feat, for Morrison emphatically announced that visitors might soon expect to be transported to the top of Snowdon aerially, for details of the scheme were soon to be issued asking for investment in shares for the project. He further suggests that 'good looking ladies will be transported free of charge'. It may be that potential shareholders were put off by this suggestion and they may have wondered who was going to decide on good looks but in any case nothing further was heard about this plan. When the mountain railway was finally brought into being some twenty years later, the fair sex had already lost its privileged position and they have always had to pay the full fare, unless they could persuade someone to pay for them.

The increase in the tourist traffic naturally led to a slow but steady rise in the accidents and fatalities on the hills; there had always been an occasional accident to local shepherds, farmers and miners who had to use the treacherous paths in their daily tasks and this despite the fact that they were experts in finding the way round the tricky routes; such misfortunes would not be included in Visitors' Books but they were the cause of some strange findings later. As recently at 1926 Arthur Lockwood was walking with some of his guests on Glyder Fach when they came across a complete skeleton, partly clothed by a few tattered relics in the pockets of which were found a briar pipe, a pocket knife, a shaving mirror, a penny dated 1898, a metal watch, a handkerchief and a waterproof. The experts decided that it was the skeleton of a man of about fifty years old and almost certainly a labourer taking a short cut across the Glyders while heading for the Eihiau workings. There were no signs of an accident and he may have died from natural causes such as a heart attack despite being apparently fit and middle aged. This body had been undiscovered for a few years, but others have been found, such as that of a woman found on the Glyders just before, which demonstrates that they can be unnoticed for a very long time; and there is not always any record of a person having been missing.

The first recorded death, that of the Rev Starr in 1846 has already been mentioned and the next one which has any record in the Visitors' Book is in 1874 when F.R. Wilton fell from Snowdon into Cwm Glas. This is one of the first climbing accidents which had a notice in the daily press, as the *London Penny Illustrated Paper* had a paragraph describing the accident and a woodcut of the top of Snowdon; today they have become a constant feature in the Dailies. In 1879 Maxwell Haseler having a winter climb on the Snowdon Massif with four friends fell to his death despite their efforts; the friends expressed much gratitude to the Owens for their great help and sympathy in their time of need.

Any academic study of the Visitors' Books is obstructed by the constant and often strange efforts at being humorous. There is great play in making entries under assumed names some of which are easy to unravel but some must leave doubts. A July 1878 entry written in a pseudo-Russian script by two men who claim to be officers of the Russian 4th Horse Guards seems unlikely to be genuine, but needs an expert to make certain that it is not authentic. But no expert knowledge would be necessary in the note on August 1880 complimenting the host and hostess in their exceptional ability in providing food and accommodation for Kufftirizoi Cetewayo, Mrs Cetewayo and also twenty five little Cetewayos!

But, of course the majority of the entries in the Visitors' Books are genuine and it is a pity that they cannot all be followed up much further for they would lead to many fascinating bits of history; for example, was the Rev A.C. O'Dell who signed his name at the end of the century a relative of Noel Odell the companion of Mallory and Irvine on their final and fatal effort on Everest, and of whom more will be told later in this chapter.

The arrival in August 1883 of two lady cyclists provided an uncommon sight for Wales at that time. The next month two travellers from Manchester, in a graphic account, gave a solemn warning to others about a very unreasonable bull they met on a walk from Capel Curig to Llanwrst; in this unsatisfactory, but happily brief encounter they were quite unable to pacify the animal even with some comforting words spoken in Welsh. So perhaps it was an early Nationalist bull who did not appreciate the foreigners' English accent.

These travellers could not have learnt the Welsh words carefully enough or did not pronounce them properly or surely they would have had results similar to those of the pair staying 1880 who wrote thus in the Visitors' Book.

Within the bounds of this hotel
  Which bears the name of Pen y Gwryd,
A black and yellow hound doth dwell
  By which my friend and I were worried.
My object is not to imply
  That he assaulted, bit or tore us,
In face he never ventured nigh
  Except when food was put before us;
But when the scent of ham and eggs
  Announced the breakage of our fast,
He came and twined about our legs
  And interrupted our repast.
We drove him from us through the door
  He reappeared; we tried the casement,
He seemed to rise out of the floor
  And importuned us as before,
To our unspeakable amazement,
  But timely succour fortune brought us
One word of Welsh we chanced to know,
  And that a fellow guest had taught us
It meant — unpleasant creature — go.
  Stranger if you should chance to meet him,
Oh! Do not pull or kick or push,
  Or execrate or bribe or beat him,
But make a sound resembling "Cwsh".

April 1884 gave rise a turning point to the Pen y Gwryd records, for that year Hugo Young, one of the hotel's most frequent guests, became completely irritated and upset with the scrawled and tattered Visitors' Book then available. Although these provided a lot of interesting information about walks, climbs and fishing exploits which could be of great use to other guests, much of the space was filled with rather silly verses, poor quality drawings, nonsense remarks and a deal of illegibility. So he presented Pen y Gwryd with a handsome, thick, leather bound volume, with first quality paper, and a strong brass lock; the whole being of a style more usually associated with the family Bible. This now famous Locked Book was intended to be kept, as indeed it was, by Harry Owen and any proprietors who followed him, and it was to be given for entries only to the chosen who in his opinion would make entries worthy of it. The ordinary Visitors' Books still remained in use, but fewer people troubled to make such elaborate comments as heretofore, tending to use merely names and addresses; but it was not until 1907 that the normal books were brought into service in which guests only gave the customary details of name, address and nationality.

On the whole the Locked Book has proved a very successful enterprise, although some details must have been lost to posterity for a number of reasons. Some of the difficulties are obvious; it relies on the judgement of the Keeper of the Book to decide who should write in the precious Book, and this may have meant that the climbers got more than their fair share as Pen y Gwryd is primarily a Climbers' hotel and it was just such technical details as many guests wanted. But it is possible that someone who wished to write about a walk was a bit shy to ask for the handsome volume. Another trouble was that Mine Host must frequently be out or busy doing something else and so the Locked Book was not always easily obtainable; but in spite of all these troublesome points, it has proved that a book of this sort can be kept free from nonsense and stupidity. Arthur Lockwood shows up very well in his personal writings for in the first place his handwriting is about the best that could be found anywhere, clear, neat and legible, and secondly he has filled pages with details of climate, weather, temperatures in various parts of the mountain range; facts which are of general interest.

When Hugo Young gave the book he wrote on the flyleaf some guidance as to what should be written in it, or rather guidance as to what should not be written in it. After this small sermon the first general entry gave an acount of a trip which illustrated well the stamina and endurance of those who went to the mountains in the days of Queen Victoria; it is a pity that only the initials are given but they are H. & C.S. and their adventures are worth looking at:

April 11th 1884 Easter. 'Ascent of Crib Goch from Cwm Dyli; thence along the ridge by Crib y Ddysgyl to the summit of Y Wyddfa, descent by Capel Curig route; views fairly good'. But this was a mere stroll and evidently only a pipe opener.

April 12th. 'Ascent of Lliwedd by ridge from Llyn Llydaw;

then to summit of Y Wyddfa. Very clear view; descent by Bwlch y Main over Yr Aran from which a magnificent view of Snowdon. Descent to Gwynant Valley along the ridge above Cwm y Llan'. Just loosening up a few of the slightly stiffened muscles!

April 13th. 'Ascent of Glyder Fawr, descent to Twll Du; fine glissade down snow slopes to Llyn y Cwn. Ascent of Y Garn, fine snow cornice near summit; continued along ridge over Foel Goch and Moel Perfedd (fine view of Elidir Fawr) to summit of Elidir Fawr. Descent to Cwm Dudodyn from where there is a good path leading to Llanberis village'.

Even for those who do not know the district a glance at the map will give some idea of the distance and terrain involved; only towards the end does snow get a mention and it must have been fairly deep in places to allow glissading. To complete three rounds such as these in three successive days over difficult country and with heavy snow conditions shows a high degree of toughness and of mountaineering skill.

It is evident that people felt that a higher standard of writing attainment was required before anything was put in the new Pen y Gwryd Bible as the arrival of the Locked Book caused great reduction in the number and length of essays and dissertations therein, for the year 1884 has but five entries while 1885 had only six. But some were not put off, in fact, they seemed to have been encouraged; the Rev Hibbert Newton, Vicar of St Michael's, Southwark, puts in a long and slightly unctuous poem; and this is followed by a long list of all the ferns found in the immediate neighbourhood of the hotel. But perhaps the best of the early ones is the full description of several walks undertaken by Mary E. Powell and Nina Lankester; these walks are fairly strenuous expeditions although today they would be called normal ridge walks and not at all out of the way for women. But their accomplishment at that period by a couple of lone ladies was a bit unusual and the description of them called forth a remark by Mary Powell that any ladies that enjoy mountain climbing can do it easily.

Then the next year sees the arrival of E. Kidson whose name shows up from now on with great regularity and who proves one of Pen y Gwryd's most staunch supporters; he starts with some fairly long essays on well-known scrambles along what are now labelled as tourist routes.

Naturally April has always been a popular month in North Wales despite the vagaries of the weather in mountain districts where spring-like days, and days of heavy snow or of blizzards can alternate with surprising frequency. But April 1887 was particularly noteworthy because of the arrival of Oscar Eckenstein who makes a note of having climbed the North Face of Lliwedd for the first time in company with Hugh Scully! Ascents of the West Face of Lliwedd had been made three or four years earlier. It is not just the first ascent which is so important but the fact that Eckenstein has the credit of being perhaps the greatest exponent of rock climbing in the country at that time; this grading has been agreed by many experts whose personal aptitude makes their opinion important, including the great figure of Geoffrey Winthrop Young, himself no mean exponent. Eckenstein's scientific approach to the subject, together with his wonderful technique on the difficult rock face pioneered the way for many towards the modern and mechanical methods seen today.

That year also saw a good account by E. Cowie of Eastbourne of seeing a Brocken Spectre; standing with his two sons on the top of Snowdon, with their backs to the setting sun their three figures were grotesquely caricatured in a cloud arising at about the middle of the Snowdon Horseshoe; the figures were surrounded by a brilliant rainbow of prismatic colours and they swelled and shrunk in size, until as the sun vanished so did they. A good many mountaineers have seen the Brocken Spectre but mostly in France or Switzerland, and sightings in this country are not very common.

In those distant days there was no organization for the rescue of those who met with an accident; should news of trouble come in or should some solitary walker or climber fail to return as expected then it fell to some hotel manager, in this case Harry Owen to gather together a search party of some sort. Many such incidents must have occurred without anyone hearing of them except those staying at the hotel concerned and description of them are rare, but one rather typical one is recorded in 1888 in the Locked Book. A certain T. Sington appears to have been rather negligently abandoned by his party while exploring Cwm y Ddysgyl and he did not reach the hotel when expected and so in the course of time everyone became alarmed. Hugh Owen from Pen y Pass gathered up E. Kidson who was at P.Y.G. and off they went together. Sington arrived back at the hotel at ten o'clock in the evening while the unfortunate searchers did not struggle back until after midnight, but when a climber volunteered to be a member of a search party this was one of the risks that had to be run.

Christmas 1887 and the early months of 1888 saw some happy events and some sad ones recorded; the sad one was the death of a long term supporter of Pen y Gwryd when Henry B. Biden died at the age of sixty. He was a man of many interests besides walking and climbing, and his sensible accounts and comments, can be found scattered throughout the Visitors' Books initialled H.B.B. and they are always informative. Christmas provided the happy event in a visit to the hotel by the great Taugwalder, a member of the family from Switzerland famous for its ability and long service as guides in the Alps. He came from Zermatt to visit North Wales and he was himself guided by Messrs Cartleighs, Wicks and Muir, but if he made any remarks they have not been left for historians to read.

And in April 1888 there took place another of the great events which carried Pen y Gwryd another step or two along the road taking it to the front among climbing centres; for staying there together were Charles Mathews, Alex Mortimer, C.R. Dent, Horace Walker, F. Morshead, L.L. Garbutt, J.A. Fort, Arthur Llewelyn, Crompton Llewellyn Davies the cream of British climbing talent, and with them were Henrik Sundt of Bergen, Norway and to crown all Melchior Anderegg the wonderful guide from Meiringen, Switzerland. An assembly of mountaineers of this country in full flower demonstrating to a couple of famous men of Europe that the hills of Britain might be small in stature, but they had much to offer to the sport of climbing.

C.E. Mathews, who spent some of the time staying at his own cottage at Machynlleth gives an amusing account of their travels, and particularly of the time when they tackled Snowdon by the customary Crib Goch route. Mathews' account runs as follows: 'I led all the way and as the snow was deep and very soft, it was not altogether an easy task. In one place I hesitated for a few seconds; Melchior instantly forged ahead and proferred his services, which I emphatically declined. No, I said, I am guide today, and you are the Herr!' Mathews was still more delighted when they reached the summit of Crib Goch 'and the cone of Snowdon rose white against the clear blue sky; Melchior, despite his faultless knowledge of Swiss mountains, said they must go back as they could not reach that further summit in less than five or six hours, to which I replied it would be less than one hour; "that" said Melchior "is quite impossible". In fact the journey took just five minutes over the hour'. From an unbiassed viewpoint it seems evident that the superb mountain expert Melchior Anderegg found the Mathews' technique a bit slow, while both of them were anxious to present themselves in the best light. Anderegg's surprisingly incorrect estimate of the time needed for the climb suggests that not only did he not know the country well but, that he had not studied the map carefully; he may have assumed a much greater drop in altitude between Crib Goch and Snowdon and anticipated a descent and ascent of fifteen hundred feet or so between the peaks instead of the simple ridge walk – simple that is for experts such as they were.

When writing of Pen y Gwryd it is not very easy to get away from climbers' adventures and dissertations even for a short time, but just occasionally one can escape and take a look from another angle.

There has always been some controversy as to whether the great William Ewart Gladstone ever visited Pen y Gwryd. Of course North Wales was his home ground and many visitors who leave the main roads will have seen the Gladstone Rock at the beginning of one of the loveliest ways up Snowdon, the Watkin Path; this rock marks the place where Gladstone once addressed a large gathering of local people when on one of his political promenades. The Pen y Gwryd Visitors' Book for July 1884 has a signature W.E. Gladstone-Harwarden; underneath this is an anonymous pencil note saying this signature is not genuine and that Gladstone never visited the hotel. There is no doubt that several members of the Gladstone family stayed at Pen y Gwryd and their signatures at a later date look authentic, but whether the W.E.G. one is, can only be guessed, and the idea of William Ewart as a Pen y Gwryd guest must remain very doubtful. There is, however, no doubt about the visit of R. D'Oyly Carte and Helen D'Oyly Carte in 1888 and again in 1895 as they signed the book, but apparently could not be persuaded into putting in the book a short extract of any of their delightful operas.

And now back to the mountains. An increasing flood of climbers becoming steadily more experienced went further and further afield in their efforts to break new ground and to try new techniques. For many years one of the striking challenges of Snowdonia was Twll Du, perhaps better known as the Devil's Kitchen; Yr Twll Du means literally the black hole and in the view of some the alternative title the Devil's Kitchen is more properly applied to the Nant Ffrancon valley for it was down this pass that the swirling storms gathered before rushing out to sea. But no one would really like to see the name removed from the striking cleft in the mountain which runs like a knife cut from Llyn Cwm to Llyn Idwal, filled for most of its length with rushing water which increased the difficulty of the most hazardous climb attempted in the neighbourhood.

As always the description given to the Devil's Kitchen by Thomas Pennant is well-worth a full quotation 'Observe, on the right, a stupendous roche fendue, or split rock, called Twll-Du, and the Devil's Kitchen. It is a horrible gap, in the centre of a great black precipice, extending in length about a hundred and fifty yards; in depth about a hundred; and only six wide; perpendicularly open to the surface of the mountain. On surmounting all my difficulties, and taking a little breath, I ventured to look down this dreadful aperture, and found its horror far from being lessened in my exalted situation for to it were added the waters of Llyn y Cwm, impetuously rushing through its bottom.'

In May 1895 Owen Glynne Jones, a master at the City of London School and the recognized leader of rock climbing for some years, gives a long and interesting essay, complete with diagram as a schoolmaster's essay should be, and showing how he attempted to climb Twll Du following a route carefully worked out but never tried by Haskett Smith. Although Glynne Jones had many first ascents under his belt he frankly admitted that he found the way too risky and had to turn back, nor could he suggest any other way up. But immediately following his lengthy account of failure is a one and a half line entry signed by Archer Thomson and Harold Hughes saying that they had completed the climb in March that year by the process of cutting ice steps up the frozen waterfall! This climb was accomplished in the year of the great frost in 1895 when it was such severe weather that the two climbers could walk straight across Llyn Idwal where the ice was seven inches thick. They had to attack what was described as a vertical bastion of ice, and their only tool for the job was a hatchet surreptitiously removed from the coal cellar of a cottage in Ogwen. It was with this weapon that they slowly hacked their way up this hitherto unconquered climb. How long it took them can be estimated by the fact that they left Ogwen at 10 a.m. and did not reach the top of Twll Du until about 7.15 p.m. so even if the method of climbing was rather unorthodox rock climbing, it was a remarkable feat of endurance. Naturally there were those who felt that this was cheating and should not count as a rock climb but the two who made it were well recognized leaders in the climbing field and they certainly showed ingenuity and courage.

It was not until three years later, in 1898 that W.R. Reade and W.P. McCullock made the ascent by normal rock climbing methods, fully described in the Locked Book. By now it must have been conquered by almost every possible way of approach, but it still remains one of the more severe climbs in Snowdonia with a mixture of troublesome rock work, loose stones and water nearly all the way to the top so that dry rock climbing is impossible and even to keep reasonably dry almost as difficult. This adventure may be thought of as the end of an epoch in climbing in North Wales; advancing techniques in rock work have brought in their train many similar great events, and every decade seems to bring forth its own exceptional climber who can accomplish what others have attempted without success for some years, for with skill and training there seems no limit to where man can climb.

Every Inn has its ups and downs and even Pen y Gwryd has not entirely escaped. But its course in many ways resembles to Trail of the Three Thousands, for it has climbed to many peaks and it has on rare occasion descended into the valleys between, but as these valleys are still a long way above sea-level, so even the lowest level of Pen y Gwryd would in many places be thought of as a high one. But undoubtedly in 1895 it reached one of the major summits for in that year the Climbers' Club was founded and its birthplace was at Pen y Gwryd. The Alpine Club was founded in 1857 as a small and select band of outstanding mountaineers, so that joining it would rank in the climbing manuals as very severe. It wished to keep its standard very high and to accept as members a number of the addicts to the recent sport of rock climbing would mean a marked change of view; looking back it is evident that the time was ripe for the formation of a club for climbers which had slightly different and somewhat more elastic qualifications for membership, and with no strict limit to numbers so that the keen and enthusiastic, even if tyros in the sport, could join and get help and encouragement from the more expert. Charles Edward Mathews gives a very clear account of the foundation of the Climbers' Club and it runs thus:

'The idea had, no doubt, its natural birth at Pen y Gwryd, its surroundings dear to many of us. In August and September most years, men who rarely met anywhere else, spent days together on the hills and found themselves at seven o'clock (more or less) round the well provided dinner table, dried, clothed and in their right minds.

'There as the inner man got what was due to him, and later, when warmth and tobacco had completed his contentment, the work of the day passed into a pleasant talk; the older men dropped an encouraging word to the beginners, difficult cases were discussed and suggestions made for the next day's climbing.

'In that congenial atmosphere where conventialities were not obtrusive and the bishop or the man of law shares the sofa with the old shepherd and listens to his opinions, men of various sorts, united in their deep love of the mountains, grew to know each other; there with the sense of association the germ of the Club struck the first roots'.

This short paragraph is the best summary that has ever been made of the whole epic of climbing and mountain walking and in those few phrases Mathews has shown for the benefit of all hill men and women the thoughts which gather together those who worship mountains. All who are attracted to the hills and valleys, in whatever part of the country and not only in Wales, will find it a perfect statement of fact; only a small minority will wish any words deleted for there are those who would not agree that those who climb are ever 'in their right mind'.

Those who met to discuss the possible foundation of a new club were all of British stock and so it goes without saying that for further planning a dinner had to be arranged and at that feast it was suggested that those who enjoyed the infrequent and haphazard meeting at Pen y Gwryd should bridge the long intervals between meetings by a yearly dinner in London. This suggestion met with a warm response and on May 19th 1897 about forty frequenters of the Welsh Farmhouse-Inn foregathered at the Monico Restaurant in London to recall old times. With the familiar and well-liked T.S. Halliday in the Chair, the dinner was followed by a full discussion concerning the possibility of forming a club for climbers of all grades and from all walks of life; naturally some expressed doubts about whether it could be a success, but the outcome was a marked desire that the Pen y Gwryd dinner having been started should not be dropped and arrangements were promptly made to hold one the next December.

And on December 6th this dinner was duly held. The date was not the best and quite a number of the Welsh Rabbits could not attend but there was a turn out of about thirty enthusiasts, who put the Rev J.N. Burrows in the Chair and he started the meeting. It was proposed by Roderick Williams and seconded by H.G. Gotch, both members of the Alpine Club, that a Climbing Club should be formed; then the replies sent by twenty absentee members of the Rabbits were inspected and this showed that thirteen of the twenty were in favour of such a club. When the resolution was put to the meeting it passed without a dissentient voice, Charles Edward Mathews was at once elected President and the Climbers' Club had started life. They had a President who as an eminent mountaineer, with an unsurpassed knowledge and love of mountains both in this country and on the Continent of Europe, so they could not ask for better leadership and he in turn was given full supporting committee:

Vice Presidents:	Frederick Morshead and F.H. Bowring.
Secretary:	George B. Bryant. Treasurer: Dr. T.K. Rose.
Committee:	Rev. J.N. Burrows, M.A., W.C. Slingsby, Roderick Williams, H.G. Gotch, E.R. Gotch, E.R. Kidson, E.R. Turner, Owen Glynne Jones, W.P. Haskett Smith; and also R.A. Robertson the President of the Scottish Mountaineering Club.

This exceptional committee had among its members a surprisingly large number of the most outstanding pioneers of rock climbing, and every name on it is one which is still honoured among climbers who know the history of their trade.

The Club then started to search for more members and all possibly interested men were circulated, giving them the bait that if they joined straight away there would be no entrance fee. The Committee hoped by this to get about a hundred members, but to everyone's surprise there were two hundred applications and surely that demonstrated how much the Club was needed. At the First General Meeting all applicants were admitted and all without entrance fee but for the future it was agreed that the entrance fee would be half a guinea and the annual subscription would also be half a guinea; this was quite a large amount in those days although a guinea is only 105 pence in decimal currency. This General Meeting had been held in the Monico Restaurant with the dinner in the Egyptian Room.

As might be expected there were some uncomplimentary remarks from the few about the formation of a new club when the Alpine Club was such a lively going concern. Charles Kingsley would have thought there were some who might be called snobs and they complained that climbing was being down-graded; but the objectors formed but a small minority. Mathews came in for quite a bit of chaffing, mostly of a friendly nature; his comrade Douglas Freshfield wrote to him a little rhyme:

Why is it to the Alpine Club,
Our C.E.M. no longer keeps?
Why should he found — himself as hub
A Climbers' Club for chimney sweeps!

Was there perhaps just a little bite in this? But no one could make a very serious objection as the enormous influx showed how much the Club was wanted and it demonstrated as nothing else could, the tremendous interest which was growing in climbing; moreover how many of these keen people could possibly reach the dignity of membership of the Alpine Club? In fact, of the original members of the Climbers' Club about one third were also members of the Alpine Club and throughout the years famous mountaineers have been proud to belong to both Clubs. When Mallory was President of the Climbers' Club he proposed Herbert Carr as a co-opted member and this has served the Club well for Carr's writings, particularly his guide books on climbs in the Snowdon region have helped greatly in the development of climbing in North Wales. Strangely enough it was at about this time that Pen y Gwryd descended into one of its valleys, and in fact it reached almost the lowest ebb, and it is fortunate that the Climbers' Club had already started there for that undoubtedly helped the hotel to keep going as a place of rest for mountaineers and climbers. The Owens had died and the hotel had changed hands several times in a short period, sometimes having absentee owners who left the running to managers and this failed to impart the true spirit of Pen y Gwryd. Not until the arrival of Mrs Lockwood, starting at first as Miss Florence Bloomfield and then later being helped by Arthur Lockwood, did the slow ascent start again and the hotel once again attained something of its former glory.

The earlier decline of Pen y Gwryd was aided by the fact that at this time Pen y Pass was having a blood transfusion and some enlargements and alterations there had considerably improved the accommodation. Pen y Pass was taken over first by Miss Pritchard, and quite soon afterwards by Rawson Owen and they quickly made their presence felt by providing the good food, warmth and pleasant surroundings required by those who had spent a cold wet day on the hills. It had also attracted Oscar Eckenstein sometimes known as the master of rock climbing, who did so much to develop the theory of the sport and to invent the craft to accompany his theory. Naturally this attracted many other experts including such people as J.M. Archer Thomson the headmaster of Llandudno School who with Harold Hughes made the first ascent of Twll Du; Archer Thomson was thought by some to be the most graceful and precise climber of his time. Among the others who clustered round Eckenstein were Professor Orton, the incomparable H.O. Jones, Leonard Noon, W.R. Reade, and H.V. Redhead. Last but by no means least Geoffrey Winthrop Young, who took Pen y Pass under his wing and for many years attracted gatherings of young climbers who went to hear his wise words, and for a short time during his reign this hotel could claim to be the centre of climbing in North Wales.

Those who have had the pleasure of reading his chapter in Carr & Lister's *Mountains of Snowdonia* will remember that Winthrop Young points out that there are times when the temptation of Gorffwyfsa proves irresistible. 'The highest roosting place in the Island and a luxurious one at that — where he was lodged upon the rim of space and spared twenty extra minutes road-trudging morning and evening'. What Winthrop Young in his modesty does not say is that it was in large measure his good fellowship and his expert knowledge of the mountains and of climbing which helped to bring forward the 'Pen y Pass Hotel' as a strong rival from the climbing viewpoint to Pen y Gwryd.

Rawson Owen was an excellent host but he did not act as guide for his guests as did his namesake down the road; in fact oddly enough in his inner soul he found it hard to understand why people wanted to climb mountains anyway. He had been a coachman and he remained an enthusiast for horses all his life, keeping a brake and pair at Gorffwyfsa, and this he often used to drive his visitors down the road to Tryfan or the Carnedd to save their legs before climbing. He leased the hotel from the Vaenol estate for nearly sixty years and there were but four years of the lease left to run when he retired. He was a very independent character of whom many amusing stories can be found.

But our right place is back at Pen y Gwryd and there are one or two loose ends that can be gathered up before getting to the year 1900. For example the tale of the gentleman from Cirencester who showed himself to be already an advanced conservationist and who was extremely upset when the new owners of the hotel put a large public house sign on the green outside the building for he felt that they had committed an abominable piece of vandalism and had shut out one of the most beautiful views in North Wales. He expressed the hope that everyone would enter a protest in the Visitors' Book against what he called this wanton and unnecessary piece of disfigurement. He went further, commenting that if there were any way of bringing the perpetrators to trial the verdict found in Mark Twain's *Tramp Abroad* would be appropriate: 'You will immediately remove all trace of your offensive work; you will pay a fine of 10,000 francs; you will suffer two years imprisonment with hard labour; you will be horse-whipped, tarred and feathered, deprived of your ears, ridden on a rail to the confines of the County and banished for ever'. So it appears that interest in conservation had started even seventy years ago; certainly the present owners of the hotel would agree with him in the dislike for such a sign although they and even the most staunch conservationists might think the suggested punishment slightly harsh. One cannot but wonder what punishment the man from Cirencester would have meted out to those who erected petrol pumps, and ugly ones at that, in some of the lovely Welsh valleys. He might have found it difficult to think up a sufficiently long, lingering and laborious death!

April 28th 1897 would now be thought a red letter day for the Women's Liberation Movement for on that day the Central Gully and the Western Buttress of Lliwedd were climbed for the first time by two women (Queen Victoria being still alive perhaps they should be called ladies). They were accompanied by two males Oscar Eckenstein and Ashley Abraham, but these experts remarked how good the women were and Miss Nicholls in particular not only needed no help but led the climb for more than half the way. This may be the first time that women led a pair of experienced male mountaineers up a difficult climb and so can be thought of as the start of a new era; an era in which women have shown clearly that within the limits of their physical strength this is a sport in which they are equal to men. In the past few decades have we seen something similar happening in the arena of the Horseshow. It is a pity that there is no mention of whether the women bravely climbed in skirts or if they even more bravely climbed without them; it was a bit early for the knickerbocker suit and it is not possible to tell which of the many subterfuges they adopted to get round this terrible problem.

But although women were starting on real climbing and were doing it well the sex war was not yet over, for in 1896 a note in the Locked Book says that 'Ladies using the Drawing Room should remember it is not a private sitting room and that courtesy to all who use it would remove the only drawback to Pen y Gwryd'. It is a pity that the writer lacked the courage or the courtesy to put his name to this comment, but it can only be hoped that a cease fire was soon established, and that there was no sex war about women using the Bar or Smoke Room.

One of the most fascinating entries in the Locked Book appears in 1891 and although it does not directly affect Pen y Gwryd it is much too good to leave out of circulation. Signed by G.A. Thorne, H. Hope, B.A., and S. Clerk, it concerns their adventures when they set out to climb Cader Idris. They left the local Inn after tea and with something of a struggle they reached the saddle, for they 'felt fairly knocked up having — most unwisely — commenced the ascent after a heavy day's walking and too much tea'. Having rested awhile on the saddle they courageously went on and gamely reached the top just at sunset; the date is not given but sunset must have been fairly late in the day. They quickly turned for home and almost at once the mist came down and they lost their track; fearlessly they still pressed on, even though at one stage they managed the classical feat of walking in a circle through the mist. But their resolution was sapped by this and not long afterwards they decided that it would be wiser to spend the night on the mountain, and at this point occurs one of the oddest entries in the book: 'Our only luggage consisted of a nightshirt and this garment was donned hoping to get some extra warmth'. It is not clear if each member of the party had his nightshirt or if one useful garment was circulated between the three of them;

nor is it made clear why they elected to carry a nightshirt to the mountaintop. Was it to fly as a banner from the top to celebrate their achievement, or was it taken to use as a flag of distress? Or had they maybe had the extreme optimism of finding a hotel or rest house at the top of Cader Idris, or the extreme pessimism of having to use it as a shroud for some failing member of the party. Anyway with its help they lasted the night safely, and starting back at break of day reaching their Inn by 6 o'clock the next morning. Their entry is followed by an entry from some kind friend. 'Moral: Don't cross mountains without compass and ordnance map'. Surely he should have added that if this trio were unable to read the map then they should carry instead a bedding roll, razor and toothbrush.

Over the next year or so the Locked Book entries show that some great men continued to visit Pen y Gwryd for purposes other than climbing. In 1897 it was visited by the historian G.M. Trevalyan, and in 1902 Mathews took with him Sir Oliver Lodge who was at that time the First Principal of Birmingham University; if Lodge had by then started his psychical research maybe he was in search of the ghost of Merlin or on the track of the Brocken Spectre. This was not Sir Oliver Lodge's first visit to North Wales for in 1885 he had carried on a long correspondence from there with Ruskin on the surprising subject of smoke abatement, on which they seemed to reach agreement – a pity it took fifty years before their ideas were put into practice.

The new century also brought in a new attitude to climbing techniques and in March 1900 there is an entry pointing out that when climbing in certain weather conditions the use of an ice axe was essential. It is the first time the routine use of this implement has been suggested, and it is included by Wilfred G. Mathews and C. Myles Mathews, both of Cambridge University and both bearers of a great name in mountaineering. As another indication of the advances in climbing methods is a steady stream of descriptions over the next five or six years telling of new climbs and of new methods of tackling old ones.

As a change in August 1904 there is most unusually a complete paragraph from a local newspaper pasted into the

Locked Book with graphic descriptions of the great storm which caused devastation that month. There was a lot of flood damage all round the County including, unfortunately, the destruction of the old Beddgelert bridge, a sad loss as it was attractive to look at and parts of it were thought to be Norman work. Tempest, thunder and flood are reputed to be constant concomitants of great occasions and sometimes to be indications of the birth of great men, so the author thinks it right to point out that this was his month and year of birth.

June 1908 shows the beginning of an entirely new venture when for the first time the Army was brought into touch with the 'Pen y Gwryd Hotel' officially. In recent times the Royal Air Force has become well attached in view of its Mountain Rescue Work but at no time does the Navy appear to have visited the area or to have taken to the pastime of climbing. It is quite understandable that in the days of sail, the Silent Service would not be expected to show interest in climbing as a form of relaxation for they had their own excitement in furling the royals in a gale of wind so that further climbing experience was considered unnecessary. Unless, as seems quite probable, the modern Government policy makes the return to the use of top-men essential, it seems about time that the Navy deserted masts for mountains and that Snowdonia saw something of the Navy.

But in 1908 fifteen officers from Camberley Staff College went to Pen y Gwryd on a military exercise, although what form this took is kept secret. It is interesting to see at the bottom of the list of officers the name of Captain Perceval; next year another fifteen officers arrived there from Camberley and Perceval had now reached the rank of Lieut. Colonel. In 1910 the number had risen to sixteen and the leader of the team on this occasion was Colonel Perceval, beside his name being written 'A plucky soldier who won the D.S.O., for saving the guns at Klip Drift.'

But this Army invasion of Pen y Gwryd continued until the start of the First War, and even in the first months of 1914 eleven officers turned up for training there and what they lacked in numbers they made up in glamour for this group included two officers from the Coldstream Guards and one from the Scinde Horse.

But before wartime is considered, there is another exceptional entry in the Locked Book; it is in the handwriting of Arthur Lockwood, and it enters the names of Winston Churchill, David Lloyd George and Harold Edwards. Lockwood assures readers that the original of this entry, that is to say the genuine signatures, had been taken out and pasted into another book by him, partly for security reasons and partly to prevent remarks offensive or otherwise being added. It is dated 1925 and signed A.L.; he was not the man to make such entries in fun and with his classical handwriting the authenticity of his entry can hardly be doubted.

M.W. Cuthbert in March 1910 claims to have been the first person to see the hotel all lit up with electric light. This was about the date that the Cwm Dyli Power Station would have started work, but Arthur Lockwood had been working on it for some time and one might have expected him to get it going at Pen y Gwryd a bit sooner.

W.E. Corlett had no reputation as a great climber but he was a most exceptional walker-explorer whose visits to Pen y Gwryd were innumerable and who covered an immense amount of ground every time he went there; his climbing ability may have been fairly ordinary but his power and endurance as a walker was exceptional. Take, for example his trips in January, 1891 when he firstly reached Dolwyddelan through a foot of snow and in a temperature of 17 degrees Farenheit, and from thence he climbed, often waist deep in snow, to the top of Moel Siabod, a journey most people find a hard slog even in good weather. He then descended to Bwlch Rhiw y Chain to find all the roads choked by snow, so he had to walk to the 'Pen y Pass Hotel' on the top of the wall for the snow in the road had reached that height. That day's exercise would seem enough to most people to last for a time, but the next day he went to the top of Snowdon by way of the shoulder of Lliwedd returning to Pen y Pass over Crib y Ddysgyl. Inconceivably this astonishing man went again the next day to the summit of Snowdon, this time by what was called the easy route, although how he found it easy is mysterious, for that day the postman from Llanberis, who like all country postmen was no weakling, took six hours to get from Llanberis to Pen y Pass along the road, normally about a two hour journey. One experienced local inhabitant estimated that it was the heaviest fall of snow since the Crimean War, presumably he meant in North Wales. One cannot guarantee the accuracy of this judgment but Corlett's walking at this time makes the Three Thousand tours almost insignificant.

In 1899 Corlett was still going strong for in March he made his two hundred and tenth climb of Snowdon, taking with him his two sons aged nine and eleven years and as there was quite a bit of snow on the mountain, step cutting in the ice was often needed; the next year he did the journey again with two boys aged nine years in addition to his own sons.

As the fame of Pen y Gwryd spread the number of foreign visitors increased. Just before the First War there was a spate of Americans, and these included one type unusual even for an American; Mr Steward from San Diego, California, who appeared in July 1911 claimed to have started a walk round the world in February 1910, with the intention of finishing his stroll by reaching Japan in January 1915. In some strange way this trip had something to do with an International Exposition which was being held to celebrate the opening of the Panama Canal. He affixed a small blue stamp beside his entry to confirm his story, although his walk is not really explained, nor is there any news to indicate if he finished the journey; maybe he was a precursor of Dr Kissenger — what a pity the latter has not yet visited Pen y Gwryd, and had a quick lunch while passing through.

Many will remember clearly the startling effect of the Second War in completely extinguishing travel and holidays for most of the citizens, and they would probably be surprised at the comparatively slight effect of the First War in this way. For about a year after August 1914 there are plenty of visitors signing the books, and only one small mention of the war when someone commented that the Germans had captured Antwerp. There was a slight falling off as 1915 went along, but it should be remembered that Pen y Gwryd drew many from Universities and the young men were in the Services and all too often were on the casualty list. There was at that time no conscription but the War was still in the stage when it had glamour and excitement, and still stirred the emotions of the young; the ardent young climber had just the characteristics which would make him prone to volunteer. When conscription started in 1916 no young men were left for holiday visits and moreover by then most folk had realized that those who foretold the finish of the War by Christmas 1914 might perhaps be wrong, and a long war was to be catered for. Moreover during the War the Locked Book was unused and there is a scarcity of entries between 1914 and 1918, and the only accounts quoted are in the normal Visitors' Books; Lockwood himself was quite hard at work not only with the hotel but he did a good deal of work with the local Volunteer Defence Force.

The Inn was hit with some force by the War in February 1915 when it was used by twenty Royal Engineers for an Army exercise, and the next month a staff sergeant instructor was in residence with four soldiers of the East Lancashire Regiment while later on he had a force of fifteen Royal Engineers to instruct; such invasions continued throughout the War and almost without exception the soldiers in training there found the hotel 'A.1' or even 'Sublime'.

January 1915 found Pen y Gwryd housing for a short holiday George Mallory and Mrs Mallory from Charterhouse School; probably the first visit of that very great climber.

The same year, no doubt because of war scares, the first register of aliens appeared at Pen y Gwryd in response to Government dictate and this register went on until 1953 when it ended abruptly but whether stopped by law or merely because the management forgot about it cannot be said with certainty. However, from then on the Visitors' Books reverted to the normal practice of most hotels giving merely name, address and nationality. The Locked Book continued in being but was kept very firmly under control and only the most important news such as first ascents or notes on climbs by well recognized climbers are to be found. It seems as though the ordinary man or woman was seldom allowed to see it, and apparently never allowed to write in it and this has proved a great loss to anyone looking for history, for although the book did sometimes get some rubbishy entries it also got very interesting ones; and although the ordinary Visitors' Books needed a long search the very occasional gem made this worth while.

August 1916 saw the arrival of another climber who in due course was to achieve fame in mountaineering circles. Dorothy Pilley of Denmark Hill, London, was one of the foremost of the women climbers; she married I.A. Richards who was a first class pioneer of rock climbing, and this encouraged her still further as a keen climber. Her writings about the subject under her new name of Pilley-Richards are most interesting, and known to all who read about mountaineering, her book *Climbing Days* being a well deserved favourite. Also she should be given the greatest credit for her stimulus in the formation of the Pinnacle Club, which is the ladies counterpart of something of a cross between the Alpine Club and the Climbers' Club. This Club was founded in the billiard room at Pen y Gwryd and more will be told about it later.

The next year shows some more interesting names; Gwladys Nonadh Odell of Conway stayed at the hotel with her husband Noel Ewart Odell who was temporarily stationed at the Royal Engineers Training Centre at Deganwy. Odell is a name famous in mountaineering circles but little known outside, and this is sad for he deserves much more fame than he gets. He was in the supporting camp on Everest with Mallory and Irvine, at a height of about twenty seven thousand feet, when his two colleagues tried the last lap and failed to return. Odell was in a complete quandary, and undoubtedly most men in his position would have thought of nothing else but to return to a lower camp to report and ask for help, but he stayed at the camp for another day and night, making several solo efforts to seek them out in case they needed help, although this meant climbing up and down at this great altitude without the modern oxygen equipment or any of the present day superb high altitude clothing. It was an exceptional effort that few could have matched, but he survived and at a ripe old age of over eighty, he still continued to attend meetings of the Alpine Club. In his exceptional endurance he ranks with another climber, also relatively unknown, the sailor/climber H.W. Tilman who has a remarkable reputation in both spheres of activity.

Owing maybe to the fact that it dispenses alcohol in sufficient quantities to produce cordiality and insufficient quantities to produce contention, Pen y Gwryd has rarely suffered from national strife, but given the golden opportunity of having to sign a Visitors' Book which for the first time had a column asking for the nationality of the signatory, trouble was bound to start. In September 1917 Owen Conolly marked himself in the book as being of Irish nationality, and not to be outdone John Jenkins of The Rectory, Bewdley on the same page claims Welsh nationality; evidently an early Welsh militant stung into action by an Irishman. From that time there is the occasional claim to hold some nationality, rather than to call oneself British as most are proud to do. Perhaps the wider view held by those who love mountains makes them understand the futility of a narrow nationalism; and also makes them realize that the greatness of Britain, in all fields including mountaineering has come from the mixture of the ingredient races.

It continues to be surprising how many visitors still patronize the hotel in the height of war: May and June 1915 shows a list of over forty guests in each of these months. 1916 showed a considerable drop with those two months having only twelve and twenty respectively, but in 1917 things started to pick up again and in May there were forty visitors while June produced over sixty. Even in the most gloomy time of the War in early 1918 when this country was indeed very near defeat and when the well-known Douglas Haig 'Backs to the Wall' appeal shook the country, Pen y Gwryd was far from empty of holiday makers. One of these holiday makers was someone who was then well-known but who is now seldom heard about — Israel Zangwill who stayed there with his wife Edith; in the first years of this century he was a well-known writer of poems and he was particularly recognized for writing tales and tragedies of the Jewish people.

The marked fall off in the number of young people going to Pen y Gwryd during and immediately after the war is understandable as all the able-bodied were serving their country, but the build up by the youth when the War had finished was disappointingly slow. In part this was due to the appalling casualty lists, for so many never returned from the War, and many more died in the horrifying influenza epidemic of 1918. Despite the somewhat hollow gaiety of the twenties it was a decade before the young men, particularly the undergraduates who used to swarm into the mountains, found time, leisure and money to get back to holidays in North Wales. Probably more students at Universities were from homes slightly less comfortably off financially, and in those days work and examination results still played an important part in the students thoughts. Then followed the great slump of the 1930s and as the country slowly recovered from that there followed improved foreign travel facilities which made trips abroad easier, cheaper and more fashionable. The less well-off student often found it possible to afford journeys to the Alps or the Dolomites which previously had been thought the province of the comparatively well-to-do, and it may be that Switzerland and Austria gained what North Wales was losing.

March 1928 another celebrity arrived at the hotel; Sir Ernest Rutherford who was still holding the Chair of Physics at Cambridge arrived with his wife; he had only the previous year gained the highest honour in the country, the Order of Merit.

The year 1921 can claim to be Women's Year for in March a selection of women who were interested in climbing met in the billiard room at Pen y Gwryd, the meeting being under the Chairmanship of Mrs Emily (Pat) Kelly. The first matter under consideration was the complaint that although women often climbed with members of the opposite sex and there was no shortage of women who could climb on equal terms with even expert male climbers, except for one or two provincial clubs, women were denied entry into many of the main climbing clubs. It was at once proposed and agreed that a climbing club for women only should be formed, and so the Pinnacle Club came into being; from then onwards this Club has grown steadily in strength and is a lively and active organization. A reasonably good standard of climbing is insisted on for those wishing to join, and all applicants have to pass certain tests.

The first President was Mrs Eleanor Winthrop Young (née Eleanor Slingsby) who also acted at Treasurer; Mrs Pat Kelly was appointed secretary, and Mrs B. Eden-Smith was made recording secretary. Mrs A. (Paddy) Wells (later Mrs John Hirst) was appointed librarian. The rest of the Committee consisted of Miss B.L. Michaelson, Miss Dorothy Pilley, Mrs Ormiston-Chant, Miss K. Ward and Miss A. Wells. The

Pinnacle Club started life with twenty full members and twenty three associate members.

Very sadly Emily Kelly was killed the following year when a rock became dislodged while she was climbing Tryfan; in 1932 when the Pinnacle Club opened their own hut in Cwm Dyli it was named after her.

She was followed as secretary by Miss A. (Paddy) Wells and in the same year Dr C.L. (Katie) Corbett became treasurer. The next President was Miss Paddy Wells who by that time had turned into Mrs Hirst.

The Miss Wells are somewhat difficult to sort out as they all seemed to have pseudonyms and the mixture of Paddy, Biddy and Trilby is not easy to fathom. However, it seems fairly certain that it was Trilby and Biddy Wells in company with Lilian Bray who were in 1926 the first women without male escort to traverse the Cuillin Ridge in Skye. For those who are not well acquainted with the mountains it should be pointed out that the Cuillin Ridge is a very different proposition from say the Snowdon Horseshoe; the latter can be easily accomplished by the tourist scrambler, but the Cuillin Ridge has in its circuit some very exposed and often rather fearsome climbing and is for the expert only.

Perhaps the various Women's Movements could notice that the introduction of women into a history book such as this does lead to complications in nomenclature. This is not, as they might claim, merely because of the change from Miss to Mrs, or even to the change from the single to the married surname; but an almost greater problem lies in the fact that so many of them prefer to be called by Christian names other than those given them at their baptism, and this, particularly in the case of two or three sisters, causes chaos and confusion. May this practice please be stopped!

Regretfully the ladies of the Pinnacle Club did not get into the good habit of having their Annual Dinner regularly at Pen y Gwryd; a surprising and inexcusable oversight! It was not until 1953 when they were under the Chairmanship of Mrs Nea Morin that for the very first time the Dinner was held at the place of their birth. From then on the Dinner has been held every alternate year at Pen y Gwryd; and, of course the Annual Meeting is always held there.

Several other members of the Pinnacle Club in addition to Mrs Pilley Richards have gone into print; Josephine Scarr in *Four Miles High* gives an extremely good account of the Club's Himalayan Expedition, and Nea Morin has written an excellent book on women and climbing entitled *A Woman's Reach*.

The future of the Pinnacle Club will be interesting to watch; it was founded in the first instance to bring together women who were interested in climbing and to foster the further development of this sport among women and it has done outstanding work in this. It is not easy to know what was in the minds of those who started the Club, but the impression seems to be that they were not in favour of segregation and had the men's clubs been willing to take women members this arrangement would have been entirely satisfactory. There may soon be the chance to know if this is a true picture for in view of recent legislation who can tell whether the Ladies' Alpine Club and the Pinnacle Club and the Alpine Club and Climbers' Club will be allowed to continue for one sex only, for it may be that all will have to admit both men and women; in this age when our rulers think that personal freedom can be achieved only by legal rigidity who can tell? It seems rather sad that if men wish to gather together and women wish to gather together for certain sports that the law cannot be made sufficiently elastic to allow this to happen.

There seems to have been an increase in the popular interest in climbing and mountaineering in recent years: exploits in the Himalayas and in other far flung places have caught the imagination of many and they have been fully written up in the daily press, so that climbs in Snowdonia appear tame in comparison although accidents in mountains still attract plenty of Press comment and when television is brought in it attracts many viewers.

But for a century before the Himalayan adventures only those particularly interested in mountaineering had the chance to read anything much about this sport. It needed a real catastrophe such as that on the Matterhorn, or an outstanding book such as Whymper's *Scrambles in the Alps* to reach the ordinary reader, but of course from its earliest days the *Climbers' Club Journal* used to detail many climbing adventures; but with regard to the sort of climbing found in North Wales the most important change has been the large and steady increase in the number of people getting keen on rock climbing and the striking change in the techniques involved. This has meant the issue of far more very precise guides giving the fullest possible descriptions of every step of the climb and the increasing demand for these guides has made them worth publishing. All those who pioneer new climbs or mark out new routes up old ones, prefer to see these printed in the official guides and this may be one of the reasons why in the post-war period there has been some falling off of the number of descriptions of climbs and other expeditions to be found in the Locked Book for no longer is its circulation big enough to spread the news throughout the climbing world. Another factor has been that it is not always possible to have someone in readiness to make sure that the book is available for those who want it, and to make sure they will put in only things that are worthy of entry.

This last thirty years saw the beginning of the slow change in the kind of visitors staying at Pen y Gwryd. In line with the increased interest in rock climbing there was a very considerable increase in the number of climbing huts available for the young to stay in, and this combined with the steadily mounting cost of hotel accommodation meant that there were fewer of the young climbers in residence at Pen y Gwryd. They still frequented the hotel for meals and for drinks at the bar, but the Locked Book was not automatically put under their noses as soon as they turned up just in case they wanted to write in it.

An examination of the figures gives some surprising results; in 1919 there was only one entry, there were none at all in 1920; two short ones in 1921, one in 1922, one in 1925, and then no entry at all until 1931. Strangely enough the falling off is in essays about climbing and that at a time when the increase in this sport was greater than ever before.

However, in 1933 several pages of the Locked Book are taken up by newspaper cuttings concerning the tragic accident in Switzerland when four masters from Eton College were killed when trying to climb Piz Roseg; they were named Howson, Slater, Powell and White and in addition to the daily papers there are pasted in the book the full 'In Memoriam' notices from the Eton College Chronicle and a picture of the mountain area where they died. Needless to say they were all climbing graduates of Pen y Gwryd. This is also true of Robertson Lamb whose death is recorded in the book at much the same time; he had climbed everywhere and was a member of almost every climbing club including the British Alpine and the Swiss Alpine Clubs.

But fortunately in 1935 the Locked Book suddenly started to come to life again; firstly with a signature and newspaper paragraph of Gladys Young, a stage star now perhaps rather forgotten but one who was well-known throughout the War and beyond for the parts she played, many of them with the B.B.C. Repertory Company.

Then it was the beginning of real keenness in the Trial of the Three Thousands for which there is a separate description in this book. This improvement in the Locked Book continued and the matters written in it certainly became more varied and hence to the non-climber more interesting.

In 1948 there is the Horseshoe Walk by Oswald Cox celebrating his eightieth birthday already mentioned, and the first entry signed by Chris Briggs as the new owner. This is a sad story for it tells of the accident and death of Paul Hermansson an experienced climber who had haunted Pen y Gwryd for over twenty years; but he slipped and fell to his death while on a solo walk on Lliwedd. His wife most kindly presented Pen y Gwryd with his very good collection of climbing books.

The 1950s the more recent acquisitions to the climbing circle started to visit Pen y Gwryd and join with the old stagers who, even if no longer climbing could not stay away. These newcomers included many names which became well-known for their feats in the mountaineering fields; names such as A.J.J. Moulam, John Disley, A.W.J. Piggott and Chris Brasher among others. Mowlem records having completed the Snowdon Horseshoe from Pen y Pass and back again in the very good time of 2 hours 22 minutes on a troublesome windy day; he claims no record for this and in any case he had no observers to watch him, but his accuracy would not be doubted and the time of 44 minutes from Pen y Pass to the top of Crib

Goch is very good going, and so is 42 minutes from the summit of Crib Goch to the summit of Y Wyddfa. In fact despite what has just been said about the change in Locked Book entries the year 1950 does show the inclusion of some new climbs. Disley and Mowlem claim a new ascent of the Ribstone Crack on Carreg Wasted and of the Inaccessible Boulder on Dinas Mot, while Mowlem with Piggott and others list several new adventures some being given fascinating names such as Shadrach, and the Custodians Creep on Pen yr Ole Wen and revolting ones such as Terror Infirmer.

A description is given in an earlier chapter of the celebration dinner given in honour of the successful Kanchengunga team. The full list of those present is in the Appendix, but extra mention may be made of two or three names; Charles Evans was at that time still working as a neuro-surgeon, but fairly soon afterwards he gave up surgical work and he was appointed Principal of University College of North Wales at Bangor a post he has held with distinction ever since. His contribution to Wales was recognized by the bestowal of a knighthood. Another worthy name is that of H.R.A. Streather, who has recently led the successful Army team on Everest; no one could ask for a better leader for such an expedition. The list also includes Joe Brown, once a plumber from Manchester, but now known as the greatest British rock climber of his age and who now owns the flourishing shops for climbing gear in Llanberis and Capel Curig.

With the rapid change of subject for which the Locked Book is well-known the next page tells of the case of R. Ingleby a Cambridge student who while investigating a rock fall at the foot of Dinas Mot on the Llanberis Pass found a large bronze axe head; he gives a diagram of his find, and included is a letter from the Royal Commission on Ancient Monuments in Wales and Monmouthshire, showing their interest in this find; they ask for the address of the finder as they wish to make an accurate record of this discovery but there is no further mention of the axe head and its later fate is still unknown.

The remarkable achievements of Eric Beard are given in the list of the Three Thousands, but it is told in the Locked Book that in October 1961 he went round the Snowdon Horseshoe from Pen y Pass and back again in a time of 1 hour 41 minutes;

again there are no checks and this cannot claim to be an official record, but his reliability has always been unquestioned and there is no reason to doubt his claim which fits so well with his other records, and in this case it can only be called phenomenal!

On September 21st 1962 there died Rawson Owen, owner of the 'Pen y Pass Hotel' for nearly sixty years and he was buried at Dolwyddelan. He had innumerable friends among the climbing fraternity and they grieved at the loss. On his death, for a very short time the hotel was run by a manager but then it was sold to the Youth Hostels Association. It has been greatly enlarged and now provides a lot of excellent accommodation for members of that Association who wish to walk and climb in the hills of Snowdonia.

One whole page of the Locked Book in June 1963 is rightly given up to the signature of the Great Tenzing, written both in English and in his native language: he was at the time staying at Pen y Gwryd for the tenth anniversary of the conquest of Everest.

At the end of August 1968 many of the hotel's guests were disturbed from their sleep by bursts of prolonged gunfire; many thought that war with the Welsh had broken out at last, but it proved to be merely the Briggs celebrating the twenty-first year of their having taken of Pen y Gwryd or rather someone celebrating it for them. The actual noise was caused by Lord Newborough and his family who, wishing to help their friends the Briggs to celebrate in style, had dragged their own cannon from the borders of Anglesea and were engaged in firing a twenty-one gun salute. Oddly enough within a few days of writing this note Lord Newborough has been getting into trouble about this cannon as some of his excitable guests at his house had just missed a passing yacht while firing it out to sea!

The Lord Hailsham Horseshoe walk in 1972 has already been detailed in an earlier chapter, but in October that year there was an unusually immense meeting even by Pen y Gwryd standards, and the Locked Book shows twenty-four unusual signatures. These include Price Thomas the Secretary of State for Wales at that time, Geronwy Roberts, the Member of Parliament for Caernarfonshire, representatives of the Welsh

Office, and of the Girl Guides, the Young Farmers' Club, Snowdonia National Park, the Royal Air Force Valley Mountain Rescue Team and others from a large variety of Clubs concerned. This meeting, which included a buffet lunch, had been called at the request of the Prime Minister Edward Heath, who was anxious to collect together a large number of the young people who were involved in all the many aspects of life in North Wales. Unfortunately at the last moment the Prime Minister was unable to attend, no doubt having trouble with his right wing or his left wing or the zealously wagging tail, and so his place was taken by Price Thomas, the Secretary of State for Wales.

The entries of Major Haro Ahluwalia and the details about his friend Harsh Bahuguna are dealt with elsewhere, but November 1872 is the date of Ahluwalia's signature in the Locked Book.

June 15th 1973 gives an entry of the death in a nursing home at Llanwrst of Major Arthur Lockwood; another occasion of great regret among the older climbers who knew him so well.

The last entry is suitably enough that of the twentieth anniversary of the successful ascent of Everest when many of the team were at a Pen y Gwryd dinner party in their honour.

This seems to bring to an end, at least for the time being the interesting or exciting extracts from the Locked Book; but it has now been returned to its home largely for the purpose of entering a very important event — the birth to Jane Briggs of a son to be named Rupert. So there is now a chance that the 'Pen y Gwryd Hotel' may for many years continue to be held by a member of the family Briggs, and may it long continue to flourish.

APPENDICES

The following appendices are almost all extracts from the Visitors' Books of the 'Pen y Gwryd Hotel', and by far the largest number come from the famous Locked Book, which has now reached the venerable age of ninety two years and which everyone hopes will in due course celebrate its century and then be given an honorable retirement in some suitable surroundings.

Appendix 1 Comprises a selection of the innumerable verses which the guests at Pen y Gwryd have disgorged over the years. An effort has been made to include most of the better poems, and to scatter in a few of the poorer ones. Any reader who might be interested could find many worse verses, suitable for inclusion in an anthology of the worst poetry in the world.

Appendix 2 Shows copies of a few of the many drawings to be found in the Visitors' Books. There are quite a number of good ones which are not included here, largely because of difficulty of transfer, and on the whole the standard of art is higher than that of poetry.

Appendix 3 Lists of plants, birds, animals and insects compiled by several of the guests at different times.

Appendix 4 The list of signatures on the ceiling of the Everest Room.

Appendix 5 Food and drink plays such a large part in any hotel that very little reference to detailed menus is possible: but the following two specimens, separated by three hundred and fifty years, and included here as being rather exceptional cases.

Appendix 6 Copy of a letter from the National Park Officer for Snowdonia giving his ideas on the origin of the many cairns put up on footpaths in the region.

APPENDIX I

JULY 1874
Been up Snowdon,
Nice ascent;
William Boden,
Burton on Trent.

T.W.C.
To wander through each dark recess
Where Snowdon stands in glory
To make the Glyders rift rocks tell
Their old volcanic story
To walk where few have dared to walk
And ride where very few ride
This is the way to use the hours
You spend at Pen y Gwryd.

And be well tired at eventide
With all your lungs inflated
With store of body's health and heart
In thankfulness elated
Home through the glowing sunset stream
To wander well assured
The happiest dinner of your life
Waits you at Pen y Gwryd.

The health to Harry Owen's face
Kind, brave and honest looking
And health to Mrs Pritchard's art
Her pleasant art of cooking.
And health to all who fear no harm
Mid rocks and chasms lurid
None but the brave deserve the fare
They get at Pen y Gwryd.

A.W. MOORE, SECRETARY OF ALPINE CLUB, May 1883

O'er Siabod's boggy height
Cheerful we came last night
With plan today tall Snowdon's peak to scale
But when this morning broke
The mists hung round like smoke
So here we stayed and penned this woeful wail.

REMINISCENCES

1856 Charles Kingsley, Tom Hughes and Tom Taylor

TT I came to Pen y Gwryd with colours armed and pencils
But found no use whatever for any such utensils
So in default of them I took to using knives and forks
And made successful drawings — of Mrs Owen's corks.

CK I came to Pen y Gwryd with frantic hopes of slaying
Grilse, salmon 3 lb red fleshed trout, and what else there's no saying
But bitter cold and lashing rain and black nor'eastern skies, sir
Drove men from fish to botany, a sadder man and wiser.

TH I came to Pen y Gwryd a larking with my betters
A mad wag and a mad poet, both of them men of letters,
Which two ungrateful parties, after all the care I've took
Of them, made me write verses in Harry Owen's book.

TT We've been mist-soaked on Snowdon, mist-soaked on Glyder Fawr,
We've been wet through on average every day three times an hour,
We've walked the upper leather from the sole of our balmorals
And as sketchers and as fishers with the weather had our quarrels.

CK But think just of the plants which stuff'd our box — (Old Yarrels gift) —

And of those who might have stuff'd it, if the clouds had given a lift
Of tramping bogs, and climbing cliffs, and shoving down stone fences
For spiderwort, saussurea and woodsia ilvensis.

TH Oh, my dear namesake's breeches, you never see the like,
He burst them all so frightful a'crossing of a dyke
But Mrs Owen patched them as carefully as mother
With flannel of three colours – she hadn't got no other.

TT But can we say enough of those legs of mountain muttons
And that onion sauce lies in our souls, for it made of us three gluttons
And the Dublin stout is genuine, and so's the Burton beer
And the apple tarts they've won our hearts, and think of soufflets here.

CK Resembling that old woman that never could be quiet,
Though victuals (says the child's song) and drink formed all their diet.
My love for plants and scrambling shared empire with my dinner
And who says it wasn't good must be a most fastidious sinner.

TH Now all I've got to say is, you can't be better treated,
Order pancakes and you'll find they're the best you'd ever eated.
If you scramble o'er the mountains you should bring an ordnance map
I endorse all as previous gen't have said about the tap.

TT Pen y Gwryd, when wet and worn, has kept a warm fireside for us,
Sock, boots and never-mention-'ems, Mrs Owen has dried for us;
With host and hostess, fare and bill, so pleased we are, that, going,
We feel, for all their kindness, 'tis we, not they, are 'Owen'.

TH Nos tres in uno juncti hos fesimus versiculos
TT Tomas piscator pisces qui non cepi sed pisciculos
CK Tomas sciagraphus qui non feci ridiculos
Herbarius Carolus montes qui lustravi operpendiculos.

TH There's big trout, I hear, in Edno, likewise in Gwynent lake
The governor and black alder are the flies that they will take.
Also the cockabundy, but I can only say
If you think to catch big fishes, I only hope you may.

TT I have come in for more of mountain gloom than mountain glory
But I've seen old Snowdon rear his head with storm-tossed mist wreaths hoary
I stood in the fight of mountain winds upon Bwlch-Cwm-y-llan
And I go back, an unsketching, but a better-minded man.

CK And I too have another debt to pay another way
For kindness shown to those good souls to one whose far away
Even to this old collie dog, who tracked the mountains o'er.
For one who seeks strange birds and flowers on far Australia's shore.

The first poem written in the Locked Book. By Hibbert Newton D.D. Vicar of St Michael's, Southwark.
Date August 5th 1885.

SNOWDONIA PERSONIFIED

Snowdonia! I sit down to write of thee,
Personified into that sort of shrew
Such as in very life we sometimes see.
Spiteful, but giving promise at first view,
To make one happy, as a man could be
Who weds her, and so weds for faithful true,

But wedded once, he finds that they unite,
To make a day of promise, black as night.

Snowdonia! What thou art I now discern,
I'll come again, when I would patience learn —
You gave me yesterday a hopeful sign —
When we were at a distance, thou went clear,
And cloudless in they aspects every line.
Like some acquaintance, ere they draw near,
Fancy that nought but goodness they discover,
I know thee better, now that I am here
So leave thee to select some other lover.

But I must say, while seated in my chair,
Not thinking of the outside of this Inn,
If fair landlady makes a lady fair,
I will admire her for what's here within.
Fair in her charges, fair for what she'll give,
At table, and, when raining, a good fire,
So join with me my friends, long may she live
For visits for both sexes to admire.

The sun went down, but still the sight
Was wonderful in strength and might;
The shades of night came rolling on,
And clouds of every shape and form.

The moon shone out her gentle ray,
As if she now would guide our way;
Adown the hilly steep descent,
And watch us all the way we went.

The stars came twinkling one by one;
They seemed like lamps of silver hung;
The gentle summer lightning flashed
And showed us where the water dashed.

Our ponies sure and firm of foot
I think of all our joy partook,

And stopped to gaze that we might view
   And praises of the night renew.

The night say we, no rather He
   Who formed these things that we might see,
And learn from all his creatures beauty
   Lessons of faith, of hope and duty.

Of faith for surely He who stood
   And formed these things for mankind's good
Is worthy of belief and fear
   Of love and lifelong service here.

With apologies to Longfellow

Pen y Gwryd, Pen y Gwryd
   High away among the mountains
High away in breezy cloudland
   Haunted by all changeful shadows
When the summer sunsets linger
   Opalescent on the Glyders
Bathing all their crags in glory
   Making earth one great sky portal;
Or the wild of rushing storm wind
   Howling in the wilderness;
O'er the cold gray stones of Snowdon
   Sweeps across to Pen y Gwryd
Sweeps across the reeking moorland
   Pipes away to Capel Curig,
Riots o'er the seething waters
   Trumpeting in hidden passes
Lost in crag and aloud and distance.

For it is from haunts of tourists
   Trim kept, clad in gorgeous garments;
Borne in cars across the mountains
   Loving coffee rooms and waiters
Lisping lazily of comfort,
   Babbling beerily of barmaids;

"Doing Snowdon" "Doing Cader"
   Hurrying home to desk and court
Ignorant of one emotion,
   Raising hearts from mountains skywards.

Date July 11th 1860

Old Jove one day from Snowdon's lofty brow
   Surveyed the world and kingdoms far below;
And some queer fancy mounted to his brain
   To taste the liquors mortals like to drain;
"Ho! Ganymede" he cried "go fetch me here
All mortals' tipples cider, porter, beer,
   Champagne and sherry, brandy everything
That's brewed on earth" so spake the immortal King;
   The page who waited on his every nod
At once flew off, obedient to the God;
   And soon around the throne in order places
The various tipples of all mortal races.
   The Thunderer tastes, but with an ugly face
Puts back each bottle in its place;
   Till suddenly, all wreathed in smiles, he cries,
While glee unfeigned dances in his eyes:
   "Ho! what is this, can mortals e'er have made
So sweet a draught without immortal aid;
   Whence doth it come?" "Why, sire as I'm a sinner
Tis what Hal Owen gives his guests for dinner.
   Tis Pen y Gwryd porter, I declare."
Jove heard and shaking his ambrosial hair,
   Pronounced it nectar of the finest brew,
And if you try it, stranger, so will you.

Undated and unsigned

He who Snowdon would ascend
   Should have with him a cheerful friend;
A Knapsack filled with bread and cheese
   Cold chicken, brandy if you please;

Or better still with Irish Whisky
That makes your inside warm and frisky.
If on the road you meet a friend
A drop of comfort to him lend;
Or if a lady cross your path
Go on your knees, take off your hat
Lay your hand upon your heart
Say you're transfixed by Cupid's dart
And that you'll love her all your life
If she becomes your darling wife.

April 1868 By J.S.B.

In coming again to a hotel like this
What thorough enjoyment one feels;
Like horses of postboy so gleeful to miss,
The lumb'ring of everyday wheels.

What joy to get rid of the smoky old town
With its harassing worry and care;
Its little men's fawning, its bigger men's frown,
Its hollowness, tinsel and glare.

What joy once again to have quiet and ease,
To leave all committee behind;
To inhale at one's pleasure the pure country breeze,
And the countrymen's appetite find.

With many such musing did 'father and me'
Our Cambrian journey beguile,
As we rambled o'er Snowdon so fresh and so free,
And chatted full many a mile.

August 1873 Extract of a poem by J.A.G. entitled A week at Pen y Gwryd

I will not occupy my time
And all too soon exhaust my rime,

By singing Mrs Owen's praise
So often sung in better days;
Of which, Oh guest at Pen y Gwryd
You must ere this be quite assured;
If you the merest glance bestowed
The offerings at the foot of Snowdon
My tale will therefore only be
Of what we did at PYG.

Tryfan
Well, first we scaled the rocky Tryfan
And found the scale a very stiffun.
We went straight up the S.E. Face,
Surmounting many an awkward place;
We clambered up a torrent cliff,
And found the peak was on our left.

Lliwedd Crags
I'll next proceed to trouble you with
Our grand attempt to get up Lliwedd
Twice we essayed and twice in vain,
So carefully slunk down again;
We spent the best part of the day
In going a quarter of the way.
I've never tried before I wist
To climb so shere a precipice.
But loth to be undone by him, we
Finally got up a chimney.

There is another equally bad and longer poem called 'Face of Snowdon from Glaslyn'.

August 1877 Rev I.F. Trent. Poem based on Psalm 121

To Snowdon's cloud I lift mine eyes
And long to see it scatter
To Snowdon's God my heart shall rise
No earthly cares shall matter.

Here in that hospitable Inn,
Secure have I been sleeping
With heavenly guards that never sin,
There watch around me keeping.

Soon up old Snowdon's rugged side,
I'll climb and never stumble
Through mist and storm my steps He'll guide
Though thunders roar and grumble.

By lonely tarn and dreary fell,
By moor and rock and river,
He watching over Israel
Will keep me safe for ever.

September 1878 Fred E. Weatherley*

You may hunt all England over
From Liverpool to Dover.
From Cumberland to Cornwall for a place wherein to dwell.
You may try the British diggings
of voracious Mrs Wiggins,
Or each London Super-Mare 'Starve and Swindle you' Hotel,
You may pitch in Nant y Gwynant
Or on Tryfan as a tenant
Or bask in sunny Bettws for many summer hours.
You may stop your jaunt or jog when
You come to Idwal or to Ogwen
Or test the Devil's Kitchen and its cool and airy Culinary
powers.

You may woo these witching wodders
The stony hearted Glyders,
Or the maids of sweet Llangollen, Dolgelly or Criccieth
Or the village fair but foggy
Where the dim mysterious doggy
Extracts the tourists coppers with his legendary teeth.

*Fred Weatherley was famous as the verse writer of many of the best known songs of the Victorian era.

Try Dolwyddelen that's so handy
For the painter's pet Mill Pandy.
Try the cockney Capel Curig or Llanberis as you may,
But of this I am assured
When you've pitched in Pen y Gwryd
You'll make your mind up quickly not to sojourn but to stay,
So here's to Harry Owen
(Be the weather fair or blowin)
And to all his honest kinsfolk long life and pleasant days
As we tramp life's rugged road on
To a grander greater Snowdon.
May we find such hearts to greet us and help us on our ways.

July 1888 J. Burgess, Sheffield

Oh weary of smoke and bad air
And weary of sorrow and strife,
And tired of the noise and the bustle and care
Of the city's unnatural life
I sighed for a few days to spend
Where natural beauty prevails,
And so to accomplish my end
I came 'mong the mountains of Wales.

Oh mountains so high and so grand
Down valleys so peaceful and fair
Delighted I rove o'er the land
Inhaling the life giving air.
And when the day draws to a close,
To finish up pleasant and well,
I seek for an evening's repose
At the Pen y Gwryd Hotel.
And get it!

September 1880 Pastor Westmonasteriemsis

Oh joyless haunts of over-busy man,
Where Westminster spreads all her crowded ways;
And din and vice and clamour mar the days,
Must I so soon go back with you again?

So soon be where the horrid curse of sin
   Festers around the feet of my sweet spire;
And to dejected hearts the full voiced choir
   Chants of the joys they scarce can win.

Let me yet drink the mountain breeze once more,
   Hear but once more the music of the burn,
Breathe thy fresh breath delicious mountain fern,
   Climb the rough rocks and hear the torrent roar.

And when by grim bedside or noisy street,
   In coming months I plod on sober round;
Oft from these hills shall many a merry sound,
   Me, unforgetful of their glories, greet.

And once again in fancy shall I stand
   High on Y Wyddfa glancing far and wide;
Or from the awful Glyders storm-rent side
   Look out upon the wonders of the land.

And oft in fancy up the valley road,
   To see good faces and grasp friendly hands;
Lingering around the happy spot where stands
   An honest landlord's hospitable Inn.

Continuation of Glyders — inserted in book, page 9

All is seen in sated wrath
   Above, around, below
As though the fiat had gone forth
   Unutterable woe.

Oh scenes so beautiful and sad,
   So broken and so great,
The likeness of a mind that's sad
   A heart that's desolate.

Now heaven's sweet light on all is shed,
   New scenes new glory yield

Eternal future seems outspread
And boundless bliss revealed.

The rock that's ringed with golden light,
The rivulet and rill;
The mountain on his daring height
The bloom upon the hill.

The deep hued lake, the distant sea
Outstretching into space,
E'en yonder solitary tree
That bends with courtly grace.

They all awake and far and wide
The prospect spreads sublime;
Till heaven from earth no more divides
The boundaries of time.

By P.J. Mavkisson

Three fishers went fishing down Gwynants fair vale,
Down Gwynants fair vale when the rain fell fast;
Each thought every fish that he rose was a whale
And between them they bagged a few ounces at last.
For men must catch and women must cook,
Though muddy the water and brittle the hook;
And the rain be unceasingly falling.

Three climbers went climbing the Glyders so high,
The Glyders so high when the mist hung dense;
Each murmured as nightfall grew rapidly nigh.
If I'd stopped down below I'd have shown more sense
For men must tear and women must mend
You don't study your clothes when you haste to descend,
And the rain is unceasingly falling.

Three travellers started the morrow's morn,
The morrow's morn, finer weather to seek;
Their pockets were empty their hearts were forlorn
They hadn't a spark of their usual cheek;

They said while preparing the start for the sea
   So good-bye to the rain that's still falling.

Things I found during my stay 1884 by S.E.C.

P lates, spoons, forks, tablecloths and beds unsoiled,
E ggs always fresh but always overboiled,
N o mutton chops but only lumps of leather,
Y ouths quite renewed by trampling bogs and heather,
G uests so gay so kind a lonely heart to cheer,
W aitresses so obliging but attendance dear;
R oast saddles charming, puddings quite a treat,
Y et butter often times too salt to eat.
D ried clothes each day in spite of daily wet,
H ostess Mrs Owen the best you ever met,
O atmeal made into cakes exceeding nice
T eetotal drinks a trifle high in price.
E ach boot or trouser torn, repaired with skill,
L ast but not least of all — a little bill.

August 18th 1885

I came in 1883
   But t'was not half enough for me;
Again returned in '84
   But still I hankered after more.
On August 1885
   And more to keep the game alive,
I ventured back and here I am
   A sadder and a wiser man.

For since last night at half past five
   The grim Crib Goch we fought and strived
To reach the haven of Y Wyddfa
   Where people can have bed and board
Six and sixpence all included
   A moderate sum but still I rued it.
For nought can half repay the scamper
   Nor solace give for Snowdon's night air.

So pregnant with much pain rheumatic
   Which came from climbing to sky's attic
If shades of evening have but passed
   Or worse than all thick mists have marred,
This was our lot last night to try
   My friend from Birmingham and I,
And now we've been and gone and done it
   We are condemned to write this sonnet.

May 1887 W.H.S.

When many folk would go a-Mayin,
   This is the very place to stay in,
The view's so grand the cooks so knowing
   There's nothing but my host is Owen.

So when you've caught and eat your trout
   And when your pleasant times run out,
You begin to think at last of going,
   You like to find that much is owing.

So there's a saw, no need repeat it
   Which speaks of cake, and then of eat it;
For feeding, climbing, fishing, rowing
   When Owen's paid, out thanks are owing.

May 1892 Arundel Begbie

The best of friend must part alas
   So we must now be going,
But e'er we leave a word with you
   My hostess Mrs Owen.

When sol came scorching on our backs
   When chilly blasts were blowing
We tramped o'er your mountain trail,
   My hostess Mrs Owen.

It's hailed, it's sleeted and it's rained
And just stopped short of snowing,
But what of that, our fun we've gained
My hostess, Mrs Owen.

By earliest dawn I've left your roof,
When cocks commence their crowing
To catch a few small scraggy trout
My hostess, Mrs Owen.

And just at dusk we ventured back
When cows begin their lowing,
But dawn or dusk are just the same
My hostess Mrs Owen.

For be it early, be it late,
Or e'en t'wards midnight growing
We've always found a welcome here
My hostess Mrs Owen.

Farewell, perhaps we'll meet again
There really is no knowing;
For my part I shall hail the day
My hostess Mrs Owen.

Your hearty hospitality
Set all our hearts a glowing
For all your kindness our best thanks
My hostess Mrs Owen.

And if again this way I come
Be sure there is no inn
At which I'll stop except this place
My hostess Mrs Owen.

I hope when we have turned our backs
You will not call our going
Pen y Gwryd's rid of rubbish
My hostess Mrs Owen.

W.J.R.

There was a young man of the mountains,
Who thought Snowdon famous for fountains,
But when he was high
He found it quite dry,
That mistaken young man of the mountains.

William Brinkton July 1897

In the days of Mrs Owen
Whom I've not the joy of knowing
God rest her soul for all that.
There was talk of ale and porter,
But no mention made of water,
Which is plentiful enough for all that.

There was talk of mountaineering
And the homely welcome cheering,
As round the kitchen chimney piece they sat.
There was talks o rocks and botany
And views when they had got any,
Which wasn't very frequently that's flat.

Then they scribbled little 'pomelette',
In praise of cookies omelettes,
And declared that muffins came so pat;
And their talk about the fishing
Sets the dainty palate wishing
For a dish of trout for breakfast or a sprat.

Oh and loud were their laudations
At the Pen y Gwryd rations
And they'd sign their noble names and all that
For a lenient inquisitor
Was every single visitor
Who came to Mrs Owen's to grow fat.

Now all you hungry mortals
  Who enter in these portals
And mind you wipe your boots upon the mat;
  Shed a tear for Mrs Owen
  And don't hurry now in going
But stay and read my verses and all that.

For give thanks to Mrs Brooks
  And some credit to the cooks
And to the fair Miss Slakes remove your hat;
  And be one and all assured
  The hotel of Pen y Gwryd
Is as good a house as ever for all that.

April 1950 D.H.K.

We have an idea that the parson's nose,
  Is rather more streamlined than some suppose;
And thus in his pages of breathless prose
  Abraham speaks of a pleasing scramble
Ladies indeed have survived this ramble;
  But do not forget that the ceaseless tramples
Of boots, not to mention the verbal ferocity
  Accompanying descents of alarming velocity
Have somewhat reduced the good cleric's rugosity.

APPENDIX 2

THE TOURISTS

E. V. FREEMAN
1875

ONLY THREE MINUTES MORE, & WE ARE THERE!!

G.H. TWIGG

DEC:19th 1903

C

AUG. 16th 1878

1

SUNSHINE THE START TEMP. 53°

2

SORROW LUNCH TEMP. 47°

3

GRIEF TEMP. 44°
MIST, RAIN PLUS

4

KINDNESS TEMP. 90°

AN ORIGINAL METHOD OF CLIMBING

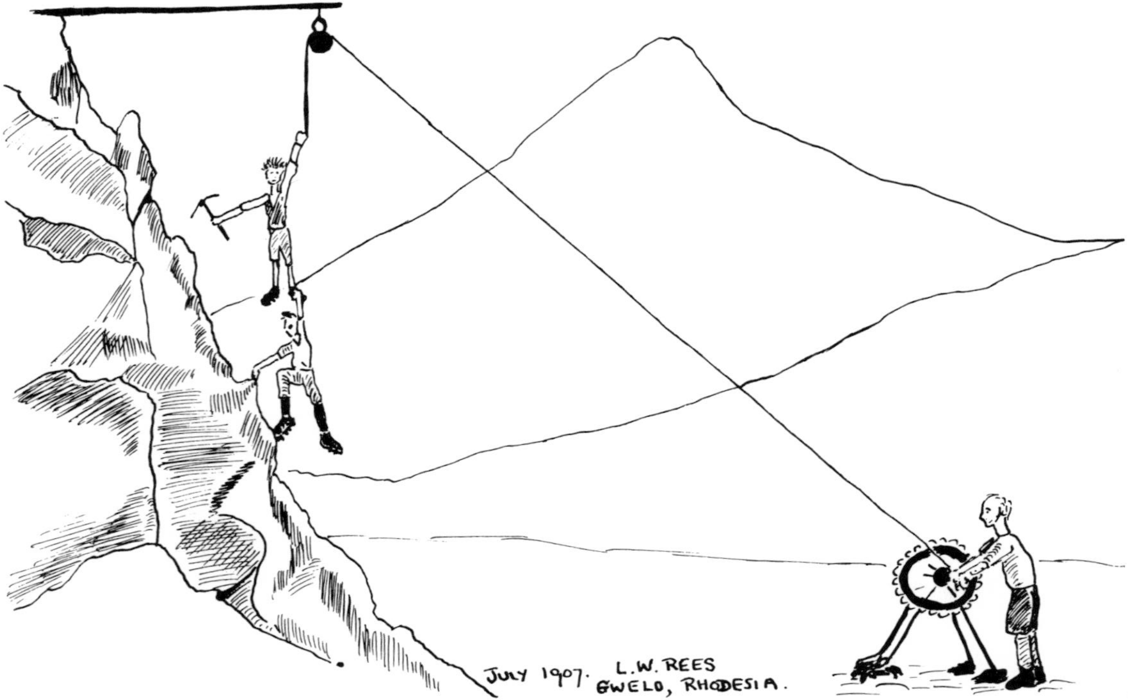

JULY 1907. L.W. REES
GWELO, RHODESIA.

W. STARLING. R.A. JULY 15TH 1888

DESCENT OF SNOWDON

C. H. HEATHCOTE

MAY 13TH 1883

H. BIDEN

AUGUST 1883 F. W. SHIELDS

PEN
Y
GWRYD
6 MILES
ANTICIPATION
REALIZATION
JULY 1900

APPENDIX 3

LIST OF BIRDS SEEN WITHIN TWENTY MILES RADIUS OF PEN Y GWRYD

Compiled by H.L. Richardson. August 1960

At or above P.Y.G. Within five miles

Little grebe
Heron
Mallard
Teal
Wigeon
Tufted duck
Golden eye
Buzzard
Kestral
Grouse
Moorhen
Coot
Snipe
Curlew
Common sandpiper
Great black-backed gull
Lesser black-backed gull
Herring gull
Common gull
Black headed gull
Wood pigeon
Cuckoo
Swift
Greater spotted woodpecker
Skylark
Swallow
House Martin
Sand Martin
Raven
Carrion Crow
Magpie
Chough
Great tit
Blue tit
Wren
Missel thrush
Song thrush
Ring Ouzel
Blackbird
Wheatear
Stonechat
Whinchat
Robin
Sedge warbler
Whitethroat
Willow warbler
Chiff chaff
Goldcrest
Spotted flycatcher
Hedge sparrow (dunnock)
Meadow pipit
Pied wagtail
Grey wagtail
Starling
Greenfinch
Bullfinch
Chaffinch
Reed bunting

Below P.Y.G. Not already listed

Cormorant
Pochard
Dipper
Field Fare

Mute swan
Whooper swan
Sparrow hawk
Redshank
Green woodpecker
Lesser spotted woodpecker
Woodlark
Rook
Jackdaw
Jay
Coal tit
Long tailed tit
Nuthatch
Redwing
Redstart
Blackcap
Wood warbler
Pied flycatcher
Tree pipit
Yellow wagtail
Hawfinch
Goldfinch
Linnet
Yellow hammer
House-sparrow

Within 20 miles of P. Y. G. Not already listed
Great crested grebe
Shoveler
Common scooter
Red breasted merganser
Shelduck
Merlin
Partridge
Pheasant
Oyster catcher
Lapwing
Ringed plover
Turnstone
Dunlin
Lesser black-backed gull (Scandinavian)
Common tern.

PLANTS

List of plants found on the ascent of Snowdon. July 16th 1861

Allosonus crispus (fern)
Arenaria verna
Asplenium viride (fern)

Cystopteris fragilis (fern)
Lycopodium clavatum)
selago)
selaginoides) Club mosses
alpinus)
Lastrea preopteris
Oxyria veniformis
Polypodium phagopteris (fern)
Rhodiola rosea (sedum)
Saxifraga stellaris
hypnoides
oppositigolia
Polystichum lonchitis (fern)
Silene acaulis
Statices var. alpinus
Thalictrum alpinus
Saxifraga nivalis (on very top of Snowdon)
Cochlearia officinalis alpina

List of Ferns in neighbourhood of Pen y Gwryd 1885
by H.B. Carlyon

Osmunda regalis
Pteris aquilina
Polypodium vulgare
dryopteris
phagopteris
Lastrea filix mas
dilatata
montana
Blecknum spicant
cristatum
Allosorus crispus
Woodsia alpina (rare)
Polystichum angulare
aculeatum
lonchitis (the Holly Fern). Local in the mountains in north and W. Ireland
Athyrium Filix Femina

Scolopendrium Vulgare
Asplenium Trichomanes
Adiantum nigrum
Viride
Ruta muraria
Septemtrionade
Hymenophyllum umbilaterade
Cystopteris fragilis
Aphio glossus
Lunaria

Also seen by John W. Hawkins in 1890

Cystopteris Montana
Polypodium phelepteris

List of Plants found in or near Twl-Du

Thalictrum aplinus
Oxyria veniformis
Pimpernella magna
Antharicum scrotinus
Circaea alpinus
Adoxa moschatellina
Plantago montena
Lycopodium clavatum (Stagshorn Club moss)
selago (Club Moss found only in Wales and the North)
alpinus (Club Moss)
Alosorus crispus (fern)
Arenaria Verna
Myrica gallus (shrub)
Meconopsis cambria
Trollius europoeus
Geum rivale
Hymenophyllum wilsonii (fern)
Polypodium dryopteris (oak fern)
phagopteris (beech fern)

Asplenium viride
Thalic trium minus
Cyotopteris fragilis
Saxifraga oppositifolia
Silene acaulis
Rhodiola rosea
Lobelia dortmanna
Subularia aquatica
Callium borealis
Saxifraga nivalis
Isoetes lacustris
Woodsea Ilvensis (rare)

NOTES ON THE RARER PLANTS

In 1878 H. Biden saw masses of Sundew open in Cwm Glas.
In 1890 'E.W.S.' saw:
Silene acaulis (Lychnis) not very common in Wales.
He noted that the Milkwort on Llewydd is white Saxifrage oppositifolia was still in flower in August 1884, usually over in June. Litorella Lacustris is seldom seen because it grows under water. Subularia aquatica (awlwort) also grows under water, rare in Wales. Lloydai Serotina only in the Devil's Kitchen, N. Wales.

BEETLES

List of the Coleoptra of the District (Beetles)

Cychrus rastratus — under stones	Beddgelert Road
Serica brunnea — under stones	Capel Curig
Geotropis verualis — crawling on road	N. of Portmadoc and Glyders
Trichinus fasciatus — on meadow sweet	S. of Trawsfynnydd
Apodernus coryli — on hazel	
Chrysorncla cerealis — on thyme	Cwm Glas. 1892
Pterostichus aettiops — under stones	Crib y Dysgyl
Carabus arvensis — on heather	Snowdon, Glyders, etc.

Carabus catcunlatus — on heather	Snowdon, Glyders, etc.
Carabus glabiatus — on heather	Carnedds
Aphodine lapponium — on sheep dung	Snowdon and Glyders
Nebria gyllenhalii — under stones	Snowdon and Glyders
Abax ater —	Tremadoc rocks

APPENDIX 4

THE EVEREST ROOM — CEILING SIGNATURES

The idea of signatures on the ceiling started with an aim to get those of all the successful Everest team: then it seemed right to add the names of those who climbed Kanchengunga, and later the signatures of many famous climbers, some of whom had been on Himalayan expeditions were included. It was then a short step to include the names of well-known athletes who visited Pen y Gwryd, and the picture was completed by adding signatures of a number of famous men and women in all walks of life who visited the Inn. The full list as it stands today is included herewith.

John Hunt
Charles Evans
Alfred Gregory
Tom Stobart
Michael Ward
George Band
Wilfrid Noyce
Charles Wylie
Tom Bourdillon
Mike Westmacott
Jack Longland
Eric Shipton
George Wood-Johnson
Wyn Harris
Vivian Fuchs
Panel of Russian Climbers.

Tony Streather
Neil Mather
John Clegg
Jo Brown
John Jackson
Tom Mackinnon
Chongpu
Dawa Tenzing
James Morris
Tenzing
Bill Tilman
Hugh Boustead
Tom Brocklebank
Charles Houston
George Lowe

Roger Bannister
Chris Chataway
John Disley
Derek Ibbotson
Sylvia Cheeseman
Madeline Wooller

Bertrand Russell
Cliff Morgan
Richard Sharp
Thomas R. Thomas
Wynford Vaughan Thomas
Hugh Weldon

Harry Llewyllyn

Peter Felix
Beverley Sisters
Petula Clarke
Jack Hawkins
John Stratton
Stephen Grenville

Meredith Edwards
John Moore
Richard Cawston
Geradine MacEwen
Donald Sindon
Robert Beatty

H.V. Morton
Alan Rowlands
Clough Williams Ellis
Al Koran
Michael Innes
Graham Chapman

This list presents an excellent picture of the whole life of this hotel; many of the names are those of climbers, mountaineers, explorers and athletes, but to this list has been added a full assortment of all other brands of mankind. The philosopher, the musician and the rugger player, the film star and the opera singer, the writer and the architect, all rub shoulders as they do on any night of the year in the Smoke Room at Pen y Gwryd.

APPENDIX 5

Earlier in the book I expressed regret that I could not give more information about the building of the numerous cairns which mark so many of the well-known routes on the mountains of Snowdonia; too late for inclusion in the text I received the following letter from Hywel Roberts B.Sc., the National Park Officer for Snowdonia and this is now included;

'As far as I know, no authority was responsible for the initial cairning of mountain footpaths, probably it was more a case of persons following the lines of sheep tracks which eventually became the footpaths, and the building of cairns was to show up the footpaths.

The first cairns built were confined to intersections with other tracks or where there was a significant change in the direction of the path.

Various organizations and climbing clubs have from time to time undertaken the building of cairns along mountain paths all over the country, but with the present day erosion on a great many mountain paths, there is no need for cairning as the line of such paths is evident from the erosion. Therefore, the co-operation of the public is being sought to stop the building of cairns, as the collecting of surface stones to build cairns accelerates erosion.

If an important intersection or change of direction needs to be shown, the Warden Service erect large free standing stones, like the seven foot monolith marking Bwlch Glas and the top of the zig-zag on the Snowdon Pyg track. Such a stone is more evident in snow than a cairn. Several other similar stones will be erected in the near future to mark important features along various footpaths.

As for the large cairn on the summit of Snowdon, one can only quote from the *Mountains of Snowdonia*, 'Rhys favours the meaning tomb or barrow and mentions a local tradition to the effect that the giant Rhita or Rhica, who was slain by Arthur lies buried on the summit'.

Second quote 'Successive tourists record the changing aspects of the summit of Yr Wyddfa. It was first described as a comparatively flat space, some 40 to 50 feet in circumference, surrounded by a low wall. A small cairn is mentioned about

1805. About 1820 the wall was dismantled for the purpose of building a 'Vile wretched hut' some 10 yards from the summit.

The large cairns and signal post seen today were erected by the men of the Ordnance Survey in 1827.'